THE OCEAN STAR BLESSING

written by Christina DiMari
art by Shannon McIntyre

Today, may you know you are a Star that is Designed to Shine.

Always *stay connected to your Source of Life &*
May the Living Water make you whole. ~
Always *travel with a Pod of people who b____ ut the best in you &*
May you be protected from t___ ___ ___oy your Dreams. ~
Always *rememb____ ___ ___ 'ife &*
May it be guar____
Always *hold on ___ ___ udversity come &*
May you be surpr___ ___ ___couragement along the way. ~
Always *Look Up u___n choosing which way to go &*
May the Bright Morning Star light your path~
Always *Believe in the infinite possibilities that are born of Faith &*
May you use your gifts to Shine Brightly for others. ~

"Christina DiMari's story reads like a novel—a gripping and powerful story of God's grace and light shining into dark corners. Stories like this affirm our faith and give us hope."

Chuck Colson
Author, *The Good Life*

Ocean Star will captivate and encourage you on your journey. Christina will have you laughing, crying, dreaming big and making an impact in your world.

Jessica McLean
Recording artist

Rays of hope shine through the pages of Ocean Star! This compelling journey inspires anyone who has ever walked in the darkness that a life of light is just within our grasp, if we will only Look Up. Christina's life proves that wholeness and healing are possible for all of us, no matter where we've been.

Jennifer Strickland
Former professional model, speaker and author of *Girl Perfect*

"The most captivating memoir I've ever read! I guess I shouldn't be surprised since Christina is about the most contagious personality I've ever met."

Bob Russell
Author, Speaker, retired senior pastor Southeast Christian Church, Louisville, KY

I love this book! Ocean Star will encourage you to Look Up when challenges block your path, to travel with friends that bring out the best in you, and to discover pearls of wisdom from mentors along the way. It will reveal the secret to becoming the whole star you are designed to be so you can pass on love, light, blessings and shine for others.

Shannon McIntyre
Pro Surfer, Co Host of Fuel TV show "On Surfari", Artist

"Christina's story and life journey deliver a message of hope, inspiration, encouragement and leave no room for excuses... Our past tells us where we came from but doesn't determine our future.. God takes us with our scars and molds us to be his stars to shine and make a difference in this world."

Tausi Likokola
Author, *The African Princess* and *The art of Beauty and Health*
Model, credits Gucci, Christian Dior
Good will ambassador, country Tanzania

"Experience beauty for ashes, oil of joy for mourning, and a garment of praise for the spirit of heaviness, as it actually transpires in the life of this young captivating writer."

Mr. and Mrs. George Beverly Shea
The Billy Graham Team

When the thrashing waves set out to destroy Christina's life, she lost some important pieces of her star, but not her heart! She found her Rock and held on tight. This book will change your life forever and leave you craving to live your life to the fullest!!

Daize Shayne
World Champion Surfer, Recording artist, Model

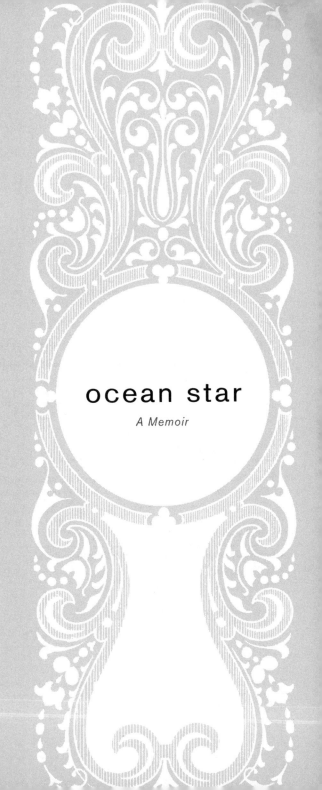

ocean star

A Memoir

Christina DiMari

Visit Ocean Star Gifts at www.oceanstargifts.com.

Ocean Star

First published by Tyndale House Publishers, Inc. in 2006. Second print run by Ocean Star Gifts in 2010. Third print run by Ocean Star Gifts in 2011.

Designed by Jennifer Ghionzoli

Library of Congress Cataloging-in-Publication Data

DiMari, Christina.
   Ocean star : a memoir / Christina DiMari.
     p. cm.
   Includes bibliographical references.
   ISBN 978-0-615-35311-1 (sc)
   1. DiMari, Christina.   2. DiMari, Christina.   3. Christian biography.   4. Female friendship—Religious aspects—Christianity.   5. Mentoring in church work.   I. Title.
   BR1725.D54A3 2006
   277.308'3092—dc22
2005025598

Printed in the United States of America

15   14   13   12   11
7   6   5   4   3

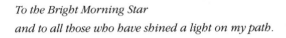

*To the Bright Morning Star
and to all those who have shined a light on my path.*

CONTENTS

LIST OF CHARACTERS

Christina and her siblings from oldest to youngest
    Angela
    Anna
    Gino
    Christina
    Carrie

Christina's parents
    Agostino and Loretta

Christina's paternal grandparents
    Frankie and Lily

Other family friends and relatives
    Karen, family friend
    Joey DiMari, Frankie's youngest brother and Christina's godfather
    Ginger, Lily's sister
    Ricky, Ginger's son

Christina's childhood friends from San Francisco
    Chip
    Rosie
    Elena
    Katie

Christina's friends in Mt. Shasta
    Tashina
    Carolyn

Christina's family
    Michael, husband
    Jake and Trevor, sons

AUTHOR'S NOTE

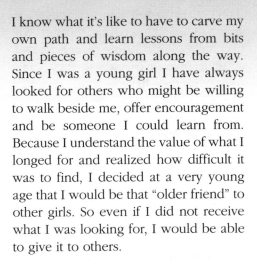

I know what it's like to have to carve my own path and learn lessons from bits and pieces of wisdom along the way. Since I was a young girl I have always looked for others who might be willing to walk beside me, offer encouragement and be someone I could learn from. Because I understand the value of what I longed for and realized how difficult it was to find, I decided at a very young age that I would be that "older friend" to other girls. So even if I did not receive what I was looking for, I would be able to give it to others.

I treat the girls that come into my life the way I would want others to treat me. I listen. I ask questions. I call out the story that is in them. When they feel heard, they feel valued. They learn from me, not by me telling them what they should do, but by sharing with them what I have done. They like to listen to my stories as well. The girls are most often looking for someone who will tell them, "Oh, that happened to me too," and "I understand what you are feeling."

The writing of Ocean Star was born out of these conversations I have had. The question the girls asked me most was, "What has helped you the most get from where you were to where you are now?" Since I learn best from listening to other people's experiences, I decided the best way I knew to share the lessons I have learned along the way was to take my readers with me, back into my story. I didn't want to tell them, I wanted to show them. I hope this memoir will become a mirror for my readers to look at their own lives: where they came from, who they have become, and who they are still yet to be.

Remember, this is a memoir, not a documentary. I have woven stories and lessons together into a story that flows smoothly from one chapter to the next in hopes to share lessons I feel are valuable for the girls who will be reading this.

For privacy reasons, names, chronology, dialogue, details and so forth have been changed. Some of the characters are the composite of two people.

Before you begin, let me ask you to hold on tight. I am taking you back to the beginning and that road can get a bit bumpy and dark at times. Don't stop. Light shines through in the most unexpected ways and the end is full of hope.

And you never know. It could be the next step on your own journey of realizing that you too, are designed to Shine!

WHAT IS MEMOIR ANYWAY?

Is it autobiography? Is it creative nonfiction? Is it straight nonfiction? Is it memory?

Hope Edelman, a writing teacher in Los Angeles and the author of *Motherless Daughters* and *Mother of My Mother*, defines memoir this way: "Memoir is an artistically rendered, nonfiction narrative about a portion of a life, based on memory and the author's interpretation of the past. As opposed to biography and autobiography, where the ultimate goal is the obvious linear truth, the ultimate goal of memoir is something much more emotional and creative and interpretive."

destiny: anna's story

Panic gripped me as I pushed my brother and sister up the stairs. I had to find a safe haven for them—an escape from the terror erupting below us in the kitchen. I motioned for them to go into the bathroom, where we huddled, wide-eyed and frightened. We waited for the silence that would signal the end of the fighting. Yet this night, silence never came.

Screams of terror and cursing continued to echo up the stairs, piercing my tiny heart. Though only four years old, I extended my trembling hands to my eighteen-month-old brother, Gino. I pulled him close to my side and cupped my small hands over his ears. Five-year-old Angela huddled close beside me. An eternity seemed to pass. The three of us clung to each other on the cold bathroom floor.

Suddenly, the sound of a siren overpowered Daddy's angry voice and Mommy's cries for help that burst from below. Torn between fear and curiosity, I quietly crawled to the top of the staircase, followed by Gino and Angela. I looked in horror at the scene unfolding below us. The living room was a beehive of activity, filled with men in uniforms like the one Daddy wore to work.

Blood covered Daddy's hands as he knelt on the kitchen floor.

"There's Daddy!" I whispered. "Why is Daddy crying?"

We watched from the darkness above as someone lifted Mommy onto a stretcher. The blanket covering her enhanced the silhouette of the soon-to-be-born child she carried.

"My baby! My baby! Don't let my baby die!" Daddy shouted as the men whisked Mommy out into the darkness to the waiting ambulance.

Daddy nervously paced the living-room floor waiting for the policemen to stop talking to each other. His hands trembled as he traced his steps over and over.

A policeman finally came over to Daddy and said, "Your wife is hemorrhaging severely. It doesn't look good. The doctor said the baby might not survive."

"No! Not my baby!" Daddy screamed desperately. "You must save the baby!"

Later that night I closed my eyes and wondered if God would give me the little sister I hoped for. The baby wasn't supposed to be born for two more months; would she live or die? In my mind I imagined the baby's life, her very destiny, hanging in the balance. There in my room, kneeling beside my bed, I gently folded my hands and whispered, "Dear God, please let my sister live."

They were only seven words. Simple words . . . and spoken by a mere child. Yet the next morning I found out my prayer was answered. My little sister, Christina, lived.

This book is her story as she remembers it.

Anna

PART I

into the chaos

I KNOW WHAT
I'M DOING.
I HAVE IT
ALL PLANNED
OUT—PLANS
TO TAKE CARE
OF YOU, NOT
ABANDON YOU,
PLANS TO GIVE YOU
THE FUTURE YOU HOPE FOR.

Jeremiah 29:11 (The Message)

believe

I grew up in the middle of San Francisco, not far from Little Italy. As a Catholic, you start out with a simple name but it gets longer over time. When you have your First Communion and Confirmation you get to choose the name of a saint to be added to your birth name. Some people even add an additional name for good luck. The irony of it all is that in Little Italy, when you're in trouble, your full name is invoked, I guess in hopes of summoning the saints to save you. I heard my full name quite a bit growing up: Christina Alisa Isabella Theresa DiMari.

My dad's parents, Frankie and Lily, came from Sicily, which is a hop across the Mediterranean Sea from the boot of southern Italy. When I was growing up, they lived in the Sunset District in San Francisco, where all the houses look as if they belong on Main Street in Disneyland. Each house is connected to the one next door and is painted a different color.

The house I lived in with my parents and siblings was white. That is, white on the outside. On the inside, it was a different story. The stuff that went on inside looked whatever the color is for wrong. It was the kind of stuff that's not supposed to be—but we didn't know that yet.

If only a few days had been difficult, maybe it wouldn't have been so hard to handle. But it went on day after day after day, the same scene repeating itself over and over again.

"Get out of here!" Dad's voice boomed. "You don't want to be a mother! Every bit of this is your fault, not mine! For cryin' out loud, I had to force myself on you to get these kids. I'm different from you. I wanted my children! I will never leave them. I'll work five jobs if I need to."

"I'll get out of here all right! I'll go straight to my father and tell him everything!" Mom screamed.

"Go ahead. What's he going to do about it?" Dad hollered, slamming some dishes against the wall. "It's no one's f— business what goes on in this house!"

"Christina, move! I can't see anything." We sat at the top of the stairs, and my little sister, Carrie, pushed me to the side so she could get a better view of the fighting below.

Mom did whatever she could to tip Dad over the edge. I wished she would leave our house for good and never come back. Dad was calm and fun, and he enjoyed being our dad. He was good—that is, until my mom did something stupid, and then everything would change, and the things he did weren't good anymore. We all blamed her. It was as if she did it on purpose to make our life sad because she didn't want to be our mother. That was one thing we knew for sure.

"Dad, stop it!" Angela yelled, stumbling upon the heated scene. Dad swung at my oldest sister, striking her. Blood ran from the back of Angela's head as she slammed into the corner cabinet. She retreated to the corner of the kitchen, crouching in fear.

Max, our German shepherd, barked relentlessly, and my brother, Gino, rushed to calm him.

A phone call interrupted the violent scene. Dressed in his police uniform, Dad's powerful presence filled the doorway as he answered the phone. Chasing all the robbers and gangsters in San Francisco aided his already athletic build. His short, dark brown hair was combed straight back with gel. Sometimes his dark brown eyes sparkled so bright the whole room lit up. Other times, like when he was flaming mad, they looked dark and spooky.

"I need to go out on a call!" Dad announced as he hung up the phone and ran out the door to his police car.

Anna immediately ran to Angela, trying to stop the bleeding on her head.

Mom grabbed my arm and dragged me to the bathroom, locking the door behind her. "This is all your fault!" Reaching for a bar of soap, she shoved it into my mouth, holding my jaw so I had to bite down on it.

I didn't understand why everything was always my fault or why I was the only one she dragged to the bathroom for a beating. After seven years of living like this, the only thing I did know was how to make sure she didn't kill me.

Gagging from the chunks of soap, I tried to spit them out onto the floor. "I'm not listening to anything you say!"

She grabbed my arms and pinned me against the wall. "I wish you were never born!"

Closing my eyes tightly, I tried not to listen to her words or look at the anger in her fiery eyes. I wanted to disappear as she slapped my face over and over again with her cold hand. The words she screamed at me were words I was too young to hear.

"You're nothing but a little s——!"

The more I struggled to free myself, the harder she struck me. I fought back so she couldn't break me. No matter what, I wouldn't let her win. I knew how to fight, but I didn't know what to do with all the hatred about to explode inside of me. So when she started beating me on my back, I closed my eyes and pretended she didn't exist, that I didn't have a mother. I did this until it hurt too badly. Until I thought I might die.

Struggling to free myself from her tight hold, I screamed, "Anna, help me!"

"No one's ever going help you!" my mother sneered as she slammed my head into the wall.

I tightened my muscles as the blow of her wooden spoon struck my small back over and over and over again.

Closing my eyes tight again, I pretended I was somewhere else, far away from her. Somewhere where she couldn't hurt me with her words, her spoon, or her hand.

"Leave her alone!" Anna screamed from outside the door. "Stop hitting her! Stop it!" Anna pounded on the door over and over, frantically turning the knob, trying to get in.

Still struggling to get away from my mother, I fell backward as Anna and my brother, Gino, managed to unlock the door. Although Anna was only eleven years old, she charged right at Mom. Gino, nine years old, stood there looking at me as if he'd seen a ghost.

"I've got to get out of this house!" Mom screamed as she pushed Anna out of the way and stormed out of the bathroom. Then she ran out the front door.

I doubled over on the cold floor, feeling as if I might throw up.

Anna's face tightened as she surveyed the marks on my body. "I hate her!" Anna yelled. "I hate her so much!" With tears streaming down my face, I latched onto Anna's hand as I had done many times before while she led me to her room.

"Don't worry, Christina. I'll protect you from her until Dad gets home."

That made me feel better. Dad was my protector. When he was home, my mom wouldn't even think about messing with me.

Turning toward the mirror, I looked at my tear-streaked face. My light brown hair was highlighted naturally with strands of yellow Anna called gold. My dark brown eyes reflected a hint of hazel green in the right light. I had Anna's thin frame, but my cheeks appeared full enough for my Italian grandfather, Frankie, to affectionately grab hold of.

Looking past my tears, I looked deeper into my eyes.

"Who's in there that is so bad?" I asked Anna. "What have I done to make her hate me so much?"

"Here. Lie down on my bed. I need to put some medicine on you."

"Ouch!" I cried as I tightened my muscles. "It hurts too much for you to touch it."

"I have to get the bleeding to stop; stay still. Close your eyes and try to go to sleep for a little bit."

"I can't fall asleep. If I fall asleep, the snakes will come after me. They come every night—big ones, bigger than my bed. They crawl under my sheets and try to choke the life out of me. I try to kill

them, but I can't. As soon as I grab one and throw it to the floor, two more appear. I can't sleep anymore. I don't ever want to go to sleep again."

Although I didn't realize it, I was holding my breath. Anna's hand gently rested on my shoulder. "Christina, is she coming after you in the night again?"

I didn't answer her. I didn't want to talk about it.

Anna knew, though, the way she knew everything about me.

After rubbing the medicine all over my face and back, Anna brushed my hair and began to tell me a story.

"In a small village out in the countryside lived five children like us. One day while the children ran in a beautiful meadow full of pretty flowers, a big, bad dragon came over the mountain. Chasing the kids, the ugly dragon bared its sharp teeth, spewing fire from its mouth. Suddenly, the kids remembered a hole in the ground by a steep cliff on the far side of the meadow. Reaching the edge of the cliff, they ducked down in the hole just as the dragon reached them. As they planned, the dragon plunged over the edge of the cliff into a deep, dark pit, falling to its death."

"Anna, I like how all the kids in your stories find a way to escape. That's it! I've got to escape! I'm going to run away!"

"You can't do that. You're only seven years old! It's going to be dark in a few hours."

"I've got to get out of here. I'm going to run away before she comes back."

Anna looked at me a long time before she stood up and marched over to her piggy bank. "I'll give you all the money I have." One by one she counted out thirty-two dollars.

I ran to my room and grabbed two books I had received from my neighbor and a strand of dime-store pearls my grandma Lily had given me for my birthday.

Anna rushed into the kitchen and threw a bunch of food into a bag. She handed me the packed bag and a warm coat and hurriedly sent me out the door. "You better go now before she comes back," Anna said, her voice betraying the urgency she felt. "Go far, so she can't find you."

I turned to wave good-bye to Anna. Standing solemnly on the

front porch, she reluctantly waved back and watched me walk down the street until I disappeared around the corner. As I looked over my shoulder studying every car that drove by, I hoped no one would kidnap me.

The smell of saltwater grew closer as I rounded the bend leading to the place that had always been my refuge.

Climbing down the steep hill blanketed with chunky ice plant, I found my way to a tiny secret alcove that had been carved out of the cliff by the strong winds.

She'll never find me here, I assured myself. Curling up with my knees to my chest, I glanced at the waves crashing onto the rocky shore of Ocean Beach.

Several hours passed as I watched families enjoy the summer activities on the beach below. Some walked their dogs. Others splashed in the waves and built elaborate sand castles along the water's edge. But soon the sound of children's laughter faded, and I heard only the solitary echo of the changing tide.

Rubbing my warm hands softly on my reddened cheeks, I tried to make the hate inside my mind and the sting of Mom's slaps go away. *Why does she hate me so much?*

My anger slowly turned to sadness as the soothing rhythm of the waves began to quiet my spirit. I reached to pick up one of the books I'd brought with me. The front cover displayed a picture of the nighttime sky, brilliantly lit up with a zillion sparkling stars. Inside the first page was the same picture as the one on the front, but here a circle surrounded one of the smallest stars. The caption read, "If God knows about each one of the stars in his universe and knows them each by name, how much more does he know about you?"

I stared at the picture for a long time. Reaching deep into my pocket I carefully pulled out my strand of dime-store pearls. Laying them on the book, I delicately arranged them to form a circle around the star.

Does God really know about me? Does he circle me down here on earth like he circled that one star way up there among the other stars? I don't feel circled. I only feel alone.

I wondered if God really knew me.

Well, if you really know me, I thought, *then you would know I'm always getting into big trouble for stuff that's not my fault. And if you were real, then you probably wouldn't let that happen to a kid. But then, maybe you're not real. Maybe you don't know me. Or maybe you live up in the stars, and you have so much to look after in the whole world that you can't possibly see everything.*

I wanted to believe God was real and that he was nice. I decided that he probably lived up in the stars. That made sense to me. That's why he didn't come and help me. I wanted to fly beyond the distant stars to where he lived. Standing up, I placed my feet carefully at the edge of the cliff and slowly leaned forward to look down at the long drop below. *If only I had wings, I could fly away from here and never come back.*

As I looked out at the wide-open water, I wished I wasn't a kid. If I couldn't fly to where God lived, then I wanted more than anything else to dive into the ocean and be a mermaid for the rest of my life.

A seagull landed a few feet away, hoping I'd give him some of my snacks. As I looked out at the waves rolling onto shore, a story began to take shape in my mind. I turned to the little bird and began to tell him my tale.

"A long time ago, I was really a mermaid girl. I spent all my time with my friend Azalia. Together we danced in the rhythm of the waves under the bright stars. There was only play, only laughing, only happiness, until one night, all of a sudden, a bad, terrible war broke out under the sea. Azalia's mommy was gone for good. I knew I had to protect my friend, or she would get eaten by a shark and die. I thought long and hard until I came up with a plan. I found a secret mountain that no one knew about but me. I put Azalia inside a cave and covered it with seaweed so no one would know she was there. Then I said good-bye to Azalia. I swam away, promising I'd come back and get her when everything was safe."

After a while I grew tired of making up stories. Sitting back down, I picked up the second book. On the cover was a drawing of Jesus surrounded by children who all looked my age. He looked straight into the eyes of one of the little girls, cupping her face with his strong, yet tender, loving hands. He gently tilted her face so she looked directly into his eyes. *I wish I were that girl,* I thought to myself. *That's what it would be like if I could fly to where God lives.*

Immediately a calm feeling swept over me. Something warm and tingly filled my face and then my whole body. Closing my eyes, I saw a blazing light. Full of wonder, I looked into the brightness and watched the light take the form of a serene being dressed in white. Pure white. His eyes were like deep blue water, and as he looked at me, it was as if everything inside of him flowed into me.

As I looked into his eyes, I sensed one simple message.

Believe.

I froze, not wanting the moment to end. *He doesn't live up in the stars!* I thought, as hope filled my heart. *He lives down here too.*

After a few moments, my eyes couldn't see the light anymore. I closed them and whispered, "Believe." With my eyes closed, the light was clear again, but this time only in my mind. When I opened my eyes everything was just as it had been before the light visited me. But the message was clear to me: I had to believe even though I couldn't see. The place inside my heart that had felt all alone now had a new friend.

Daylight faded. *Everything's going to be all right,* I coached myself as I wrapped my arms more tightly around my knees, trying to stay warm. The big orange ball gradually dropped from its lofty place in the sky and sat slightly above the water's edge far out at sea. I watched the sun slowly disappear into the water as if it were tired and wanted to go to sleep. I rubbed the sleep out of my eyes and fought the urge to close them.

Nightfall finally won its battle with the receding daylight.

"I don't want to be here anymore," I whispered, staring out at the ocean. "Now what am I going to do?"

I didn't want to stay at the ocean all night, but I didn't want to go home either. Wrapping my coat around my shoulders, I tried to make the shivers go away. I didn't want to cry. I wanted to be tough. I pressed my hands against my eyes and bit my lip, but it was too late. Water filled my hands and streamed down my cheeks.

"I forgot to ask Anna," I said aloud to the stars above, "after I escape from the dragon, where do I go once I'm free?"

CHAPTER 2

shades of white

After Dad had found me shivering in my hiding place the night before, he promised to take me for a walk on the beach the next day when he returned from his work at the police station. I sat on the front steps of our house waiting for Dad, elbows propped on my knees and my head resting in my hands. We never talked about what happened in the house. I didn't understand much except it was clear that Mom hated me and Dad loved me. That's all I knew. He was my father, and without him, I was lost. We both believed all the screaming and fighting was Mom's fault and jumped at the chance to get far away from her.

As soon as I saw him driving up the street, I ran to greet him, and off we went to the beach. Walking barefoot in the sand and listening to the waves rolling into shore calmed Dad and me and seemed to carry all our troubles away. The wind blew, and I brushed the sand out of my eyes. Dad reached for my hand and tenderly covered it with his. His warmth flowed all the way under my skin. I knew he would take care of me forever.

The beach stretched for six miles from Fort Funston, where we started walking, all the way down to the Cliff House, where the seals gathered on the rocks a short distance offshore.

Once in a while a ship passed far out at sea, triggering memories for Dad of the time he had spent in the navy. As we walked, he told me stories of places he had visited, people he'd met, and the life he had hoped for when he got out.

Gripping my hand in his, he smiled at me. "There was nothing I wanted more than a little girl to go walking on the beach with, my little Bella."

"You mean *run* with!" I shouted, splashing water as I raced down the shoreline.

"You can't run forever!"

"Yes, I can! I can run and never stop. Not ever."

"Well, you are one fast runner!" Dad said as he passed me.

"One day, I'm going to beat you in a race!" I burst out as we collapsed on the wet sand laughing, each trying to catch our breath.

A short distance down the beach, we watched some surfers catching huge waves on their surfboards. I stared, awestruck, as they paddled out past the first set of waves into the deeper water. Then we watched them get on top of a wave and ride it all the way to shore. "One day, I'm going to learn to surf just like them," I announced confidently.

I glanced up at Dad and caught him fixed in a daze, watching me with a tear or two welling up in his big brown eyes. "Bella, you better slow down. I don't know about that. Girls surfing? There are a lot of sharks out there. Maybe you'd better watch the waves from shore!"

"No way. I can't wait to get on top of the biggest wave out there! Don't worry about me. Anyway, you'll always protect me."

"Yeah, you can count on me," Dad said with a big smile. "We better get back to the house. I want to check on Anna's dress for her First Communion next week."

A few minutes after we arrived at the house, the shouting started. We were in our bedrooms upstairs but could easily hear our parents yelling in the kitchen.

"That dress looks three sizes too big for Anna!" Dad hollered. "She can't wear a hand-me-down. Angela's a whole head taller than her and bigger. For cryin' out loud, go buy her a dress that fits her!"

"She's spoiled rotten! There's nothing wrong with her dress!" Mom yelled back. "She's only going to wear it for one day. Leave it be. It's none of your business what dress she wears!"

"It *is* my business," Dad shot back. "You don't care what Anna's going to feel like having a dress hanging all over her. What do you do all day? Do something useful with yourself! This dress needs to be altered."

Anna came down from her bedroom to check on Gino, Carrie, and me when the screaming started escalating out of control. Gino's room was next to the one I shared with Carrie, but on nights like this, Anna often made him come in our room so we'd all be together.

Quietly, she listened through the crack in our bedroom door, all the while telling us not to worry. She saw Dad walk up the stairs and heading down the hallway toward us.

Trying to calm himself as he approached our rooms, he called out, "Anna, where are ya?"

"In here, Dad; I was checking on the kids."

"Anna, you like the dress the way it looks on you?" he asked in his strong Italian accent, holding the Communion dress in his hands.

Anna shook her head slowly but responded firmly, "No, it doesn't fit me right."

"That's it!" Dad announced. "Tomorrow after work I'll pick you up and take you to someone myself who will make this look right for you. You got this special day coming, and she wants you to look like you got a white sack of lace hanging from your shoulders. I'm never going to figure that woman out!"

Before he walked out into the hallway, he turned and looked at me. A warm smile spread across his face. "Bella, Bella, Bella!" He kissed his hand and blew it to me as he walked out the door. *"Buona notte."*

I melted when Dad treated me like I was the one he liked most. It was like medicine on the wounds I received from my mother. I needed to know that my life mattered to someone, that I wasn't just a little piece of trash that was never going to amount to anything. Dad's words made me feel special.

The day before the ceremony, Dad came home from work with

the dress, all excited. "Anna, Anna, Anna! *Presto, prestissimo!* Come quickly!"

I ran down the stairs after Anna when I heard Dad calling.

He held her dress up like a display in a store window, his eyes filled with pride, as if he had sewed it himself. "Hurry," he said, beaming. "Slip it on. Make sure it fits!"

Mom walked up from the family room, shaking her head and flinging her black hair out of her eyes, as if she didn't see why he went to all the trouble. Dad sat in his brown suede recliner in the living room. He leaned forward, fidgeting with the arm cover, waiting for Anna to come down from her room with the dress on. I sat on his lap while we waited.

Anna came down the stairs, looking like a bride about to get married in her beautiful white dress. Dad beamed with pride as we stood there looking at her. "Now, that's my girl! You look absolutely beautiful!" Nudging me he asked, "Doesn't she?"

The next morning Dad's parents came to the house before the Communion celebration. Frankie didn't like any of the names kids called their grandparents, so we called our grandparents by their first names. Frankie and Lily drove up in their brown Chevy for the big day. We all knew to get out of the way when Frankie drove. Pulling up to the curb he inevitably rolled his tire up over it to make sure he parked as close as possible so he wouldn't be sideswiped by other cars speeding by.

The whole neighborhood seemed to show up at church for the ceremony. With guests around, Mom and Dad were on their best behavior. People stood in the back and all up and down the side aisles by the confessional booths. Gino sat next to me and jabbed his elbow into my side. "Hey, look! There goes Father Lorenzo into the door of the confessional. Nobody better go in there now, or they'll be in big trouble."

"How come?" I asked.

"'Cause he gives the longest punishments," he answered with a stern look and fear in his eyes. "He'll make you say a hundred 'Our Fathers' just for saying a tiny white lie."

"What's a white lie?" I asked.

"It's when you say the truth but twist it a tad bit so ya don't get in trouble."

"How does he know if you're telling the truth or a twisted truth?"

"They know all the bad stuff about you even if you don't tell them. That's their job."

"Well, I'm never going in there!"

Gino laughed. "When they say it's time for your First Communion, you have to go to confession. You don't get a choice."

As the kids, all dressed in white, made their way up the aisles to the front pews of the church, I gazed around the church at the life-like statues. We only went to church a couple of times a year, and I was starting to have so many questions.

Looking up at Dad, I whispered, "How come they got all those fake people in here?"

Dad leaned over and whispered, "They're here to watch over ya."

"How do they watch you if they're not real?"

"Shhhhh, look for Anna," he instructed, putting his fingers to his lips.

"How come Anna's dressed in white?" I pestered Dad. "They all look the same. I can't find her."

The priest came out to start the ceremony. His long, golden robe hung to the floor. Carrie stood on the pew and held on to Lily's shoulders.

"When's he coming?" five-year-old Carrie asked repeatedly.

Lily tried to lift her to let her see the priest over all the adults' heads, but she kept asking, "When's he coming out?"

I leaned over, "The priest is there! He's the one with the big hat on."

"No, not him—Dod!" she said, looking toward the altar. "When is Dod gonna come out?"

Frankie started to laugh. "God? God doesn't come out. Only the priest does."

Looking up at Dad, I said, "I thought you said God lives in church. If he lives here, how come nobody ever gets to see him?"

"God doesn't talk to people like you and me. He only talks to the priests."

"Is that how come the priests know about how bad we are? Does God tell them?"

Mom leaned over from the other end of the pew. Her face was all crinkled up, and she firmly scolded, "Stop talking in church!"

Dad leaned forward to look at Mom at the far end of the pew. With an audible voice he snapped back at her. "You got ears like an elephant. Leave her alone. She's not talking to you! If Christina wants to ask me a question, she can ask me whatever she wants!"

Lily leaned over and gave me a dirty look as if I ought to have known better. Frankie got a quirky smile on his face and tried to hold back his laughter.

After about an hour, I finally spotted Anna as she joined the processional out of the church. Afterward I asked her, "Why do you have to do all that anyway?"

"Now that I'm old enough to have my sins forgiven," she began, "I get to wear this white dress to show I'm pure white inside."

"You mean they made you go in the confessional today? Father Lorenzo is in there!"

"No, not today. We all went yesterday, so we'd be pure in church today."

"You mean you didn't think a bad thought between yesterday and today?" I asked.

Anna looked at me matter-of-factly and said, "Nope."

"Well, what if you get all clean and then you do something bad again?"

Shrugging her shoulders, she answered, "I guess you get a shade of white, but you're not pure white anymore."

"Oh, I get it," I stated confidently. "It's a good thing you don't turn totally black all at once." Then I asked hesitantly, "Anna, am I going to stay all black until my First Communion?"

Deep in thought, Anna scrunched up her nose. She was sure the answer was yes, but if she told me so, she knew I'd worry. She couldn't say she didn't know because Anna always knew something about everything. Finally her face relaxed. "Christina, you're probably not really black. You're just a darker shade of white. Then when you get to have your Communion, you'll get pure white like me."

Anna got pulled along outside with her classmates for pictures.
I walked back inside to find Dad. Lily stood in the back lighting
candles, and Dad sat in the last pew talking with some man. While
I watched them talk, I made sure I kept my eye on the confessional
booth. *Will the people look more afraid when they come out than
when they went in?* I wondered silently. Dad and the man ended
their conversation. Dad handed something to him.

Sitting down in the pew, I asked, "Dad, you ever go into the
confessional?"

Jolted by my question, he straightened his back and tightened his
lips. His narrowed eyes shifted to mine without turning his head.
"What are you asking me that for?" he asked defensively. Then with
a wave of his hand, he confidently assured me, "Sure, I go in there
all the time."

"What for, Dad? You never do nothin' bad."

CHAPTER 3

flying like an eagle

All five kids scrambled out of the old brown-paneled station wagon and raced up the twenty-two steps to the wrought-iron gate that guarded the entrance of Frankie and Lily's house in the Sunset District. Dad often dropped us off to spend time with our grandparents while Mom was out doing whatever it was she did. Dad, their only child, waved good-bye and drove off to work. Peering through the bars of the gate, I saw Frankie's tall, thin frame through the small window next to the front door. His olive skin and light brown bristly hair gave the impression he worked out in the sun every day.

Lily, two heads shorter than Frankie, stood next to him, eager to welcome us. She wore an apron around her robust waist. Her light-brown hair was colored with streaks of strawberry blond. Lily's eyeglasses, framed with light blue metal rims, looked like they were made out of the bottoms of old soft-drink bottles. The thick glass magnified her ocean blue eyes, presenting the illusion they'd pop right out of her eye sockets. Her left eye shifted sometimes while she talked, making it hard to pay attention to what she said.

Some of the kids kept their eyes on the ring of keys in Lily's hand, wanting to be the first to get in the gate. I fixed my attention

on Frankie's and Lily's faces, on their welcoming smiles, knowing they'd be happy to see us. After each one of us got through the gate, we kissed Lily on the left cheek and then the right. Once through the front door, the whole gang took a sharp left, following their noses to the kitchen. I made a hard right and sat down next to Frankie by the front window. Our two chairs looked identical, covered in a lime green fabric with tiny white flowers. A red candy bowl full of caramel-covered marshmallows sat on the small glass table between the chairs.

"Where ya been? China?" Frankie asked me in his strong Italian accent.

"No, Frankie," I said with a smile. "But one day I'm going to go somewhere far away!"

"Yeah, I believe it. All that running away you do, one day you're going to run too far. Then what are you going to do when your father can't find you?"

Relaxing back in the chair, I answered him in a manner I knew he understood. I put a smug look on my face, straightened my back, and looked at him out of the corner of my eye. "I guess I'll just take care of myself."

We looked out the window for the afternoon without either of us saying a word. Frankie drifted into a world of his own, lost in his thoughts. I called his chair "the disappearing chair" because that's what he did there.

I gazed at his face, wondering what he thought about. I didn't assume he was curious about what I was thinking. I think he was curious as to why I liked him so much. I didn't really know why. I just did.

"Why don't you go play with the other kids?" Frankie asked. "What do you want to sit here with me for?"

I put a smug look on my face, straightened my back, and looked at him out of the corner of my eye. Without saying a word, I shrugged my shoulders as if to say, "I don't know, but I'm going to keep on doing it whether you like it or not."

He usually chuckled to himself. He knew I understood him.

Lily poked her head in the living room and said, "Christina, you're the girl Frankie never had. You look like your old grandfather. The two of you sit there all day. Why don't you get up and make yourself useful in the kitchen?"

I stood up and looked in the mirror. "Do you think I look like you, Frankie?"

Standing up, he reached for my cheeks and pinched them tightly, "That's-a-my girl. You come with me. Let's go make some spaghetti sauce."

Frankie thought the bigger the mess he made, the better the sauce tasted. I hated the mess. Mesmerized by Frankie's ability to be lost in the joy of his creation, I wondered how he managed to be unconcerned about the disarray around him. I grabbed a wet cloth to clean up.

"Christina, forget about the mess. You watch me," he shouted, waving his hand in the air. "Then one day, you'll be able to make the sauce yourself. Put the washcloth down. Relax! Enjoy your life!"

I stood on a chair in the middle of the kitchen and pretended to be Maria Callas, singing on some big, fancy stage in a piazza in Florence, Italy.

Frankie pulled me down. "Come here. I want to show you my new jacket I bought."

I followed him down the hallway, and he opened the closet where he kept his clothes.

All his favorite plaid sport jackets and polyester pants hung neatly in a row. He favored clothes in shades of brown and olive green, with the exception of this new blue suede jacket. He took the jacket off the hanger and proudly put it on over his white suspenders.

"What's the matter with you?" Lily hollered from the kitchen. "You forgot about your sauce. It's boiling over and making a mess all over the kitchen."

We walked into the kitchen to see the sauce splattered all over the walls. Frankie kept his new coat on for the rest of the day.

While I was cooking with Frankie, I heard Lily coming up the hallway, singing a happy tune. She peeked her head halfway in and motioned to me with her finger to quietly come and follow her.

Lily resumed singing and delicately took small dancelike steps toward her bedroom as I followed close behind. Her dress wasn't

quite long enough to cover her sagging nylons, which collected at the bottom of her ankles. Once in the bedroom, she quietly shut the door behind us. Her puffy hands squeezed my arm as she leaned her body close in a show of affection. "Now Christina, shh, sit down there. I've got a little something special for you."

I sat on the big bed, my legs dangling off the edge. Lily's fingertips gently rubbed together with excitement as she disappeared into the walk-in closet, still humming her tune. I heard rustling around in the dark and then the creaking of boards being lifted. She then slid the clothes back to their original places and came out of the closet, looking like a child up to something mischievous. She grabbed both my hands in hers, slipped something into my palm, and folded my fingers tightly around it.

Winking at me, she disappeared down the hallway singing. Once she left, I opened my fingers to find she had placed a bill in my hand. My eyes grew wide at the sight of five dollars. In 1968, that made me a rich seven-year-old.

My brother and sisters waited to pounce on me as I came out of Lily's room. "How much did you get?"

I tucked the cash deep into my pocket. "Fat chance I'm telling. Lily told me not to tell, and I'm not telling."

Angela snapped back, "Since when do you ever do what you're told?"

"Don't worry about it. She gives us all the same amount," Anna said. "Let's race our bikes before Dad comes to get us. He told us to be ready on time because Mom plans on having some of her relatives over for dinner."

Riding bikes in San Francisco felt like being on a big roller coaster. Up and down the steep hills we raced for about a quarter mile all the way down to the finish line.

Anna, the official referee of the race, hollered after me, "Stop, Christina! You stay here with me and help me see who gets to the finish line first."

"No way. I'm going to be in the race!" I said, as I pedaled faster, trying to catch up with the others before she stopped me.

"Don't start yet!" I shouted. "You better wait for me!" Angela and some of the neighbor kids rode what I called "big kid" bikes. Ten-

speeds! I rode Anna's old hot pink bike with green and yellow daisies decorating the long, narrow seat.

Gino made sure everyone waited for me. Angela lined us up
along the top of the hill. Our final goal appeared so far away that
when I strained really hard to see Anna, she looked small enough
for me to hold in the palm of my hand. Gino made sure he started
next to me.

"Go as fast as you can to get up your speed," Gino coached me.
"Then somewhere about the middle of the second hill, lift your
hands in the air and pretend you're an eagle."

My adrenaline pumped extra hard as Angela yelled, "Ready! Set!
Go!"

We sped off in a flash. Halfway down the first hill, I focused my
attention on pedaling superfast. If I got my speed up by the second
hill, I'd get to fly like an eagle. By the time I approached the second
hill, the other kids raced toward the final stretch to the finish line.
Seeing them far in front of me pushed me to pedal faster. As I
started down the second hill, I lifted my hands off the handlebars
and raised them to the sky, shouting, "I'm an eagle!"

The wind coursed over my entire body. I took flight to another
place, even another time. Only I flew too fast.

In a split second, I frantically switched from soaring like an eagle
to controlling a bike behaving like a high-spirited horse. The bike
wobbled and swerved back and forth. Struggling to keep it upright,
I gripped the handlebars tightly, willing myself to stay on course.
The old man backing out of his driveway thirty yards down the hill
didn't see me. My dreams of flying high came to a sudden stop as I
smashed into his green Ford sedan at full speed.

Everything went dark as my body crashed to the ground. I
faintly heard Gino screaming, "Christina got her head run over by
a car!"

It seemed as if I were lying in the dark for a really long time
until my eyesight came back all blurry. Through a haze, I saw Dad
running toward me in slow motion. "Oh, my baby, my baby. What
happened to Christina?" I looked to my side and noticed Anna sitting next to me. The world spun in circles, making me dizzy. Anna
made funny faces at me, trying to get me to laugh.

"I got to feel it, Anna." I said. "I got to feel it real good." Anna smiled and patted my arm. Her eyes told me she knew what I meant.

Dad plowed past everyone and scooped me up in his arms. "Bella, Bella, Bella, you're going to be okay!"

My head did not exactly get run over by the car, but it sure felt like it. Dad rushed me to the hospital. I ended up with seventeen stitches across the top of my right eye. I looked like Captain Hook with an ugly patch covering half my face.

When I walked into our house, Mom glared at me. "What did you think you were doing riding with all the big kids? This is going to mess up all my plans for the evening."

I didn't pay any attention to her. Neither did Dad. He packed me an overnight bag and brought me back to my grandparents' house where I'd spend the next few days. It took many years to realize what a safe place their home actually had been. You can't always understand that kind of thing when you're just a kid.

All of us liked different things about being with our grandparents, but we all felt the same when it was time to go home. Each of us, in our own self-taught way, had to gird ourselves, preparing our hearts and minds for the inevitable return to the awful reality of life at our house.

I never could figure out why my mom was so mean to me or why I always seemed to bear the brunt of her anger. It was only much later that I understood why she was all tangled up in her own pain and that somewhere deep inside she blamed me.

CHAPTER 4

falling

Five years passed in a blur as we lived in the ever-present fog of tension, anger, and violence in our house.

My oldest sister, Angela, now seventeen, made sure the multi-colored embroidered sign hanging on her door faced the right direction. From my room on the second floor I could read it clearly: "Do Not Disturb!"

Do not disturb what? my inquisitive twelve-year-old mind wondered. "What are you doing in there?" I hollered.

Angela yelled back, "What's the matter with you? Can't you read? It says, 'Get lost!'"

"It does not!" I stated firmly. "It says, 'Do Not Disturb.'"

Right then the door opened as she stuck out her flushed face. "Read my lips: Do Not Disturb!"

I flinched as she slammed the door in my face. I knocked on the door, but she didn't answer. I knocked again.

"I told you not to knock," Angela yelled.

"I'm not knocking for you," I yelled back. "I'm knocking for Anna! It's her room, too, and it's not her sign. So if I'm knocking for Anna, I don't have to look at your stupid sign!"

Anna opened the door.

"What are you doing in there?" I asked.

"I'm trying to sew a dress. I got invited to the prom by the quarterback of the football team. Mom said if I want to go I need to buy the dress myself. I don't have much money so I decided to try to make one. I also made Dad this Hawaiian shirt. Do you like it?" she said handing it to me.

"Wow, what a trip! You made this yourself? He's going to love it."

Later that day she gave it to Dad. He put it on immediately. The crooked pocket she sewed on the chest for Dad's Marlboro cigarettes gave the brown Hawaiian shirt unique character. Each evening when Dad came home, he put on the shirt with a pair of light brown pants. His cigarettes continually fell on the floor. He retrieved them, put them back in the crooked pocket, and patted his chest, saying, "This is the best present anyone's ever given me."

Dad's job demanded more time away from home since he'd become a lieutenant in the police department. One day when he was preparing to leave for work, he saw me rushing around the house getting ready to leave.

"Are you late for something?" Dad asked.

"I'm already supposed to be at the beach. My training for cross-country running starts in about fifteen minutes. I'll never make it on time."

"Wait a minute, I'll make a call." He dialed the police station. "Do you think you can cover for me? I'm going to be about twenty minutes late." Hanging up the phone, he looked at me and smiled. "Get in the car. I'll take you on my way."

"Oh, great. Thanks!"

I expected him to be at work until midnight, but when I came home I noticed his car in the driveway. I looked everywhere for him. Finally I found him sitting on the back-porch stairs, smoking a cigarette. His face was swollen from crying. Rubbing his eyes, he mumbled something under his breath over and over again.

"Dad, I thought you went to work. What's the matter?"

"You saved me!" he blurted out. "My baby! You saved me. I could be dead!" He sobbed uncontrollably, rocking back and forth.

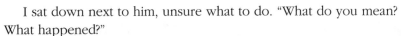

I sat down next to him, unsure what to do. "What do you mean? What happened?"

"They came looking for me," he sobbed through his tears. "But they killed my friend Lieutenant Soldari instead. He was sitting at my desk covering for me. It's my fault he's dead! I was supposed to be there. It was supposed to be me!"

I didn't understand what had happened and I wanted to know more. Dad abruptly stood up. "I've got to go. I've got to find whoever did this."

"Dad, you'd better not go anywhere!"

He walked to his room to gather his things. Reaching into his closet, he retrieved his gun from its hiding place. He opened a drawer and pulled out a handful of bullets. Then he kissed me on the cheek and hurried down the stairs.

"But, Dad, where are you going?"

"Stay here until Anna gets home. When all the kids get home, tell 'em not to leave. I'm sending a squad car over immediately to stay with you kids until I get back," he ordered as he got in the police car and sped off.

Ten minutes later, a squad car with two police officers pulled up to the house. They tapped the phone line, walked around the house, and sat at the kitchen table talking to each other. I heard one of them mention my mother's name, but I couldn't understand their comments. My mom never seemed to be home.

I looked out the window nervously, hoping the other kids would get home before dark. Anna arrived first and the others followed soon after. Anna sat at the kitchen table with the police officers, asking them questions. I listened from the adjoining room.

"There are some problems down at the station. Your dad's going to be gone for a few days. A policeman will be staying with you kids around the clock. We'll be picking you up from school and taking you straight home. For the time being, we don't want any of you alone at any time."

I stared at the ceiling most of the night, trying to make sense of what happened. The policemen talked about a rebel group that came into the station and opened fire. *Why would someone want to hurt Dad?*

A few days turned into weeks. When Dad came home he was obsessed with capturing whoever killed his friend. He taped pictures of the suspects all over his office walls.

* * *

While it would be many years before I learned all the details, whatever happened that night changed Dad. The things we used to do together didn't happen anymore. When he freaked out, instead of taking me with him, he left alone. He didn't come home until really late at night. He told us he'd started working another job doing some work as a private investigator.

Sometimes I would come home from school and sit for hours watching him make charts, just to spend time with him. When not drunk or flaming mad at someone, he appeared blank. Unreadable. Unresponsive. He was lost in the battle going on inside his mind.

What's happening to Dad? Is he going to shut me out forever? I wondered. He grew more and more distant, like the setting sun disappearing below the cold ocean waters beyond the San Francisco Bay. Mom had long ago detached herself from all of us, so I didn't expect anything different from her. I didn't want anything from her. But without Dad I had no parent. I wasn't willing to let him slip through my fingers.

The deeper he sank into a downward spiral, the more I blamed my mother for tearing the life out of him.

With each passing day, a deepening sadness filled his eyes. I watched helplessly as his drinking continued to increase. The death of his friend threw him into a deep depression. This only escalated the constant fighting between him and Mom.

One evening Anna made dinner for the family, planning to serve it at 5:30 p.m. sharp as Dad liked. Dinnertime arrived. Dad fumed that Mom was not home. She had told him she would be home from her new job at 5:00 p.m.

The five of us took our places. Dad, still dressed in his full police uniform, sat at the head of the table. Anna had prepared a huge meal of spaghetti and meatballs with garlic bread. Dinner was ready to be served.

"Anna, bring the food to the table," Dad said firmly.

The food smelled so good. The aroma of garlic and olive oil filled the kitchen. My stomach growled as Anna placed the food in the center of the table. Dad's nerves sliced the air like a knife. He sat tall and abnormally quiet. He never let us eat a meal until we said grace, but this time he didn't pray. We waited for a signal. None came. Each of us looked down at our empty plates. Every once in a while we peeked up at each other through the corners of our eyes.

The clock read 6:00 p.m. Anna's cold meal sat on the table. Each of us sat with our hands folded on our laps waiting for Dad to say grace so we could eat. No one fidgeted with their place settings or squirmed in their chairs. As each minute passed, Dad's anger grew. *If Mom leaves for good, maybe Dad will never get mad again,* I thought to myself.

At 6:30 p.m. Dad slapped the table hard and said grace. Anna served us as we reluctantly began to eat the cold meal that no longer looked appetizing.

"Anna told me you got the letter saying your grades are not good enough to get into Saint Ignatius High School. Is that true?" Dad pointedly asked Gino.

Gino hung his head low, not wanting to look up at Dad. Seeing the despair on Gino's face, Dad continued. "I don't want to see any sad faces. If you're not willing to do the work and get good grades like Anna, you don't deserve to go to a good school."

"Well, if I can't go to Saint Ignatius, where am I going to go?" Gino asked timidly.

"You're going to Franklin High, and that's the end of it!"

The rest us sank in our seats.

"Dad," I said hesitantly, "the bad kids who carry guns to school and beat the daylights out of kids for no reason at all go to Franklin High."

Angela straightened her back and challenged Dad. "How's Gino supposed to be any good at golf if he has to play on a stupid team like Franklin High?"

"That's all he's good enough for."

We all looked at Angela, hoping she would stop challenging Dad

so openly. Right then, Mom came prancing in the front door, tipsy and with a flushed face.

"Oh, it's too bad I missed dinner," she blurted out, glancing our way.

Dad scooted his chair from the table, rose abruptly to his feet, and stormed downstairs to the family room.

After dinner, Angela planned to go out for the evening. Anna, wanting us all together, told the rest of us not to go outside. We all knew what came next.

"Loretta, where have you been all night?" Dad yelled from behind the built-in bar, releasing a string of curse words we were used to hearing by then.

"I went out for a drink with some friends," she jeered as she walked halfway down the steps to where Dad was standing.

Dad's eyes lit up like two flames of fire. "I'll bet you were out running around with Lenny! If I ever catch you with that man, I'll smash his face in, and you won't ever know what happened to him."

My mother brushed him aside. "Oh, you're jealous," she said laughing.

I thought Dad might kill her right then and there. Pointing his finger in her face, he yelled, "You're a slut like you have taught Angela to be. You're nothing! You hear me? You're nothing but a whore. You're worthless!"

Shrugging him off, she yelled back, "Oh shut up, Agostino! Leave me alone. I'm not listening to anything you say."

Slamming his drink against the wall of the bar, he dragged Mom the rest of the way down the stairs. "You will listen to what I say! Your father called here today looking for you. You can't fool anybody. Your own parents know you're no good. What did you tell them, huh? He asked me questions. The nosy—"

"I'm not telling them anything!" Mom insisted.

"You tell them everything! Our family's none of their business! No one believes anything you say anyway. You live in a stinking fairyland. Snap back to reality! You're ruining any chance your kids have at a normal life. Your own son can't even get into a decent high school. He's flunking out of school. How do ya like that? Go tell all your friends that Gino's going to Franklin. How's that going to make you look?"

"He needs to figure it out for himself," Mom blurted out. "It's not my problem if he wants to be a screwup."

Dad's face reddened as he clutched Mom by both arms and shook her vigorously. "What in the name of God is the matter with you?" Dad spun her around and slammed her body against the side of the bar, knocking over an open bottle of vodka.

As the fighting continued, we withdrew to our rooms, hoping to disappear. I kept the door open a sliver, peering out to see what would happen.

Meanwhile, Angela was getting ready to go out with her boyfriend. As Dad walked up the stairs from the kitchen, Angela tried to sneak past him and out the front door.

"And where do you think you're going?" he demanded, grabbing her arm.

"I am going skating!" she said boldly.

"Who are you going with? C'mon, tell me. Is it Jim Bollini? Is he picking you up? You're nothing but a whore, just like your mother!"

Before Angela could escape, Dad grabbed a roll of duct tape from the kitchen drawer. Tearing off her shirt, he slapped her chest repeatedly until it turned crimson red. Angela tried with all her strength to push him off but fell backward under the force of his blows. Angela's face tightened as she cried, "I hate you! I will always hate you!"

With a roll of duct tape in his hand Dad pinned her down, wrapping her torso with tape and concealing her flesh. "If you want to go out with him, you'll have to go like this," he yelled, pushing her to the floor. "No boy is going to touch my daughter!"

Max started barking loudly. In a rage, Dad kicked him into the corner. "Don't hurt the dog!" Gino yelled, as he frantically ran down the stairs.

Seeing her chance to escape, Angela scurried upstairs to her room, slamming the door as her "Do Not Disturb" sign fluttered to the floor. Dad ran up to the second-floor landing, standing just inches from my bedroom door.

Huddled in our room, Carrie and I heard Angela open her door and bravely walk back down the stairs. I opened my door a bit farther and peeked out again.

"I'm telling you, you're not going out with that boy," Dad barked as they stood in the hallway nose to nose.

Angela lunged at Dad. Losing his balance, he tumbled backwards down the stairs. Angela whirled about and raced up to her room.

I stood speechless at the top of the stairs looking at Dad's strong and powerful body sprawled out below me. Barely able to move, he groaned with despair, aimlessly reaching for something or someone to help him.

The light from the hallway fixture reflected the words on his police badge proudly displayed on his chest: "To Honor and Protect." *Who?* I silently wondered. *Not us.*

The image of my childhood hero now lay shattered before my eyes as I watched Anna gently lift Dad's head. The last light of hope I had that he could make everything better slowly flickered out.

CHAPTER 5

merry christmas

Two years later, Dad planned to take Anna and me for some last-minute Christmas shopping downtown. We bundled up in warm coats and strolled along Market Street looking at the elaborate holiday window displays. Toy trains whistled softly as they wound their way through colorfully wrapped packages and disappeared into tunnels of pure chocolate. Stuffed animals with large red ribbons reminded me of my childhood shopping trips with Dad.

San Francisco in December was often chilly. Rarely, however, did it snow. That year, a seemingly miraculous light dusting of snow briefly blew through downtown. The swirling, pure-white flakes cascaded around the three of us, creating an almost magical calm in our lives for a few short hours. Dad had a bounce in his step as he hummed his favorite tune and said hello to strangers passing us on the sidewalk.

"What do you think, girls?" Dad asked, spotting a stylish brown suede dress in a department-store window. "Do you think your mother will like this?" Anna and I glanced at each other. Our eyes betrayed our real opinion that the dress looked ugly.

Dad's eyes sparkled like a kid's at Christmas as he made the purchase. Heading out the door with his special gift for Mom in his hand, Dad said, "Okay, my two Bellas, let's go get a Coke and a doughnut."

Stopping for a snack at the corner doughnut shop was a must on any shopping trip downtown with Dad. Sitting in the window booth, we made small talk while sipping our drinks and munching on doughnuts. Continuing another tradition he and Frankie loved, Dad pulled a wad of bills out of his pocket and spread the money out before us like a fan.

"Go ahead," Dad began. "Close your eyes! Both of you. No peeking! Pick one and see what your lucky bill is." With our eyes squeezed tightly shut, Anna and I both pulled a bill. "I got a hundred!" we shouted in unison.

Dad sat back and smiled so big we thought his face would split. "Don't you girls ever forget how much your daddy loves you."

We smiled back at him. "Don't worry, Dad, we won't," Anna said warmly.

About an hour later, Dad made another purchase at a small store down the street.

"Look!" I whispered to Anna as Dad pulled out his big wad of cash. "They're all hundred-dollar bills!" Dad was always flashy like this. It was his way of trying to make everyone okay. When he wanted to cheer us up, he often gave us money or bought us presents.

It was Christmas. Dad was happy. Time stood still. As we walked together down the crowded street, my world seemed peaceful, safe, and beautiful.

The calm came to an abrupt halt the following afternoon when it was time to decorate the Christmas tree.

"Ah, to h—— with the lights!" Dad shouted to no one in particular.

"What's the matter with the lights?" Mom asked, pulling an ornament from one of the boxes strewn about the floor. "They worked great when I took them down last year."

"Worked great? I don't know if the d—— things work 'cause they're all tangled up! I'll never understand what's the matter with you. Why can't you put this stuff away neatly, so I can make some sense of it when it's time to pull it out? For cryin' out loud, it's the same thing every year!"

Each of us desperately hoped Dad could keep control. *Take a deep breath, Dad,* I thought to myself. *C'mon, don't lose it.*

Picking up the lights, he hurled them from the living room, sending them crashing into the kitchen cabinets. "Ah, you kids do it yourself!" Dad roughly shoved Carrie aside as he stormed down to the bar in the family room to cool off. Mom took off up the stairs to her bedroom. Repeating the same scene from years past, the kids were left to decorate the tree on our own.

Our conversations were cautious and uneasy during the rest of the week leading up to Christmas. Dad's mood swings were part of our everyday life, but I wished he could keep it together for Christmas. Didn't he understand how his bad moods filled the whole house with darkness?

I overheard Angela and Anna talking about how as soon as Anna graduated from high school this spring, the two of them were going to take off to San Diego for college. I gulped hard. *Gino's sixteen, I'm only fourteen, and Carrie's twelve. What will we do without Anna? I never thought about her leaving before.*

* * *

Christmas morning found the entire family seated in the living room waiting to open presents. When my turn came to open a gift, I chose the smallest box under the tree with my name on it.

"What did you get me, Gino?" I asked, eagerly tearing the paper from the tiny box. "Ohhhhh, Gino, I love it!" I said, slapping his arm affectionately. As I lifted up a delicately braided necklace, my eyes sparkled with joy at the pure gold surfboard dangling from the end of the chain.

Dad's turn was next. He methodically opened the box and lifted out a quilt that Anna had made just for him. He wrapped it around himself, saying, "This is the best present anyone's ever given me."

Anna and I held our breath as the moment arrived for Mom to open her gift from Dad. My mind flashed back to the picture of Dad's sparkling eyes as he picked out the dress he assumed would be perfect. Opening the package, Mom slowly held up the dress. "You think I'm going to wear this?" she said, scrunching up her nose.

Disgusted, Dad waved his arm at Mom and mumbled, "You don't like the dress? Return it!"

Why couldn't she simply pretend she liked it? I fumed to myself.

Dad tried to keep his cool for the rest of the day, but the tension level throughout the house continued to increase with each shot of whiskey he consumed.

After dinner, most of us returned to the living room to gather up our gifts.

"So tell me, what don't you like about the dress?" Dad asked Mom as she sat in the living room. "You don't like the color? Or you don't like it because I gave it to you?"

Mom stood up. Reaching for the dress lying across her recliner, she glared in Dad's direction. "I don't like anything about it!" she shouted.

"Oh yeah? Well, I don't like anything about you!" Dad volleyed back.

"Then don't buy me any more dresses that make me look like I'm a housewife!"

Anna, Gino, and I stood in shocked silence as Mom spun around and tossed Dad's gift into the well-stoked fireplace.

The rage Dad had managed to keep submerged below the surface suddenly boiled over. Without thinking, he picked up the closest object to him and slammed it against the wall. I watched in horror as Anna's gift to me of stained-glass artwork, opened just hours earlier, shattered in a million pieces. All five kids bolted for the stairs as Dad grabbed Mom, throwing her all the way through the kitchen doorway. Perched on the landing we watched with knotted stomachs as Dad dragged Mom down the stairs to the family room.

The chaotic exchange drove Max, our dog, into a barking frenzy.

"If that stupid dog doesn't shut up, I'm going to kill him!" Dad threatened.

"He wouldn't bark if you didn't scream so much!" Carrie sassed as she scrambled down the stairs to try to calm Max down.

Without warning, Dad lashed out at my little sister, Carrie, kicking her hard in the stomach as she passed by him. Immediately Carrie doubled over, wailing at the top of her lungs.

Anna bolted down the stairs to Carrie.

"Don't hurt Max! He's not your dog. He's mine!" Gino shouted, running to Max.

"You no-good pothead!" Dad shouted. Grabbing Gino by the hair, he dragged him into the bathroom, shoving Gino's face in the toilet. Gino thrashed about as Dad mercilessly held his head under the water.

"This is where your head belongs! If I ever see you smoking that stuff anywhere near my house again you'll never see the sun!"

"Dad, leave him alone!" I screamed, running down the stairs. "Let him go!"

Dad finally yanked Gino's head out of the toilet and threw him to the floor, leaving Gino choking and gasping for air.

"Get out of this house and leave us alone!" Angela shouted from the top of the stairs.

"Your own son's a pothead!" Dad sneered at Mom.

"It's not my problem if he wants to take drugs," Mom blurted out as she tried to escape.

Dad reached for her hair and pulled her back down the stairs.

"Get your worthless hands off me!" Mom yelled. "Is this the kind of Christmas you want your kids to remember?" Slapping at Dad's face with both hands, Mom struggled with all her might to break free. "You're a freaking maniac!" she screamed.

"I'm going to kill you!" Dad threatened as he slammed Mom's head against the stairs.

Anna ran to Gino's room, grabbed Angela's old baseball bat, and flew down the stairs at Dad. "Let her go! That's enough. Let her go!"

Swinging at Dad with the bat, Anna narrowly missed hitting him on the side of the head. Startled, Dad lost his balance, slipping on the stairs.

"Mom, get out of the house now," Anna ordered. "For once in your life think about how your actions are going to affect us! He's going to kill all of us if you don't get out of here."

Anna grabbed Mom's arm and pulled her up the stairs. Dad, struggling to his feet, clumsily lunged at Mom's leg, determined not to let her leave. Anna brought the bat down hard across Dad's back in a desperate attempt to loosen his grip on Mom. Once more the hardwood weapon found its mark. The second blow across his upper back sent Dad tumbling down the final few steps to the floor below.

Anna scurried up the steps, dragging Mom with her out the front door. "Run . . . now!"

Why doesn't Mom just learn to keep her mouth shut and stop antagonizing Dad, I wondered. It didn't take much to keep Dad happy, but I also knew it didn't take much to send him over the edge. My mom seemed so determined to do whatever she could to keep him agitated. *Doesn't she care that one of these days he might get so mad he could kill her . . . or us?*

As Mom stumbled down the sidewalk, Anna flew back in the door. "Get all the way upstairs now!" she silently mouthed as she motioned for us to head for our hiding place, the third-floor bathroom. We huddled on the cold bathroom floor after locking the only entrance to our tiny hideout.

A horrific silence descended upon the house. Each tension-filled minute that passed seemed like an hour. Finally, Anna crawled over to the door, quietly unlocking the only barrier protecting us. Without a sound, she slowly disappeared into the hallway.

Desperate to know Dad's whereabouts, Anna crept to her old vantage point at the top of the stairs. Horror filled her face as she saw Dad loading his gun. Anna knew what she must do. Slipping into her bedroom, she quickly dialed the police.

"This is Anna DiMari," she whispered into the phone. "My dad's a cop. He has his gun out and I think he—!" Before she gave the dispatcher our address, she heard noises from below. Dropping the receiver, she whirled and bolted back to the bathroom.

Anna quietly slipped back through the door to four sets of frightened eyes staring up at her. White as a ghost, she whispered, "Dad went into his bedroom and grabbed his gun! I saw him put the bullets in. Everyone lie down as flat as you can. Don't make a noise!"

Carrie began to cry. "Shut up!" I ordered. "He's going to know we're up here!"

Anna leaned over to cover Carrie's mouth with her hands as she whispered in her ear. "Be tough! Don't cry! Everything's going to be all right."

Precious seconds passed as the torment of the unknown gripped us. We all held our breath, petrified. Then it happened. Two deafening gunshots blasted from the floor below us.

Five hearts almost stopped beating simultaneously as we wondered, *Did Dad kill Mom? Will he come after us next?*

"Don't move!" Anna ordered. "Don't make any sounds at all. Whatever you do, be as quiet and still as you possibly can."

I closed my eyes tight. I didn't want to see my dad when he stormed into our hideout like he had done in the past. I didn't want to see him swirl his gun in the air the way he did when he was drunk and mad and freaked out. I closed my eyes tighter and tighter until I could start to see a light, deep inside the middle of the darkness in my mind's eye.

That was the only way I knew at the time to find the light that had come to me when I ran away nearly seven years earlier. I had to find the light. It was my only escape.

I couldn't hear Anna's voice anymore telling everyone what we should or shouldn't do. I went inside the light and waited to see if I would live or die. The quiet lasted longer than normal.

No sign of either parent.

No footsteps coming our direction.

Only the five of us waiting together to know what would happen next.

I don't know how long it was before we started to hear deep voices talking and footsteps moving about the house. It seemed like an eternity. Finding the nerve to venture outside our refuge one more time, Anna crawled out to the hallway. "It's the police!" she gasped. "You guys can come out."

One by one each of us descended the stairs to the living room. The blinking lights and glitter of our Christmas tree flickered out of place amongst the broken glass and remnants of Mom's smoldering dress in the fireplace. The gaping hole blown through the front door stopped us in midstride. The realization of how narrowly we had avoided a similar fate left me chilled inside.

Our parents were long gone.

Anna immediately began to field questions from the police while Angela and Carrie sat solemnly on the brown sofa. Gino and I

noticed the family-room door slightly ajar. Curiosity drew us down the bloodstained steps to the surreal scene below. Angela's baseball bat lay on the family-room carpet. Dad's brown sweater was spread across the bar counter beside a broken martini glass. Vodka dripped down the side of the bar from the broken bottle on the countertop. Max was sprawled out on the carpet with blood dripping from his neck. He was dead.

Gino ran to Max. "That f— man! I'll never talk to Dad again for the rest of my life. I swear it on my life, Christina—not ever!"

I stood in stunned silence surveying the wreckage while Gino fell to his knees before his dog.

A firm hand on my shoulder startled me back to reality. "You kids shouldn't be down here." The policeman gently led us back upstairs.

As we sat in the living room together, the police questioned each of us. "Do your parents fight like this often?" a detective asked.

"Yes!" Gino answered without hesitation. "That's all they ever do is fight."

"Have any of you ever been hurt?"

Carrie started sobbing. "I'm afraid he's going to kill me. Sometimes when I'm home alone, he . . ." She couldn't talk through her tears.

After about an hour of questioning, the two policemen prepared to leave.

"Kids, that patrol car out front will be staying there all night," one officer said in a confident voice. "Your grandparents will be here shortly."

"Do you know where Dad is? Is he okay?" I asked anxiously.

"We'll let you know as soon as we know anything," the other officer replied as they headed down the front-porch steps.

"I'm worried about what's going to happen next," Anna said, pacing the living room. "The police know Dad used his gun in the house. That's going to put all the blame on him. This whole thing is going to come down on Dad."

Gino stood up. "What are you worried about, Anna? If Dad gets put in jail, it means we're finally free. For once I can come home without being scared for my life!"

"I agree," Carrie quietly added. "Anyhow, my friend Suzie's mom told me to move in with them."

"It's about time they throw him in jail where he belongs," Angela seethed. "We should've told the police a long time ago how bad it has been around here with him."

"I can't do that!" I protested. "I can't say it was all Dad's fault. I'm not siding with Mom. No way! It's all her fault he flips out."

Everyone's gaze fixed on me. I shrugged my shoulders as tears welled up in my eyes.

"I'm totally confused," I admitted to no one in particular. "I've got to get out of here."

CHAPTER 6

my dolphin pod

"Come on, Gino," I encouraged, elbowing him gently in the ribs. "Remember what Anna told us. We've got to be like the heroes in the story. We'll find a way to survive until we get out of here."

A long, disappointed sigh rolled from Gino's lips. "You're only fourteen years old; you have four more years of high school before you're free. Anyway, who are you fooling? We knew all along Anna was the only real hero."

"You're wrong, Gino. A hero is someone who looks up long enough to know there's a better way to go. Anna looked up. She found her way out by studying for college. We can't go the way she went because we're not smart enough. We have to find another way. But we will, Gino; I'm sure of it."

Angela and Anna stood in the driveway, packing up their car for their big move to San Diego. The dreary, foggy day cast a shadow over our house and my soul. Sitting on the front steps of the house in the rain, Gino and I dreaded the farewell only moments away. I thought about all the lectures Anna had given my friends and me about staying pure and not letting boys take advantage of us. She scared us into keeping them at arm's length by showing us disgusting pictures of all the infections we could get if

we fooled around. I hated that she was bossy and always told me what to do, but now that she was leaving, I wished she would stay.

I wanted to be happy for her, but my stomach twisted in knots as I watched her put her belongings into the car. Anna always had a plan. Up until now, her plans had always included me. This time was different. On her road to freedom, she only possessed one extra ticket, and she'd given it to Angela.

Anna stowed the last box in the old blue Pontiac while Angela impatiently banged on the horn. Anna turned toward us, uncertain what to say. "I'll . . . call you soon . . . okay, guys?" Solemnly nodding our heads, we stood on the porch, unable to move. Anna, momentarily frozen, appeared unsure what to do next. She slipped her mood ring off her finger and tossed it to me. I caught it and held it tight. Slowly reaching for the car door, she slid into her seat. Angela pulled out of the driveway. Hands appeared from each window as they vigorously waved good-bye. Anna was gone.

* * *

Carrie moved over to her friend Suzie's house. Mom disappeared for the most part, working her new job. Dad was supposedly on probation, trying to get his act together. Gino and I were on our own.

Although I had been repeatedly suspended from grammar school for poor grades and bad language in the classroom, I escaped with my eighth-grade diploma by the skin of my teeth. I then enrolled in the all-girls Catholic high school Dad made me attend.

After homeroom attendance was taken, my best friends, Elena and Katie, and I often snuck off campus, heading for the beach to get high. We had a "go for it," living-for-the-moment attitude that dictated our daily routine, and we rebelled against anyone trying to put a damper on our fun. My friends and I made up new names. They called me Breezy. It fit me perfectly, as all I wanted was to feel free to live my life the way I wanted without anyone telling me what I should or shouldn't do.

Our friend Rosie joined us sometimes, but she had a double life. She lived on the edge yet maintained excellent scores on her report

card. Her brains helped me get by so I didn't get kicked out of school.

One day Gino met us at the beach with his friend Chip, one of the hotshot surfers at Ocean Beach.

"Hey, Christina!" Gino hollered as they strutted toward us. "Chip brought an extra board. Are you up for your first surfing lesson?"

"Definitely!" I said.

Chip taught me how to pop up on a surfboard and how to ride the baby waves. After I gained some confidence, I convinced Chip to paddle out to the big swells with me. I spent the rest of the afternoon listening to him teach me the ins and outs of surfing. Most of the day I wiped out but had a total blast doing it. From that day forward Chip and I thought of one another like brother and sister. Spending endless hours together on our boards in the water, we talked about everything. Sometimes we cut our water adventures short because Chip would tire easily due to his recent cancer treatments.

Hanging out with Chip and my girlfriends at the beach, I was introduced to a strange new group of people—the hippies. Their old Volkswagen vans displayed painted flowers and "Peace, Love, and Joy" signs. From a short distance, I would watch them dance, barefoot and uninhibited, to their wild music. Though Gino and Katie thought they looked freaky, I was curiously attracted to their free spirits.

A few weeks after we discovered the hippies' beach hangout, I was feeling extra brave—probably because I was a little high on Gino's potent Hawaiian hash. I grabbed Rosie's arm and headed toward the hippies. Rosie and I giggled nervously as we approached the parking lot where their vans lined up facing the Cliff House, a historical restaurant built into the cliff overlooking Ocean Beach.

"Hey, what's happening, kids?" a ponytailed guitarist slurred as he swayed rhythmically to the offbeat music blaring from a nearby monitor. He winked at us as we walked toward a crowd of hippies dancing in the sand. Making our way to the center of the group, Rosie and I began to dance as if we'd known them all our lives.

"Hi, I'm Maggie," one of the girls offered. She grabbed our hands and led us to her van. Orange-flowered material covered the rear windows. Long mattresses on the floor replaced the rear seats.

Maggie sat down and pulled out a stack of record albums. Music filled the cramped quarters as she pointed out all her favorite songs.

"This song's called 'Ripple,'" she said, brushing her long blond hair.

"I totally love this music!" I said. "Who's the band?"

"The Grateful Dead," she replied, licking something off a piece of paper. "Want some acid?"

"Uh . . . sure, why not?" I said with a smile, looking hesitantly at Rosie.

"What will it do to us?" Rosie asked.

"It'll take all your troubles away, sweetie!" came Maggie's melodic reply.

After a few awkward moments of silence, I made up my mind. I took a hit of the LSD she offered. Following my lead, Rosie did the same.

Within moments, brilliant vistas of color swirled throughout the van. Looking at Maggie, I noticed that her feet had turned into lizards. Four hours later, I staggered to my feet, hitting my head on the ceiling.

"Uh, we'd better go, Rosie," I slurred. "I told Gino we'd only be ten minutes, and I think we've been in this van for two days."

Still nodding her head to the music, Maggie smiled. "Come back and visit anytime. You girls are great dancers! Come party with me again."

"That will be so much fun," I said as we stepped out of the van.

"Hey, you girls want a dog?" a voice from behind me asked.

The guy who played the guitar now sat next to a huge box in the back of his van. Inside the box yelped three tiny husky puppies. I lifted up one of the soft balls of fur, cuddling it close against my neck.

"Okay, I'll take this one," I said, holding it up.

"What are you going to call him?" Rosie asked.

Maggie cranked up the music in her van. I knew the song—it was the first one she'd played for us.

"Ripple!" I shouted.

"Life's a trip; enjoy the ride!" the guitar player hollered as he hopped in the driver's seat of his van and drove away.

My dog and my new hippie friends gave me two more good reasons not to be in school. Doing scarcely enough work to get by, I often cut classes and took off for the beach with Ripple. He was my constant companion. Ripple ran at my side as I took my daily run, and he lay patiently on the sand while I surfed the water at Ocean Beach.

In the months that followed, Maggie took my friends and me to every Grateful Dead concert within driving distance of the Bay Area. At one of the concerts, a band member noticed Rosie, Elena, and me dancing. A photographer happened to be in the audience and took several pictures of us dancing in front of the stage. We were surprised but thrilled to find our picture in the music section of the newspaper the next day. For three fourteen-year-old girls, that was the pinnacle of life.

Dancing at concerts with the band lured us down yet another risk-filled path. Enchanted by the spotlight, we decided we needed to upgrade our attire. We envied the dresses our hippie friends danced in and decided it was time for a shopping trip. I became the ringleader in teaching my friends how to steal whatever they wanted. The day before a concert at Berkeley, Rosie, Elena, Katie, and I wandered down the aisles of one of the biggest clothing stores in the city, collecting our favorite outfits. In the changing room, we nonchalantly slipped the new clothing on under our street clothes and simply walked out of the store. "This store is enormous. They won't miss a few dresses," we told ourselves. "Besides, we need to look good at the concert tomorrow night."

I was overwhelmed by the free-for-all backstage party at Berkeley. We were hanging out with the movers and shakers—everybody who was anybody in the San Francisco music scene! Our hippie friends had succeeded in guiding us through a new gateway of escape in our constant search to avoid the boredom of our daily lives.

* * *

Haight Asbury, a street in San Francisco, became one of our favorite places to hang out with our hippie companions. Bobby, the guitar

player who gave me Ripple, had been flirting relentlessly with Rosie for several weeks. I intervened one evening when Bobby began to make his move right there on the crowded street. Torn between wanting Bobby's attention and feeling slightly uneasy, Rosie was taking no action to stop his aggressive advances.

"Hey, Rosie!" I yelled, firmly grabbing her arm. "C'mon, we've got to go!" I headed in the other direction with Rosie in tow, stopping about twenty feet away from a somewhat startled Bobby.

"What did you do that for?" Rosie protested.

"Rosie," I insisted, "don't let him put his hands all over you!"

"Why not? He told me he loves me!" Rosie replied, obviously upset that I'd ruined her plans for the evening.

"He doesn't love you. He's only going to use you!"

"You don't know Bobby like I do. He's promised we'll be together forever."

"Don't be stupid, Rosie! Bobby's like any other guy. If you put out a little bit, then what are you going to do when he wants to go all the way with you?" I challenged. "What will you do if you get pregnant? It's hard enough to take care of yourself, much less a baby! You better think about what you're doing," I said, thinking about Anna's words of warning before she left.

"Christina!" Rosie whispered, pulling me into a doorway. "We already did. Last night . . ."

"What? Are you crazy, Rosie?" Smacking her hard on the shoulder, I scolded, "Don't let him get away with that. Don't forget what Anna told us before she left. You're going to get yourself all messed up if you don't put up some boundaries."

Rosie's face suddenly changed. "What's up with this? Are you my mom?"

"Rosie, I—"

"Just forget it," Rosie yelled over her shoulder, running up the sidewalk. "Bobby is waiting for me; I'm going back!"

Anger and disappointment swept over me as I watched Rosie disappear into the crowd to look for Bobby. He hadn't even waited for her.

In spite of my increasing animosity toward Bobby, Rosie and I quickly patched things up. We continued to hang out with Maggie

and her friends at the beach. Their carefree lifestyle became increasingly attractive to me.

By the time we were juniors, Rosie and I often talked about going on a road trip with them across the country, certain we'd leave all the trouble of home behind us.

We talked of this more and more after Rosie's dad died in a car accident. Rosie had been late returning home one night, and her father went out to look for her. As he was rounding a curve, a drunk driver slammed into his car, killing him instantly. Rosie's mother reminded her often that if she had come home on time, her father would still be alive.

"Why does Mom blame me for Dad's death?" Rosie sobbed to me one night. "I was only a few minutes late. I didn't know he would go out looking for me. How was I to know he was going to get killed?"

Rosie wept bitterly. "I try to do everything right for her, but I know I'll never be good enough."

I felt like Rosie had come into my life for a reason. I was able to relate to her struggles with her mother. She couldn't get her mom's critical words out of her mind. Even though my mother's words tried to fill my mind, I had learned how to ignore her.

I tried to pretend I didn't hear my mom talking to her friends, telling them I was on drugs and how I was never going to amount to anything. How it didn't matter if I even went to school because I was so stupid I'd probably never graduate anyway.

I wanted to teach Rosie how to ignore her mother too. I knew it was the only way she was going to make it.

"Rosie, you've got to tune your mother out. You don't need her," I said as we watched the waves crash onto the beach in front of us. "You know deep down that your dad's dying wasn't your fault. Even if your mom hates you forever, you can't let her define who *you* are. Look at you! You have so many great qualities!"

Wiping her tears away, Rosie choked out the words, "I don't know why I care so much about what she thinks of me. It seems like ever since I was a kid, she has wanted me to be perfect. Even though I get straight As, all she ever does is put me down. For once, I'd like her to tell me I did something right—that she is proud of me."

"What if you wait forever and she never says anything nice? Then you've wasted your whole life waiting for something that is never going to happen. That would be the biggest bummer of all."

Reaching my arm around Rosie's shoulder, I pulled her close to my side while she bawled her eyes out.

"You know what the problem is with our mothers?" Rosie said. "They don't know the difference between good words and mean words."

"Yes, they do," I said. "They just don't choose them."

"Not only do they want to tear us down, they don't ever see the good in us. Doesn't it bother you all the times you win a cross-country race and there's no one to say, 'Way to go! You did great'?"

"Yeah, I guess it does a little bit, but I try not to think about it," I admitted, taking a deep breath. "I tell myself not to want something I don't have. Instead, I try to be thankful for what I do have. I like when you and Gino come watch me. My friends are all I need. I don't need anyone else."

Katie and Elena caught up with us to watch the sunset. As the sun was about to drop below the horizon, the four of us stood at the water's edge and let the rising tide wash over our bare feet. Ripple dug furiously for sand crabs by our side.

Elena interrupted our contemplation. "Look! There's a dolphin pod in the roll wave down shore!"

We ran down the beach until we could see them clearly.

"Wow! I've never seen a dolphin pod in real life!" Katie exclaimed.

"Me neither," I admitted.

We stood side by side and relished the joy of watching the pod effortlessly surf the roll wave.

Elena broke into a wolf howl, hoping to connect with the dialect of the dolphins. We all bent over laughing. Then we listened.

There was magic in the air. Something we'd never experienced was happening between the dolphin pod and us. The quieter we became, the more we felt it. The dolphins knew something that we needed to know. I wanted to know what it was.

Beyond the expanse of what I knew my world to be, I looked at the dolphin pod and saw its symbol of hope.

"That's it!" I exclaimed. "We'll be like a dolphin pod. We'll travel together like they do. And we can protect each other from all the sharks that want to tear us apart."

It was clear that my friends understood what I had seen in the dolphins.

"I read that when one dolphin in a pod is injured, two healthy dolphins immediately come to help. They swim under the dolphin in trouble and support her with their flippers. Then they bring the dolphin to the surface so she can catch her breath," Katie added excitedly. "They help each other when times are tough."

"It's like they have a strong connection with each other," Elena said. "They know how to be friends—just like we do."

"Yeah, they don't leave each other when the going gets tough," I said. "Instead, they show up for each other. See, Rosie, I was right. We've got each other. You don't need your mother!"

CHAPTER 7

broken pieces

As I prepared to leave for the beach one afternoon, a police car pulled up in front of the house. I peered out the living-room window, and my stomach churned as I watched two policemen help Dad out of the back of the car, escorting him up the sidewalk toward the front door. For the past two years I hadn't seen much of dad as he tried to get his act together.

Torn with conflicting emotions, my first thought was to run to the door to meet him. *Do I really want to see him?* I asked myself, my heart pounding like a drum.

As the trio reached the steps, I realized for the first time that my fear of Dad loomed stronger than my desire to be with him.

"Gino, Dad's here!" I hollered up the stairs. Gino locked himself in his room.

As I opened the front door, my eyes immediately locked with Dad's.

"Your daddy can't live here no more, Bella," he sobbed. "Your mother got a restraining order against me. They say I can't see you kids no more. I'm doing better, though. I just needed some time to work things out. I think I'll die if I have to live alone."

I wanted to tell him not to leave. I wanted him to go back to

being the father I knew as a child. I wanted him to be happy again.

The policemen followed Dad to his room. I stood in the hall as he packed his clothes into a brown suitcase.

I watched helplessly while Dad closed the lid of his suitcase. One of the policemen nudged him to hurry up. Dad lifted the over-stuffed case off the bed and headed toward me.

"Don't forget your daddy loves you, Bella!" he said through choked tears. Wrapping me in his embrace, he kissed my forehead. "I want you to come live with me," he whispered quietly in my ear.

Dazed and numb, I followed them downstairs and silently watched as they walked out the front door. I knew he wouldn't be coming back, not ever.

The door slammed shut behind him. I leaned against the wall and slid down to the living-room floor. A deep sadness filled every place inside my body. For the first time in years, I let the tears pour out. In a minute, with the packing of a suitcase, my already mixed-up world turned pitch-black.

A few days later I turned sixteen. A birthday card arrived from Dad with five one-hundred-dollar bills in it. He also included his new address and phone number. The last two sentences on the card jolted me: "Bella, please think about living with your dad. I don't think I can go on if I have to live alone."

Gino and my sisters had written Dad off by this time, but I couldn't do it. I wasn't sure why we had this special bond, but I knew I was the only one who could help him.

I went to the beach to think about what to do. My tiny alcove in the side of the cliff had become like home to me ever since the days I would run away as a small child. Over the years I ran away more than a hundred times, and I almost always went to the same place.

There, a comforting peace covered me as I breathed in the refreshing air laced with seaweed and salt. Seagulls sailed in the wind, eager for any trace of food. I stretched out on the cool, green ice plant that blanketed the hillside. With Ripple cuddled beside me, I rested my head on my arms and gazed down to the beach below from my lofty hiding place.

I thought about a dream I'd had the night before.

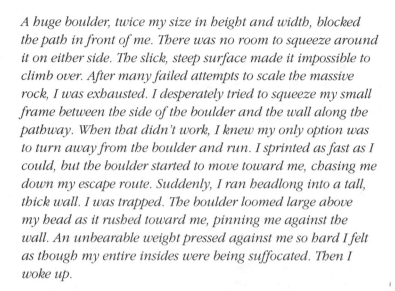

A huge boulder, twice my size in height and width, blocked the path in front of me. There was no room to squeeze around it on either side. The slick, steep surface made it impossible to climb over. After many failed attempts to scale the massive rock, I was exhausted. I desperately tried to squeeze my small frame between the side of the boulder and the wall along the pathway. When that didn't work, I knew my only option was to turn away from the boulder and run. I sprinted as fast as I could, but the boulder started to move toward me, chasing me down my escape route. Suddenly, I ran headlong into a tall, thick wall. I was trapped. The boulder loomed large above my head as it rushed toward me, pinning me against the wall. An unbearable weight pressed against me so hard I felt as though my entire insides were being suffocated. Then I woke up.

My dreams often helped me understand how I felt about what was going on in my life. This dream came over and over again. At the time, it was a way for me to express the pressure I felt to take care of my dad while not knowing what to do with my life. I felt trapped, hemmed in on all sides.

The peaceful ocean lay before me as far as my eyes could see while the sun warmed my entire body, but I wanted more. I begged the sun to shine its light inside me and not abandon me to the approaching darkness.

For hours I tried to figure out what to do as I watched the waves roll into shore. Eventually the invitation of the water became irresistible. Ripple swam with me in the small roll waves close to shore. I let each wave carry me wherever it wanted to take me. Engulfed in nothing but water, I felt nurtured and completely relaxed. In the rhythm of the roll wave I didn't have to worry about where I had been or where I was going.

I felt that as long as I could get on my board and be in the water, I would be able to make it through this season of my life, a scary time that seemed determined to crush the life out of me. For me, the ocean symbolized openness and life even when my world felt as if it was closing in around me.

* * *

A few weeks later I met Chip to surf. Trying to ride the waves lifted me to the realm of pure freedom. Multiple shades of blue blended with the continuing rush of pounding waves. For those few hours, nothing else in the whole world mattered.

"Let the wave pick you up," Chip coached.

"I'm trying. But every time I miss the wave, I get hammered before I can get positioned again."

"Paddle faster."

"I'm paddling as fast as I can. The waves are coming in so close together."

The waves grew larger. We pressed past the bigger waves to get to deeper water. As a huge swell crashed down upon us, we gripped our boards and flipped upside down under the wave. Our boards floated on the surface above us while we waited until the rush of the water swept overhead, glancing off the bottom side of the board. As the rush released, we rolled back, gasping for fresh air.

Unexpectedly, the current began to change. A huge swell peaked in front of us, coming in faster than we had anticipated. We rolled under our boards hoping the swell would wash over us, but we timed it wrong. The massive wave crashed down on top of us with full force. The power of the water threw us off our boards and into a tailspin deep under the crashing wave.

Searching for the surface, I knew I'd lost my bearings. I broke through the surface just as another wave crashed down and ripped me into its vortex. I wrestled with the water, trying to get free from its grip. I held my breath as long as I could until my head finally broke the surface of the water again. Gasping for air, I struggled against the pounding waves to get back on my board.

I realized I had been pulled into a riptide. I remembered what Chip had taught me: *Stay calm. If you fight it you'll get pulled under. Look at the water. If you swim parallel for a while you'll get out of its grip. Once you're out of it, swim to shore.*

In only a few minutes the strong current swept me south toward Fort Funston, separating me from Chip. He made it back to shore

while I paddled vigorously, trying to break free from the current's pull. I feared becoming food for a shark that might be hiding in the darkness. Finally out of the riptide, I caught a wave that carried me safely back to shore.

Dizzily walking out of the water, I shook my long golden hair out of its ponytail and gazed up at the bluff. I'd made it to shore right below the cliff that guarded my favorite spot in the hillside.

As I looked down at the sandy beach, I heard Dad's voice filter through a distant memory in my mind. "Slow down, Bella, you're running too fast. I can't keep up with you anymore." I tried to shake off the image.

Suddenly my heart started pounding. *Is that Dad's car?* As I strained to see in the dim light, I saw a car that looked exactly like Dad's in the parking lot overlooking the beach.

I panicked. I stood as close to the cliff's surface as possible and hoped it would conceal me until I could figure out what to do.

Leaning my surfboard against the side of the cliff, I carefully climbed up the steep hill. Once on the path, I sneaked around and hid behind some thick bushes a few yards from the parked cars.

As I peered through the leaves, my heart skipped a beat. *It is Dad's car, and he's in it.* I saw him bury his head in his hands. His sobbing was barely audible over the sound of the ocean waves breaking onto the shore below.

Did he see me? I wondered. *Was he watching me surf?* I sank to my knees and stayed behind the bush. Closing my eyes, I tried to block out the pitiful scene playing out before me. Part of me wanted to go to him. I wanted to be his little girl again.

I looked down the bluff and thought back to a time ten years before when we had stood there together. Dad, strong and hand-some. Me, small and spirited. We walked barefoot in the sand, lis-tening to the waves roll into shore carrying all our troubles away. The wind blew, and I brushed the sand out of my eyes. Dad reached for my hand and tenderly swallowed it in his. His warmth flowed all the way under my skin. I knew he would take care of me forever.

I opened my eyes, and I knew those days were gone for good. *I don't know who he is anymore. I don't know if I can trust him. I don't know if he is bad or good.* Confusion swept over me. I needed to break free from the turbulent waters of his tormented life.

I slowly turned and walked away. I made no contact with Dad after that. I would count on no one but myself and my friends. Yet as I did, a wave of guilt heavier than Dad himself threatened to push me under with every stroke I swam away from his side.

* * *

I found Chip on the beach, and soon our friends showed up for our nightly ritual of watching the sunset together.

We all paused in silence, getting ready to count down the last seconds of the sun's final descent. Together, we counted slowly out loud, "Ten, nine, eight, seven, six, five, four, three, two, one. Gone."

Breaking into a good California beach-bum howl, we held hands and started dancing wildly along the shore to the music of Bob Dylan pumping from the hippies' vans.

Minutes later, we stretched our feet into the coming tide as the horizon blazed with spectacular streaks of purple and orange. The sea that hours earlier had raged around us settled into a steady, calm rhythm. I wanted to capture the scene spread out before me and hold on to it.

Ripple trotted past us with a big starfish flopping from his mouth. We all laughed at the funny sight. It reminded me of a story my dad told me when I was a kid. I told what I could remember to my friends.

"A long time ago the nighttime sky was filled with bright, shining stars. All we had to do was look up to their light to help us find our way. There were so many zillions of stars to look up to that no one ever got lost. Then one day, some of the stars forgot how to shine for each other.

"One by one, many of them broke and fell from the sky. They landed in the sea. Some people call them starfish, but they're really ocean stars. They're on a journey to learn how to get put back together again. Once they do, they turn back into a star, shining for others the way they were designed to. So if you ever find an ocean star, make sure to be kind and gentle. It's trying to find its way home."

Elena gasped. "Go get the starfish!"

Chip and I almost tripped over a sand castle a few children were building as we chased after Ripple to rescue the ocean star. Taking it out of Ripple's mouth, I brushed off the sand and marveled at the multitude of patterns depicting its life's journey.

"Chip, part of it is broken, but it's still alive," I observed.

"That's what's so cool about a starfish. As long as it's in the ocean, connected to its source of life, it will grow back any piece that gets damaged along the way."

"Wow, that's so amazing!" I said, admiring its intricate design. "If only it were that easy for us. We'd just live the rest of our life in the water."

"Not a bad idea," Chip said with a chuckle.

"Hurry, throw it back in the ocean!" Elena hollered, catching up to us. I clutched it in my hand like a Frisbee and flung it as hard as I could, sending the ocean star back to sea.

CHAPTER 8

look up

I spent the next two years of high school wandering from one seem-ingly thrilling adventure to another, including skiing, surfing, and cross-country running. I worked a few jobs here and there that pro-vided enough spending money for most things I needed. Rosie, Elena, Katie, and I kept hanging out with the hippies at the beach. I continued to numb my emptiness with drugs and sought on-the-edge experiences that provided an exciting reason for living. I had no curfew and followed no rules. With my father out of the house, my two oldest sisters away at college, and my youngest sister living with a friend, Gino and I were left pretty much to ourselves. My mother worked downtown and lived her own life completely detached from us. That was fine with me—the less I saw her the better. At least that way I didn't have to listen to her critical words. I came and went as I wanted, and no one ever knew the difference. But the freedom I had craved only turned into the bondage of forced self-sufficiency.

With only a few months until high school graduation, I often wondered if I would even graduate since school had always been my lowest priority.

Ripple and I often headed off to Lake Tahoe in my old red

Volkswagen. I passed the ski-instructor courses and often worked the slopes on the weekends. Ripple even went to the slopes with me and became the mascot of Heavenly Valley. More weeks than not, I skipped school on Mondays to stay up on the mountain to ski.

During one particular weekend, I won the first round in the ski competition for my level. To participate in the later rounds, I had to miss an entire week of school.

Monday morning, I woke up as usual to take my five-mile run before heading off to the slopes for the next round in the competition. Ripple and I started running along a path by the lake. As we rounded a bend, three guys on bicycles came speeding toward us. I dove to the left into the bushes. Ripple veered off the other direction into the road.

Suddenly a car slammed into him, throwing him across the street.

"Ripple!" I screamed.

I looked around, desperate for someone to help me. The empty roads echoed my scream. Walking out to the middle of the road, I burst into tears. I gently picked up Ripple's bloody, limp body and carried him to the edge of the running trail.

"Ripple, you can't die!"

Burying my head in his soft fur, I forced myself to face the truth before me. He didn't move. He didn't make a sound. My faithful friend was dead. Despair welled up inside me as tears poured from my eyes onto his lifeless body lying in my lap.

That evening, I buried Ripple down by the lake across from the ski resort. I marked his grave with a cross made from sticks and sat down beside it. Holding the green bandana I used for his collar, I said my last good-byes.

Skiing in the competition all day and getting high that night helped numb the loss of Ripple. But neither drugs nor placing second in the final competition staved off the sadness I felt. Gino's phone call Thursday night only deepened the pit I found myself in.

"The principal's not going to let you back in this time!" Gino blurted out over the phone. "You've been expelled! Now what are you going to do?"

"Big deal! Everything is such a bummer right now. . . . I'm really thinking about staying up here."

"Come on, Christina, you've been gone over a week. Besides, I don't want to bum you out anymore, but Chip's not doing well. He went back in the hospital. He needs you to come back and cheer him up."

Although I didn't let Gino know it, being expelled from high school, coupled with hearing the news about Chip, shook me up.

As I thought about flunking out of school, I began to feel like a total failure. I realized I'd blown it. I suddenly found myself wishing I knew someone who could help me figure out what to do. I wished I could go home and find the lights on and someone I liked waiting for me. But I knew that darkness filled the house—and no one was home.

I headed back from Tahoe the next morning hoping to cheer up Chip. Gino met me on the front steps of our house as I carried my skis up the sidewalk. One look in his eyes betrayed that something serious had happened.

"Christina, I don't know how to tell you this. Chip's sister called. Chip died this morning."

The words sounded hollow in my ears. Slowly sitting down on the front steps, I cupped my head tightly in my hands. Gino sat beside me in silence, his eyes filling with tears.

"Why? Why did God let Chip die? He was so young," I cried, wiping the tears from my face. "He was my friend, Gino." Burying my head in my hands, I wept for what seemed like hours. Gino put his arm around me and sat by my side.

"Why is life so hard?" I asked through my tears. "How come all this bad stuff keeps happening? Did I do something wrong, Gino? I don't understand!"

"I don't know why," Gino admitted reluctantly. "I don't know why life is so hard either."

"Gino, I don't know if I can handle this! I feel like my brain is going to blow up."

"The only thing I know to do is get high and try to numb the feeling. There's nothing else we can do."

Later that day, Miss Bianchi, my senior counselor, called the house and asked me to meet with her that afternoon. Before now, I had not been cooperative with her or any of my other teachers. I

didn't trust Miss Bianchi. In fact, I didn't trust anyone, especially women.

Why does she want to see me now? I wondered as I arrived outside her door.

I nervously sat down in the blue chair facing her. I didn't really like her short haircut or preppy clothes. She got up and walked around her desk to sit in the chair right next to mine. I felt uncomfortable having her so close. Scooting my chair over, I took a deep breath and asked, "Why did you want to see me?"

"Christina, I know this is a rough time for you. I'm sorry to hear about Chip's death. I know he was a close friend of yours. Why don't you take the next couple of days to be with your friends? Then I'd like to see you here first thing Monday morning. We are going to come up with a plan for you to get your diploma."

Although I didn't really understand why, I nodded my head in agreement.

After the meeting ended, I drove to the beach, hoping the breeze and surf would wash away the pain of losing Chip and Ripple. Cranking up one of Chip's favorite songs, "The Times They Are A-Changin'," I drove through Golden Gate Park to my ocean haven. Skirting the water's edge, I ran mile after mile, thinking I'd never stop. Bob Dylan's song about change played over and over in my head.

Why can't anything stay the same? I wondered. *Why does everybody end up leaving?*

Yet the more I thought about it, the more I realized I didn't want anything to be the same. What I really wanted was for people to change, not leave. But I couldn't change people. I couldn't change my situation. I could only change me.

* * *

Monday morning I kept my meeting as promised with Miss Bianchi. True to her word, she mapped out a plan of action for me. She asked me to do the impossible—study! Every teacher gave me a certain amount of work that needed to be done by graduation. If I completed the work, I would satisfy the requirements and graduate with the rest of my class.

"I don't know if I'll be able to pass," I said hesitantly.

"How do you know?" Miss Bianchi responded. "Up to this point it doesn't appear to me that you've even tried. I have a feeling you are capable of a lot more than you think you are."

Chills ran up my back as her words found their way inside my heart to some potential she knew I possessed. She put it out there on the table, and I could almost see it.

She gave one more stipulation before she set the plan in motion: "You must agree that you will go to college," she told me.

"College?" I balked. "Are you kidding? I figured it would be a miracle if I could graduate from high school."

She took out a big map of California to show me some of the junior colleges around the state. "Are there ski resorts near any of those?" I asked curiously.

"There's one in Mount Shasta, which is five hours north of here."

"It's a deal," I said, picking up a red pin and sticking it in the map. "I'll go there."

The next three months I "lived" in the library. Rosie often met me there to work on her graduation speech while I attacked my schoolwork with newfound determination.

"Mom gets drunk almost every night," Rosie confided one afternoon as we plodded through our studies. "Every time I walk in the door she reminds me that I've ruined her life."

"You need to get out of there, Rosie."

"But, Christina, what if she's right? I can't get her words out of my mind. If I were never born, Dad would still be here, and Mom's life would be perfect. Sometimes I feel like it would be better if I simply disappeared."

"Rosie, you have *got* to tune her out. You can make it without her. Life will get better. You'll see."

Two weeks before graduation, I actually felt as if I would receive my diploma. I worked diligently to fulfill all my requirements by the end of the three months.

That Monday morning, I couldn't wait to see Rosie to tell her how much work I'd finished, but she didn't show up for our regular rendezvous before the homeroom bell rang.

About a half hour after class began, Miss Bianchi appeared at the

door and motioned for the teacher. After a short discussion, Mrs. McCall asked me to follow Miss Bianchi to her office.

"Christina, I want you to sit down," Miss Bianchi said gently.

Taking a chair by her desk, I wondered if I wouldn't graduate after all.

"I have terrible news," Miss Bianchi said quietly. "There's no easy way to tell you this. Last night, your friend Rosie committed suicide. They don't know if drugs were involved."

"What? What did she do?"

"She jumped from the Golden Gate Bridge."

I sat frozen in the chair, unable to move or speak. I wanted to throw up.

"Christina, do you know what caused Rosie to do this?"

Mountains of frustration and anger exploded from deep within me. "Yes, I know!" I screamed. "Her mother drove her crazy! When Rosie's dad died in the car accident, her mom put all the blame on Rosie. She made her crazy!"

Miss Bianchi stepped close to try to calm me. I jumped from the chair and stormed out the office door.

"I've got to get out of here."

"Stop! Talk to me! Do you have anyone helping you?"

"Helping me with what?" I sassed. "I don't need any help!"

Miss Bianchi hollered down the hallway after me, "Help with your life, with school, with what you're going to do next year?"

I angrily turned to face her. "No! I can take care of myself. I'm used to it!"

I ran down the hall and out the main doors of the school. My old Volkswagen painted with large daisies found its way to Baker Beach, south of the Golden Gate Bridge. As I stood alone in the shadow of the mighty expanse, questions flooded my mind in torrents.

"Why do women have children if they don't want them?" I shouted for all to hear.

Overcome with the image of Rosie near the edge of the bridge, I could almost see her mother standing behind her shouting negative remarks. Each critical word pushed Rosie closer and closer to the edge until her mother's voice finally shoved her over.

"No! Rosie, don't jump!" I shouted toward the bridge. "Don't give up! Don't listen to her!" I pleaded until tears burst out and I could barely breathe.

Weak in the knees, I found a large rock and sat down. Burying my head in my lap, I sobbed, aware only of the unbearable reality that Rosie had killed herself.

"Why did you give up, Rosie?" I cried. "You should have tuned your mother out. You can't let yourself feel those feelings if you're going to make it!"

I faced the bridge again. "Couldn't you see your life mattered?" I whispered through my moans. "Your life mattered to me, Rosie," I assured her as I weakly pounded my chest with my fist. "Your life mattered to me."

Tears flowed freely as I gazed at the instrument Rosie chose to end her life. Emotionally drained, I sat at the water's edge wrapping my arms around my knees. The morning and afternoon drifted by barely noticed as I struggled to come to terms with the reality that I'd never see Rosie again. I cried and cried until I thought I'd never stop crying. But then I stopped. No more tears came—only a paralyzing sadness like a dark, heavy blanket wrapped around my soul. As I stared blankly at the waves rolling into shore, I lost myself in the soothing motion of each swell, hoping its nurturing comfort would wash away my weighty burden with its changing tide. I sat alone at the water's edge watching the horizon until the last traces of daylight had drained away.

The clear blue sky formed a crisp backdrop as the huge orange ball ever so gently touched the surface of the ocean far in the distance. Ripple was gone. Chip was gone. Rosie was gone. As the sun began its descent below the horizon, the sound of my solitary voice echoed eerily off the water as I slowly counted out loud alone. "Ten, nine, eight, seven, six . . ." I stopped and then began again. "Five, four, three, two, one. Gone."

I stretched out my legs to allow the soothing water to touch my skin. I closed my eyes. I wanted to be gone too—somewhere far away from all the pain and emptiness and confusion.

The walls I had built around myself to tune out the negative voices started to crumble with Rosie's choice to give up. Was I fooling myself?

Was I really bad and not worth anything? Would it have been better if I had never been born? Did my life matter to anyone?

That's ridiculous! If my life matters to me and me alone, that should be reason enough to live.

I resolved to build the walls higher and thicker. I tuned out the negative voices behind the gate and threw away the key. I wasn't going to listen to them.

As I lifted my head, I noticed the sun had painted a kaleidoscope of color across the sky. Shades of brilliant orange, pink, and purple filled the heavens as if an artist had painted a brilliant masterpiece there. The deeper the sun slipped below the water, the brighter the colors glowed in the sky above.

As I focused on the majestic strokes spread across the horizon, a peaceful feeling that I recognized swept over me. Closing my eyes for a moment, I felt a serene presence standing in front of me. I listened.

Calming words of hope found their way deep into my heart: *Don't focus on the darkness of the disappearing sun. Look up at the color I can paint with your life.*

As the last remnants of color faded from the horizon, the first stars of evening dotted the darkening sky. I thought about all the stars that had lost their light and fallen from the sky.

"I promise you, Rosie, if I ever figure out how to put all the broken pieces back together again, I will be a star that shines for others so that other people like you and me will have someone who is willing to be a light for them. Whatever I do, I'll do it for both of us."

* * *

Elena convinced me to go to a concert the following weekend. Looking into the eyes of those dancing around me, I saw people stumbling blindly down a road leading nowhere. There was no light in their eyes. There was no purpose to their lives.

Do they know where they're going? Do they care? I wondered.

Every once in a while a hippie friend pinched me, startling me out of my deepening thoughts. "Lighten up! No need to worry. Let the music take all your troubles away."

I smiled back, knowing a shift was taking place inside of me. My path was drifting from this place. What did I want anyway? I didn't know. I only knew I didn't want to be numb.

A better life resided out there somewhere. There was no one guiding me, so I determined to guide myself.

A few weeks later, the moment of truth arrived. I stood in the procession line at my high school graduation ceremony, waiting for my name to be called so I could receive my diploma. Every teacher had passed me except my English teacher. She insisted the quality of my work exceeded my capabilities and that I must have had a friend do it for me. If she decided not to pass me, I couldn't receive a diploma.

Careful not to get my hopes too high, I trudged forward in the long line. I wore the strand of dime-store pearls that Lily had given me as a child. Lifting my hand to the beads around my neck, I nervously ran my finger over each one as I waited to hear my name.

"Christina Alisa Isabella DiMari." The sound of my name snapped me back to the present. I took a deep breath and stepped forward to take my diploma. I smiled at Gino as I walked back to my seat. Elena and Katie waited nervously, wondering if I'd get it after all. Nonchalantly, I looked down and opened up the bright red cover. It was empty.

Oh no! I thought silently. *All that work for nothing!*

As we stood for the procession out of the huge cathedral, I bit my lip and avoided eye contact with anyone, for fear I'd start crying. But when I stepped into the sunlight, I saw my counselor running up the steps as fast as she could, frantically waving a big piece of paper.

"I've got it," Miss Bianchi cried. "I've got it! It took some work to convince the board that you really did do the work, but I did it!"

"Are you sure?" I asked. "Oh, thank you!"

As I looked into her eyes I gathered strength from her faith in me. Somehow Miss Bianchi was able to see past my struggle to survive. She didn't see the loser that my mother saw. She saw something else, and I wanted to see it too.

All my pent-up anxiety and emotion burst forth. I found myself

laughing and crying all at the same time. Elena and Katie ran to my side, shouting loud enough for the whole city to hear.

"Yeah, baby!" Gino howled, running to lift me up in a bear hug. He spun me around. "You did it, Christina!" he shouted, giving me a high five.

In many ways, earning my diploma gave me the assurance that my life had some direction. Perhaps this represented my ticket out of the maze I had wandered through for many years.

Grateful Dead's song "Ripple" encouraged me as well. The lyrics spoke of a road that would not be easy to travel between the dawn and dark of night. Sometimes you have to take that road even if it means you must travel it alone.

Perhaps the road that lay ahead symbolized the bridge between the darkness of my past and the dawn of a bright future. Even if no one journeyed with me, I determined to find the bridge alone. I repeated the words that would throw a beam of light onto my dark path as I traveled onward from this place: *Don't focus on the darkness of the disappearing sun. Look up at the color I can paint with your life.*

CHAPTER 9

life's a trip

"Where've you been—China?" Frankie asked as I bounded up the steps. After my family blowup, I went through most of high school without seeing much of my grandparents. It felt good to be with them again, even if it was just to say good-bye.

"No, Frankie, for the first time I really am going somewhere!" I told my grandfather with excitement. "I leave for college tomorrow."

"All the way to Mount Shasta? Don't you stay gone too long," he said with his usual smirk.

As Lily squeezed me hard in one of her trademark hugs, she whispered, "Write me a letter when you get there, Christina."

Frankie waited for me at the front door. I tenderly kissed him on each cheek, then turned and dashed down the front steps as Gino and Anna pulled up in Gino's brand-new, shiny black Mercedes to pick me up for lunch at Fisherman's Wharf. I laughed at Gino's flashy appearance. He looked so much like Dad, but he hated Dad. I kept my thoughts to myself.

Anna had come home from San Diego to say good-bye. Gino had taken off from his job as a wine distributor to meet us for lunch.

Snacking on fresh shrimp, Anna brought us up to date on her life in San Diego, where she worked as a nurse at Children's

Hospital. We were a captive audience as Anna told us story after story about the children she worked with in the pediatric intensive care unit.

"Last week I took care of a six-year-old girl named Leah," Anna began. "She had a tumor wrapped around her trachea and struggled with her breathing. The doctor and I explained to her parents that the morphine dose Leah needed to control her pain was so large that soon she wouldn't have the strength to continue her labored breathing. We had to tell her mom and dad that Leah would probably die soon." Anna paused momentarily to compose herself.

"Her parents went in and sat with Leah, explaining to her that she was going to get to go to heaven and see her grandma and grandpa really soon. Leah understood she was going to die. Later that day, her mom and dad went down to the cafeteria to eat. Leah asked if I'd climb into bed with her and hold her. We're trained not to get emotionally involved, but I lay beside her in the bed. She wrapped her arms around my chest and tucked her head gently into the groove of my neck. I held her close. A few minutes later, she looked up at me and whispered, 'Anna, they're here to get me. I'm going to go see my grandma and grandpa now.' I asked her, 'Who is here to get you?' She smiled softly. Then she said, 'The angels. They're at the end of my bed. Two of them came to get me.' She hugged me as I looked down to the end of her bed. I didn't see anyone. When I turned back to look at her, she died, right there in my arms. They took her."

Tears streamed down our cheeks as Anna finished the story. I wondered what would happen to me when I died. Would angels be there for me?

Listening to this story brought me back to my own experience as a child. I had always believed in God, but I didn't really understand how believing in him made all that much difference to us while we lived on the earth. Deep down, I think Gino wanted to believe in God, too, but he got all tangled up in blaming God for my parents' bad choices. Anna didn't blame God. She was more like me. We simply didn't really know how believing in him could make our life any different in the day-to-day stuff.

Anna loved what she chose to do with her life. She'd moved to San Diego, finished nursing school, and now helped children in crisis at the hospital. Her stories sparked something inside me. *Perhaps someday I'll help little kids as well,* I thought to myself.

At the end of lunch Anna leaned forward and looked Gino and me straight in the eyes. "I'm worried about you two."

"Why?" we both asked defensively.

Focusing on Gino, Anna said, "You know that guy last year who overdosed on drugs? You think that's not going to happen to you. But I'll bet you he didn't think that would happen to him either."

"I'm not going to OD," Gino blurted out.

Sitting back quietly in my chair, I listened as Anna continued. "That guy couldn't find the door to freedom because he got into the habit of knocking on the only door he saw—drugs. He couldn't see that drugs would never provide a permanent escape. They tricked his mind into thinking he'd escaped, but every time he came off the high he was right back where he started. Think about a person who suffers from kidney failure. After dialysis cleanses his system, he begins to feel good. But as soon as the benefits of dialysis wear off, he feels miserable again, not to mention that he's in danger of dying. His only hope for a cure is a transplant."

Gino and I both looked at each other and started laughing. The analogy was way over our heads.

"Oh, Anna, I don't need a transplant!" Gino mocked.

"I'm serious," Anna said. "You need to fix the original problem, not merely relieve the symptoms. That's how you are with drugs. All that pot you smoke, the cocaine, and whatever else the two of you are taking is messing you up. You do it to give you temporary relief from a life you want to run from. If you keep taking drugs, you will drive yourselves right down a dark path, and you'll never find your door to a better life. It's time to figure out how you want to live your life. No one can make you stop doing drugs but yourself. The choice is up to you."

I knew Gino needed that lecture. He partied really hard almost every night. But my situation was different. I had been smoking marijuana pretty much every day throughout high school, but I never really thought much about it or thought it was something bad. I figured at least it wasn't LSD or something that could kill you.

The drugs I take aren't hurting me, I thought silently, trying to reassure myself. *I only do them to have fun. Besides, I can't ski unless I'm high. It's all part of the experience. Anyway, I'm heading off for college. I'm making good choices.*

Gino smirked and started singing a song about how he didn't know where he'd be tomorrow or if he'd ever make it home again. We all started laughing as the tension broke.

"You better listen to me, Gino! I'm serious!" Anna ordered, trying to regain her composure.

"Oh, Anna, relax!" Gino scolded. "You're not my mother."

"Yeah, well, you better listen to me because I'm the closest thing you've got."

The next morning, I found myself in Elena's old blue Volkswagen. As we headed north on Interstate 5 I began to understand how Anna had felt when she found her ticket out of the past. *Now it's my turn,* I thought.

Cranking up the tape deck, we belted out our favorite song by the group Little Feat. We rolled down our windows and shouted the lyrics to "Spanish Moon."

Four hours later we gassed up in the small town of Dunsmuir, California. As we got back on the road, I spent the next fifteen minutes checking our map, making sure we were heading toward our destination.

"What's that?" Elena asked, pointing ahead. The cloud cover broke to the north, revealing spectacular scenery before us.

Looming some fourteen thousand feet above the plains and foothills of Northern California stood Mount Shasta. Awesome in its enormity, this remote sentinel of snow and granite had at its base— among other things—the college I'd pegged with a red pin in Miss Bianchi's office months before.

As we drove into the small mountain town, I immediately felt at home. The locals looked like hippies who had migrated right from Haight Asbury in San Francisco to this quaint community nestled on California's northern border. Old buildings housing health-food stores and New Age bookstores lined the street.

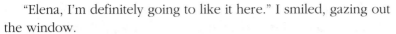

"Elena, I'm definitely going to like it here." I smiled, gazing out the window.

"Shoot, I wish my job didn't start tomorrow," Elena complained.

"I know. I wish you could stay up here and go to school with me."

Our final stop was one exit north. As the town of Shasta disappeared in our rearview mirror, two sets of eyes excitedly peered forward looking for the Weed exit.

"There it is!" I shouted. "Weed! Can you believe I'm going to college in a town named Weed?"

We giggled the rest of the way down the exit ramp. Minutes later Elena dropped me at College of the Siskiyous's main building. Although it was hard to say good-bye, Elena had to return to San Francisco to get ready to start working at the art museum the following day. As she drove away, she leaned out the window and shouted, "Life's a trip!"

I smiled, then added the finishing line to our dolphin-pod trademark saying: "Enjoy the ride!"

With seven hundred dollars in my pocket and a bag in each hand, I walked into the admissions office.

"May I help you?" the lady at the desk queried.

"I'm enrolled here to start school," I answered. "I just got into town. What do I do now?"

"Who's your counselor?" she asked.

"I don't know."

"What's your major?"

"I don't know."

"Well, usually new students are matched with a guidance counselor to decide their course of study," she replied, trying to contain a smile. Stepping around her desk, she led me out her door and down the hall to the drama classroom. Mr. Barnes, the drama instructor, also doubled as one of the guidance counselors.

Three hippie guys in their late twenties hung out in his room.

"Christina, this is Russell, Dave, and Howard," Mr. Barnes began. "They're friends of mine who work with me in the drama department."

"Drama?" I replied. "I don't want to be in—like—plays!"

"Well, what do you want to study?" Mr. Barnes questioned.

"I don't know. I think you're the guy who's supposed to show me my options."

Half an hour later, I'd chosen my classes: cross-country running, skiing, jazz dance, outdoor survival, nutrition, and world religions. I couldn't believe no one cared that I didn't schedule any math or science courses. Miss Bianchi had helped me apply for a grant that provided all my school expenses for the year. Life looked good.

"Where are you going to live during the school year?" Mr. Barnes asked as he finished up my course plan.

"I don't know. I hoped to figure it out when I got here."

"The dorms are full, but we've got a spare room for rent at our place," Russell offered, speaking for his two roommates in the room. "It's small, but it only costs thirty-five dollars a month."

"That sounds great!" I said. "I'll take it."

The room was very small, hardly big enough to fit a small mattress and a trunk of clothes. One tiny window thankfully allowed some morning sun into my small "cave."

Russell, Dave, and Howard were the most eccentric three guys I had ever met. I hoped I would be safe living in their house.

During my first months of school I enjoyed meeting new people and exploring mountain trails. After the first snow of the winter, I attended a huge outdoor ski party at the base of a nearby ski resort. The sound of Grateful Dead tunes blared from the speakers as I rode the chairlift up the mountain.

"Oooow! I love this music!" the girl next to me howled.

"Me too," I said with a smile.

We shared a little about our lives. I told her about my dog and how I had named him after the Grateful Dead song "Ripple."

"They're playing up in Seattle next month," she mentioned. "Do you want to hitchhike with me up to see them?"

"Uh, yeah," I said hesitantly, not having hitchhiked before. By the time Tashina and I reached the summit, I knew I'd found a new friend. An instant connection flowed between us as though we'd known each other forever, even though we'd just met. She looked like she could be my sister. Her long brown hair shimmered in the sun as she got ready to ski down the mountain.

Once off the chairlift we stood on top of the mountain for a few moments and took in the breathtaking view in all directions. The royal blue skyline created a crisp backdrop for the stark white-covered slopes. The bright sun danced off the fresh-fallen powder. Snow-flecked trees carpeted the mountainside, glistening in the brilliant sunlight. The sun's warm rays penetrated my skin and rejuvenated my body. The scent of pine trees filled the air. Snow falling from the towering trees, standing like warriors of a distant land, broke the calm silence of the summit.

I'd imagined this moment my entire life. The vista spread before me sealed a promise of hope within my heart. Perhaps my life really could find a fresh start. I embraced my new beginning with a joyful, adventurous spirit.

As we made our way to the steep edge of the mountain, I couldn't wait to fly.

Two ski patrollers scanned the run as we approached our launching point. "You girls ready for the ultimate risk of your life?"

"Yes!" I announced without hesitation.

Looking in every direction, Tashina said, "It doesn't look like anyone's even gone down this run yet."

"Plenty of people came to check it out, but their nerves got the best of them," the buff ski-patrol guy said.

"Yep. Too many people deciding to play it safe," Tashina said, pumping up her nerves.

"Life's too short to play it safe," I said. Slipping the tips of my skis over the rim of the peak's crust, I turned and smiled. "Sometimes you've just got to go for it!"

With the rush of adrenaline bursting through my veins and one push with my poles, I launched myself over the cliff, flying into the air and down onto the soft powder below. The snow under my feet cushioned my skis as I sliced through the brisk alpine wind. Down through the open bowl I flew, blazing my trail down the ungroomed side of the mountain like a streak of lightning.

Tashina and I seemed like one soul living in two different bodies. We quickly became best friends, enjoyed our classes and skiing, and dove into the rapidly growing health-nut craze. Often our adventurous spirits felt stifled living in the small mountain community. We squeezed our own fresh juice, threw some clothes and pot into a backpack, and hitchhiked to the closest Grateful Dead concert playing west of the Rocky Mountains. Our adventures on the road provided us with ample opportunity to widen our horizons and meet a variety of interesting people along the way. Tashina was overly trusting of people, but I was overly suspicious, so as long as we stayed together, we kept each other safe.

By the beginning of the second semester in early January, Tashina and I had found a tiny cabin to rent close to school, dated a couple of ski bums, and enjoyed being roommates.

In mid-January, the jazz dance team I performed with invited me to audition for a production of *The Crucible* in Ashland, Oregon, about an hour north of Weed. I landed the lead role of Abigail, a woman accused of being a witch during the Salem witch trials in Massachusetts. Tashina and I decided it would be fun to practice our parts together. We agreed to meet in a wooded area in the afternoon to work on the choreography, scene changes, and our lines. At dusk we built a fire to help extend our practice time. As the fire blazed, we danced around it, chanting our lines and hoping to get more "in character."

Tashina's mom was a churchgoing Christian woman and warned us not to chant lines that were of the "dark side." When she came to town to visit her daughter, she told us that we needed to call upon God's angels to protect us until we could finish that horrible play. At first we laughed her off, but as it came time to chant our lines, she got us spooked. We decided to take her advice and called out for angels instead.

After about an hour, we decided to pack up and head back to town, where the New Age bookstore was throwing a block party complete with music and dancing. Many of the locals had come to live in Shasta because they believed the mountain had special healing powers. Ohana Nanda, one of the many spiritualist leaders who lived in the area, met us as we walked down Main Street.

"Who were you girls dancing with up in the woods?" Ohana Nanda asked in a serious tone.

Tashina and I gave each other a strange look. "What do you mean?" I asked.

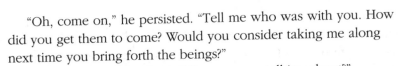

"Oh, come on," he persisted. "Tell me who was with you. How did you get them to come? Would you consider taking me along next time you bring forth the beings?"

"You're crazy!" I laughed. "What are you talking about?"

"A friend of mine saw you dancing around the fire with four men dressed in white," Ohana Nanda explained. "Tell me, is it true? Did they appear and dance with you?"

Tashina and I laughed so hard we almost broke into tears. "No way. You can't possibly believe that!" I said, barely containing myself. "We were only practicing our parts for a play we're in."

"Have no doubt about it," the spiritualist sternly warned us. "Four beings danced with you girls in the woods. They could have been from the spirit world, but you were not alone."

The week after our encounter with Ohana Nanda, Tashina and I were working in the school cafeteria, where part of our job included tending the salad bar. A girl named Carolyn, on the opposite side of the salad bar, filled her plate while looking at us. Without any warning she leaned over and pointedly asked, "Whose side are you on?"

"What are you talking about?" I asked.

"Simple. Are you on God's side or Satan's side? There are good spirits or angels that belong to God, and there are bad spirits or demons that belong to the devil. We all must decide at some point during our lifetimes which side we will live for. You know, like Bob Dylan's song says, 'You've got to serve somebody.' Well, whose side are you on?"

"I don't know. I've never thought about it before," I responded, somewhat taken aback by her question. "I guess I'm on God's side."

"That's where the devil wants you—guessing but never knowing. If you were on God's side, you would know it. You would know it like you know I am right here talking to you. You would know he's walking with you and watching out for you wherever you go."

Wow! I thought to myself. *That's really heavy-duty.*

"Come on," Tashina said as she pulled me to a different part of the room. "Don't listen to her; she sounds just like my mother. I had to listen to all that mumbo jumbo my whole life. All that hellfire and brimstone scaring you into believing in God could make you fanatical!"

Over the next couple of weeks I couldn't stop thinking about the spirits Ohana Nanda talked about and what Carolyn told me. If there was a way to be sure I was on God's side, I wanted to know what it was.

CHAPTER 10

follow me

Months passed quickly back in Shasta as we neared the end of our school year. Some sort of shift was taking place inside of me although I couldn't explain it very well.

"I don't know," Tashina sighed. "We've been such great friends this whole year, but I feel like you're changing more than I want to. You have all these ideas and plans about what you want to do and where you want to go. I don't think like that. I want to enjoy one day at a time."

"I want to enjoy each day also, but I'll enjoy it more once I get where I'm going."

"Where are you going?" Tashina asked. "What do you want that's so different from what we have now?"

"I'm still not sure. I want something else, but I'm not really sure what it is. I totally love it here in Shasta. But I feel like I'm on a journey, and I haven't gotten where I'm going yet. Anyway, Tashina, this is your first year on your own. I can see why you want to go with it and have fun. I've been on my own since I can remember. I'm ready to find meaning and purpose in life beyond solely having fun and living one day at a time."

Tashina looked at the ground for a while. "What do you want to do?"

"The only thing I know how to do now is ski! I don't know what else to do."

"Oh, lighten up!" Tashina said with a smile. "We're only eighteen. It's not like our lives are almost over. You need to stop thinking about where you're going and instead enjoy living today."

I shook my head in disagreement.

"Tashina, if I do that, I'll be no different tomorrow than I am today. I want to be different. I want you to be different too. We need to look ahead and see how the choices we're making today are affecting where we're going tomorrow."

I was tired of living my life with no direction and purpose. There had to be more.

"Oh, come on!" she said, leaning her head on mine. "Let's go do something wild and fun before you get all straight and boring on me."

I went to my last Grateful Dead concert the next weekend. Tashina moved in with some friends closer to school. With spring in the air, I decided to live in my tent and practice what I learned in my outdoor survival class.

I set up my new home on Lake Siskiyou by the mouth of a mountain stream fed by the melting snow from Mount Shasta. I loved it there. The sound of the water represented change, cleansing, and going forward to something new. The majestic fourteen-thousand-foot peak greeted me each morning as I crawled from my green two-man tent. In the stillness of any moment, the sounds of the wildlife echoed off the water. The fragrance of the pine trees blew in the wind and made every breath fresh with new life. The crystal clear lake shimmered in the early light of dawn from the melted snow high on the mountain. It wasn't the ocean, but it was clean, clear water and a peaceful place to live.

When he learned that I was walking or hitchhiking the couple of miles to school, Ohana Nanda, the spiritualist leader Tashina and I had met, donated an old bicycle to me for transportation.

During the final months of the semester, I spent most of my time at school or out on the slopes. My college course in world religions only served to fuel my growing interest in learning about God.

Carolyn, the girl I had met in the cafeteria, was in my class. As I got to know her, I realized she wasn't as hard-core as she first came across. We enjoyed long conversations about spirituality. I believed in Jesus, but somehow I ended up coming to the conclusion that he had left me just as everyone else had. I wanted to find him again.

"The Bible is a good place to find some answers," Carolyn reminded me one evening as I sipped my hot herbal tea. "You may never figure it all out in your head. It takes faith and trust to believe, and that comes from the heart."

Then she read me Proverbs 3:5-6: "Trust the Lord completely; don't ever trust yourself. In everything you do, put God first, and he will direct you and crown your efforts with success" (TLB).

"I do believe. I just have some questions."

"Why don't you come to church with me? My pastor is really cool. You can talk to him."

"I don't know, Carolyn," I said hesitantly. "Me and church don't go together. I usually feel worse leaving than when I came in."

"Well, I want you to know you are welcome to come with me anytime."

"Okay. I'll think about it."

The following Sunday I decided to give Carolyn's church a shot. It wasn't easy, but I convinced Tashina to come with me.

We walked to the far end of the lake to hitchhike the couple of miles to the ranch where the church group met. The people who owned the ranch had built a small church on the property for a local congregation. Wearing hippie chic dresses, we hesitantly ascended the steps of the building. Pulling open the rough-hewn pine doors, I felt welcomed immediately as several people extended warm greetings to us.

So far, so good, I thought as I sat down in a chair next to Tashina.

A man in his late twenties walked to the front of the room. Sitting on an old wooden stool he strummed his guitar and began to sing: *He gave His life, what more could He give? . . . Oh, how He loves you and me.*[1]

My eyes filled with tears. The emotion stirring deep inside my spirit brought me back to a time when I was younger, sitting at the beach and watching the sunset in the days and months after Chip and Rosie died.

The man with the guitar sang several more songs. As I looked around at the small congregation, I could see that these people sang and talked as if they knew God personally. I wanted to know him that way too.

The pastor, a man about thirty years old, walked to the front as the last song ended. "Have you ever wondered if God knows who you are?" he began. "Have you ever wondered if he cares about what happens to you? In Psalm 139, God tells us he knows when we sit and when we rise, when we go out, and when we come in. God searches the depths of our hearts."

I hung on his every word. I wanted to replay each sentence in my mind again and again. Borrowing a pen and paper from an older lady sitting next to me, I scribbled frantically, trying to capture every word.

"God has not lost track of you," the pastor continued. "He does not live in some faraway place, unaware of who you are. This psalm says he hems you in, before and behind, and he created your 'inmost being.' Have you ever looked up at the nighttime sky and wondered if God thinks about you? He knows each of the countless stars in the sky so intimately that he has named each one. Not one of the most distant stars has been forgotten or misplaced. That is how God looks at us on earth. He knows each one of you seated here today. He knows you so well and so personally that he calls each of you by name. He is calling you because he wants you to know him. . . ."

As the service ended, I sat stunned, trying to take in all I'd experienced and learned in less than an hour. Then I noticed the pastor walking toward us.

"Hi, I'm Pastor Gary," he said, extending his hand. "Is this your first time here?"

"Yes," Tashina said excitedly. "This is way better than any church I've ever been in."

"If you want to know God," he said, smiling, "you won't find him in this building." Handing us each a Bible, he tapped on the

tattered copy under his arm. "You will find him in here." Then he pointed to his heart and said, "And you'll find him in here too."

* * *

Spring was beginning to transform the landscape. I sensed a transformation taking place in my heart as well.

A few weeks after we attended church for the first time, I went for a late evening walk. I wrapped my warmest coat around my shoulders and stepped out of my tent into the brisk night air. Mount Shasta stood before me like a strong sentinel guarding my home in the woods. The faint tinge of smoke from a far-off fireplace mingled with the refreshing scent of pine. Lake Siskiyou stretched out behind me like a giant plate of glass, forming a perfect mirror image of the vista that surrounded me.

As I walked along a snow-packed road deep in the woods, I tilted my head back as far as I could to behold the countless brilliant stars stretched across the sky.

God, I know you're real. I'll never forget when you came to me as a child. I'll never forget taking my pearls and forming a circle around the star on the book I was reading. You told me that you circled me. You came and told me to believe. I do believe, God, but I want to know what I believe. How does believing that you are real affect my life here on earth? Will you please come to me again and teach me?

In an instant, his presence could not be missed.

I slowly dropped to my knees and closed my eyes.

Something warm and tingly filled my face and then my whole body. With my eyes still closed, I saw a blazing light, dazzling like a pure crystal with multitudes of dimensions. Full of wonder, I looked into the brightness and watched the light take the form of a serene being dressed in white. Pure white. In my mind I saw Jesus standing before me. With strong yet tender hands he reached and touched my face. His eyes were like deep blue water, and as he looked at me it was like everything inside of him flowed into me.

Light flooded the places deep within my soul. The same wondrous light that had come to me as a child came again. This time, it

came as an invitation to enter and explore the depths of God's love. I surrendered to the rhythm of the wave and allowed the Spirit to take me to the deep dimensions of who God is and how I could know him. Deep in the center of the light I saw a cross. For the first time in my life, I believed that he died on that cross for me.

"Where are you when I don't see you?" I asked.

I'm everywhere.

"Where do you live?"

I want to live in your heart.

"In *my* heart? My heart is all busted up and broken in a million different pieces. I don't think you'd want to live there."

I knelt on the dirt path for the longest time. I thought he would leave, but he stayed. Blazing light permeated from deep within his being, flowing over me as waves of endless light. I continued to kneel before him, basking in a kind of acceptance I had never experienced before.

Then I heard him say, *I'm going to put the broken pieces of your heart back together again.*

"Okay, that would be good. How? How are you going to do it?"

Piece by piece.

I saw Jesus holding the broken pieces of my heart in his hands. Then I heard music in my mind like I'd never heard before.

> *Come to me, my child, there's no need to be afraid.*
> *I will walk with you awhile, till your darkness starts to fade.*
> *When your sun will set no more, and your light shines bright*
>   *as day,*
> *I will always be with you. I will never go away.*
>
> *A crown of beauty I will give, after all the ashes burn.*
> *Oil of gladness I will pour, when the path of mourning turns.*
> *A garment ringing of praise will replace all the despair.*
> *The broken pieces of your heart, I will tenderly repair.*

"What do I do now?"

Jesus' two-word reply was simple, yet full of wonder and possibilities as it resounded clearly in my heart.

Follow me!

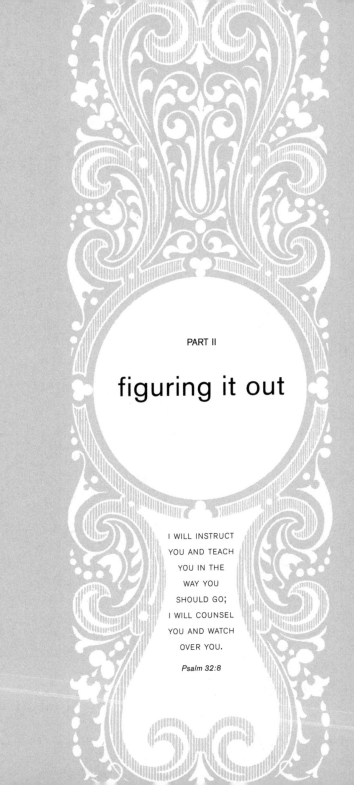

PART II

figuring it out

I WILL INSTRUCT
YOU AND TEACH
YOU IN THE
WAY YOU
SHOULD GO;
I WILL COUNSEL
YOU AND WATCH
OVER YOU.

Psalm 32:8

a fresh start

In my dream, I saw myself leisurely walking through a meadow. Out of nowhere a bird landed on my shoulder. As I looked at it curiously, I realized something wasn't right. It was a dove, but it was yellow, not white. Suddenly, blazing light flashed through the clouds like a streak of lightning and filled the meadow. The land rumbled underneath my feet. The blinding light slowly transformed into waves of flowing majestic fabric, unfolding out of the sky. I stood spellbound, waiting to hear what God had come to say. Out of the light came a voice that was both strong as thunder and gentle as a lamb. "Stay pure," it said. Only two simple words, yet they pierced through my being and nearly knocked me off my feet. I heard the voice first with my ears; then the vibrations of the sound filled my spirit and my soul until the current flowed all the way through my body. Just as quickly as the light burst into the meadow, it dissolved before my eyes. I looked at the dove. It was white. Then I heard the same voice, this time whispering in the wind, "You'll know when it's right, when the dove is white." The dove left my shoulder and flew up into the sky until I could see it no more.

Just like that I woke up.

I began to realize that "following him" meant making some pretty hard choices. When I thought about standing before the presence of God, there were many parts of myself that had that "yellow" feeling, the feeling that something wasn't quite right. The dream helped me understand that the intuitive gut-level feeling I had was really the Spirit of God leading me toward living a life that was pure in his sight, and I began to feel his delight when I chose to do right. As I began to feel his pleasure, I was motivated to continue to align my life with what I knew was right.

The first change I made was my attitude about smoking pot. I tried to imagine what God thought about me smoking it. In my mind I heard these words: "I'm not asking you to be perfect. I'm asking you to be pure. Don't get these two confused. This is not about keeping rules; it's about letting my light shine through your life." When I imagined myself getting high, all I could see were clouds of smoke filling up my body and my mind. For me, that visual helped me make a clean break with everything that clogged up or clouded my body. The night I realized this, I flushed all my pot down the toilet and never touched it again. I'm not saying I wasn't tempted to, because I was . . . many times. But I chose not to.

That yellow feeling kept coming up. When it did, I asked myself what I needed to do differently. Soon after the dream, I felt yellow every time I got dressed because almost all of my clothes were stolen. I came up with this wild idea to give away everything I ever stole. Once I began to do that, I felt totally free. My job at the cafeteria enabled me to slowly replenish my clothing. But soon I found I'd attracted a few secret angels on assignment. Without giving away their identities, some individuals from church randomly left me special notes like: "I want you to know that God has a plan and purpose for your life. Keep on following him!" Inside the note the secret person would often stash some cash.

Another note read, "If you want to have a relationship with God, you need to put forth the time and energy it takes, like in any relationship. I want you to see that God asks a lot of you. In your devotion to him you will find protection. His love is deeper and wider and broader than the ocean. As you continue to explore who he is, you will find that no matter what you go through, he will walk through it with you."

Although I was making some major life adjustments, the rush I felt from being on a journey with God and knowing that my life mattered for a bigger purpose captivated my heart. I wanted to play a vital role in helping others find hope.

As the summer approached, I was looking forward to a trip to Europe with Elena. We'd been planning and saving for this trip since we were young.

Tashina and I wondered what our lives would be like after my trip to Europe. Not knowing if I'd come back to Shasta or when we'd see each other again, we promised to keep in touch with each other no matter what. So much had happened to me so quickly, I could hardly take it all in.

Knowing I had some unfinished business to take care of before Elena and I took off on our trip, I hitched a ride with a friend back to San Francisco. I hadn't seen anyone in my family for more than a year. Anna planned to come up from San Diego to see me.

As we rounded Mount Tamalpais, the Golden Gate Bridge came into full view. I rolled down my window, letting the cool ocean breeze blow through my hair. I smiled as I thought of all I loved about this place. Then I saw her. The image of Rosie standing near the edge of the bridge about to jump flashed through my mind as a painful reminder of all that I'd tried to leave behind. I wanted to stop the car and grab her, pulling her to safety. But then, right before my eyes, I saw her jumping. Leaning out the window I looked down at the water below only to see waves chopping in the wind. My stomach churned. Looking up at the majestic golden arches I treasured, I realized at that moment they would forever be different. That bridge would always carry the memory of Rosie.

Trying to shake off the bad memories, I focused on what needed to be done prior to my trip to Europe. First, I withdrew some money from the bank and went straight to the department store I had stolen from while in high school. I asked to see the store manager. She almost fell over in disbelief when I handed her a huge wad of cash, hoping to make restitution for what I had wrongfully taken two years earlier.

Later in the afternoon I hooked up with Anna and Gino. Together we went to see our grandparents.

"Where've you been—China?" Frankie asked, his eyes dancing as he spoke.

Frankie wanted to know all about what I was up to. I liked that.

"Are you going to call your father while you're home?" Frankie asked.

"I don't know, Frankie. I'm thinking about it."

"He doesn't know why no one will call him. You're the only one who really loves your father. You better call him," Frankie persisted. "That old mother of yours turned you against him, didn't she?"

"I don't know, Frankie. It's been three years since I've seen him," I said, dropping my gaze to the floor. "It's all so confusing. I don't really know what to do."

"Go ahead and call him right now. Here's his number. See if maybe he'll meet you for lunch," Frankie prodded.

"If you call him, I'll go with you," Anna offered, overhearing our conversation.

Hands trembling, I picked up the receiver. *I can do this,* I told myself as I dialed the number. Anna stood next to me watching as Frankie nervously paced the floor.

Two rings. Three rings. Four rings.

"Hello?" a voice answered.

"Dad, is that you?" I asked, even though I knew his voice.

"Bella, Bella, Bella! My Bella!" he shouted with joy. "I knew you'd call me again someday." He wept. "Your daddy misses you so bad."

"Dad, I'm at Frankie and Lily's. Anna is with me. I'm calling to see if maybe you want to have lunch with—"

"Stay there!" he interrupted. "I'll be right there. I'll come and get you right now." The phone went dead.

I hung up the receiver. Anna looked at me anxiously. "What did he say?"

"He said he's coming right now."

Anna looked at me in disbelief. "Now?"

Frankie broke into a big smile. "That's good. Your father's going to be so happy now."

"Yikes! We need to tell Gino," I warned. "He's going to freak out."

Gino had already overheard. He hadn't seen Dad since the night we thought Dad was going to kill all of us.

"You're not going to catch me dead around here if that man's coming over," he said firmly, grabbing his car keys and heading for the door. "Call me later. I'm out of here!"

A half hour later Dad arrived. My heart felt all confused as he walked through the door and lifted me into a bear hug. I smiled as he hugged Anna too. Dad hurried us into the car, eager to take us out to lunch.

Anna and I slid into the half-moon-shaped booth at Corrozi's Italian Café. Dad sat down on the other side of the crescent, leaving me squeezed in the middle.

Dad didn't seem well. His dark brown eyes betrayed a glazed, faraway look. His cheeks appeared puffy and rounded. His strong athletic build now carried at least an extra thirty pounds.

"I've been assigned a new position at the police station," he offered, doing his best to give us an upbeat report. "I'm doing mainly criminal investigations and homicides. I'm also dating a nice lady I met at work," he added. "She's pretty, and we get along really well. You know, she's not like your mother at all. You will like her; I'm sure of it. Everything's going great for your dad."

Anna and I saw right through his stories. He appeared desperately lonely. No words came to my mind. I didn't know what to say to him.

Tears welled in his eyes as he looked at us.

"I miss you kids!" he cried, his voice cracking. "You're all I got! I can't bear living my life alone," he continued, sobbing. "All those years I worked hard to support my family, and now I've got nothing. No one talks to me anymore. I don't know why no one will talk to me."

Listening to Dad, my heart sank. I could almost feel his hand in mine and the cool, wet sand between my toes as we walked the beach together. Once more, I wanted to look up into his strong, vibrant face, to see laughter dance in his eyes.

As we chatted and ate together on the overstuffed red-vinyl seats in the old diner, I realized that Dad longed to pretend nothing had changed. But it had. The little girl he desperately wanted to hold did not exist anymore. I had been forced to grow up without him many years before. I had had to learn to make it without anyone, even him.

"Enough of this," Dad abruptly announced, blowing his nose so loud the whole restaurant glanced our way. "Anna, I want you to tell me all about being a nurse. What do you do? What happens when a person you're supposed to be taking care of dies?"

As Anna told some stories, Dad looked at her in silence for a long time.

As I looked at my dad I could see he wasn't well. He didn't look healthy. Something was wrong. I didn't want to think about him dying. *I wonder if Dad ever thinks about the afterlife? his own death? where he will go? Does he see demons or angels?*

"Anna, you can still be a doctor if you want," Dad said, tears filling his eyes again. "I always thought you would make a great doctor. You always took good care of your brother and sisters."

Anna smiled softly as she glanced my way. The look in our eyes betrayed the thoughts we left unspoken: *Why in the world had the weight of raising us lain on Anna's shoulders when she was just a kid?*

I wanted Anna to know God so she could see that he would take care of her. Since she was always the one who took care of us, she never got to experience what it was like to have someone take care of her. I wanted my dad to know God so that his broken heart would be healed. I wanted my brother to know God so that he would finally have a Father who would love him. Over the next few months, I shared with all of them, hoping they would see and understand what I had come to know about God. Instead, they just looked at me as though I had lost my mind. The more I tried to explain, the more I turned them off. It frustrated me that they couldn't see what I could see. Then God whispered in my mind, *They won't see through words; they'll see through your life.*

CHAPTER 12

letting go

At eighteen years old in 1979, Elena and I took off for an adventure around Europe for six months. Following that, I dropped everything and took off for the Philippines to live in a remote jungle region doing mission work. In all of my travels I often felt drawn to help the abandoned children and young girls I saw in orphanages, as well as those struggling to survive in the streets.

What will happen to them? Tears welled up in my eyes as I cross-examined myself. *Are they strong enough to make it? Who will come to help these little girls?* The questions rang deep within me. I thought of the Scripture verses in Psalms that meant so much to me: "Though my father and mother forsake me, the LORD will receive me" (Psalm 27:10) and "Defend the cause of the weak and fatherless" (Psalm 82:3).

"Perhaps I can do something more," I said aloud to no one in particular. A small seed of an idea began to take root in my heart.

The following January I enrolled in Simpson College, a Christian liberal arts college in San Francisco, focusing my studies on how to help "at risk" children around the world. I was captivated by stories of American missionaries like Elisabeth Elliot and Amy Carmichael. As I read how these women had served God by helping children, I knew that was how I wanted to live my life.

After school three days a week I volunteered at a shelter for children. The level of abuse they suffered broke my heart. I understood their pain. When hands designed to protect and nurture children are used as weapons, terrible scars, both seen and unseen, are left behind.

I realized that I could build bridges with these children because I was familiar with the places they went to disappear. I wanted to teach them how to disappear just enough to protect themselves, yet not so far they would forever be lost inside. Working at the shelter made me aware that although I harbored unpleasant memories of my own, many others experienced so much worse than I had.

* * *

As I continued to grow spiritually, I repeatedly read that God was my Father. But I didn't want God to be like Dad. I didn't want to feel responsible for God; I wanted him to take care of me.

I began a deeper journey of learning how to look to him for guidance and purpose. As I did, my heart overflowed with inspiration: I could in turn make a difference in the midst of so much suffering in the world! That excited me.

But another voice competed for my attention as well. *Who are you kidding? God doesn't have a plan for you.* The voice continued the attack, accusing me. *How could he possibly use you? You're not good at anything.*

I knew this voice—it was my mother's. I'd tried to tune it out my whole life. Every time my thoughts haunted me with how I was never going to amount to anything or that I was worthless, I trained myself to replace her critical words with words from God. I repeated a favorite quote over and over again: "I will instruct you and teach you in the way you should go; I will counsel you and watch over you" (Psalm 32:8).

I continued my studies with a renewed determination. When the school quarter ended, one of my professors personally handed me my grades. I slowly opened the folded piece of paper. My eyes lit up. "All As!" *Wow!* I thought to myself. *I've never seen an A in my life—at least one that wasn't sports related.*

My professor looked at me with a "What are we going to do with all that exuberance of yours?" kind of look.

"Christina," he said, "you need to think about channeling some of your enthusiasm into practical experiences beyond what you are already doing at the shelter downtown. I'd like you to seriously consider sharing your story at a youth conference I'm putting on next month."

I went to the beach to pray and think about the idea. As I sat alone in my cubbyhole I thought about something my professor had shared in class. "God searches the earth for those who will be willing to shine for others. He searches for those who will say, 'Here I am. Use me.'"

Throughout my growing-up years, this was the place I had come to get away from all the turmoil of my world. The memories that bothered me almost seemed to be tucked away in the walls of the cliff. I didn't want to think about my life experiences— it was too painful to go there. I wanted that part of my life to be washed away with the changing tide. I reasoned that God wouldn't be able to find anything in my past to use me for, so he would need to create something new. I was open to what that could be. I believed that God specializes in making something out of nothing. I wanted to seek new opportunities to grow and new challenges to stretch me.

As I stared at the ocean, I felt as if I was being invited to take a journey. Everything in me filled with excitement. I raised my hands to the heavens and said, "If you by chance are looking at me, if you see any way I can be helpful, I'm all yours!"

In the next few months I spoke at several youth events, encouraging kids to look to God as their source of life and to live their lives in a way that was pure before him. In addition, I continued to volunteer at the shelter as well as teach several young girls how to integrate art and creativity on their spiritual journeys.

* * *

My college was located close to Frankie and Lily's house, so I dropped in for lunch at least once a week. Three days after

Valentine's Day, I pulled up for my regular noontime visit. Oddly, I saw Frankie standing in front of the window as I got out of the car. He never did that; he always sat in his chair while waiting for me to arrive.

I wonder if something is wrong, I thought, stepping onto the sidewalk. The door of the house flew open, and Frankie scurried down the stairs.

"Your father's had a heart attack!" he shouted. "We've got to get to the hospital! Go in there and help Lily. She's all turned around. I'll get the car."

"Heart attack?" I asked, wide-eyed. "When did it happen?"

"I don't know nothing!" he stammered. "We've got to get to Mercy Hospital."

Fifteen minutes later, we burst through the hospital doors only to find out we couldn't see Dad yet. The three of us sat in the waiting room for more than an hour watching the hands on the clock slowly mark off the minutes. Finally, the doctor stepped through the doorway. "Only one of you can come in at a time," he said quietly, motioning for us to follow him. "You'll only be able to stay a few minutes."

"You go on in, Christina," Frankie choked out, dabbing the corner of his eye. "Your dad will want to see you."

Dad opened his eyes and smiled when I crept in. He looked pretty good in spite of the jungle of clear tubing, white hospital tape, and wires attached to his arms and chest.

"Come here, Bella," he said in a weak voice. "I had a big scare, but I'm going to be all right."

Wrapping my arms around his neck, I whispered, "Sorry, Dad, that you were all alone."

Tears poured out of me like they did the day he left our house.

The doctor informed us that Dad had suffered a massive heart attack. Over the next ten days, I went to the hospital every day. I sang songs to him with my guitar or read him the newspaper while he rested.

One afternoon as I sat next to him reading a book, he broke the silence. "How's your mother?"

"I don't know. I never talk to her."

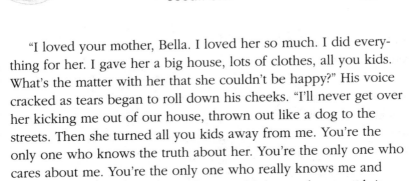

"I loved your mother, Bella. I loved her so much. I did everything for her. I gave her a big house, lots of clothes, all you kids. What's the matter with her that she couldn't be happy?" His voice cracked as tears began to roll down his cheeks. "I'll never get over her kicking me out of our house, thrown out like a dog to the streets. Then she turned all you kids away from me. You're the only one who knows the truth about her. You're the only one who cares about me. You're the only one who really knows me and knows I'm good. You're the only one who knows how much it hurts for your dad. My Christina. You'll never hurt your daddy, will you, Bella?"

"No, Dad. You know I love you," I said gently, taking his hands in mine. "I know you're good. I don't care what the others think. I know you're good."

We sat in silence for a long time. I held his hand and gazed out the window at the city spread out below us. I couldn't avoid him this time. Dad had no one else but me to share his burden, so I had to embrace it. I decided to take care of him.

The doctor expected to discharge him from the hospital on the following Friday, the same day I planned to leave for a white-water adventure in Canada that a friend had invited me on months earlier. We intended to be gone four days. Frankie and Lily agreed to pick up Dad, take him to his apartment, and keep an eye on him.

"You sure you don't care if I go?" I asked, standing beside his bed, clasping his hand.

"No, forget about it," he insisted. "You go and enjoy yourself. The doctor says I should be fine. For cryin' out loud, they've kept me tied up in this place long enough. I've got things to do."

"Dad, I . . ."

"You call when you get back," he said, smiling. "I am going to be fine. Now don't you worry about nothing while you're gone."

I gave him a big hug and turned to leave. Stopping in the doorway, I turned back. "Love you!" I said, blowing him a big kiss.

Friday night our plane landed in the remote mountains of western Canada. A handful of good friends joined me for a fun time of rafting. We were in a beautiful area, a place where a person could feel so free, so alive. Yet that feeling of freedom still eluded me. My body had journeyed to Canada, but I felt as though my heart had remained at Mercy Hospital.

How can I carry Dad, yet carve out my own life as well? I wondered silently the night before our rafting trip began. In the past, I would have numbed this burden by losing myself in drugs. With the weight of my dad's needs heavy on my heart, I felt tempted to join my friends for a little "escape." They got high every night. It would be easy to say yes.

"Stay focused," I muttered under my breath. "You made up your mind when you left Shasta to stop doing drugs for good."

As I had many times over the past year, instead of turning to drugs, I trusted God to sustain me and help me take care of my dad.

On Sunday night, I received an urgent message asking me to please call my sister Carrie.

"Hey, what's up?" I asked as she answered the phone.

Carrie's voice shook. "I hate to be the one to call you, but Anna isn't home and I can't track down Gino. Frankie called bawling his eyes out, wanting to know how to get ahold of you. He carried on about Lily and kept telling me, 'Get Christina to come home!' I couldn't get him to tell me what happened. I kept asking, 'Is it Lily? Is she okay? What happened?' Finally Frankie started screaming so loud into the phone I had to hold it away from my ear. 'No, it's not Lily,' he said. 'It's your father. He's dead!'

"Dad died, Christina! He died. You better come home right away!"

The words echoed around inside me like someone yelling in an empty stadium. *That can't happen!* I screamed inside. *He can't die. I told him this time I would help him!*

"Dad suffered another heart attack this afternoon," Carrie continued. "He called the doctor, who told him to lie on his bed until the paramedics arrived. Dad must have known he was going back in the hospital. He packed a small bag and went down the stairs to wait for them. He never made it all the way down. The paramedics arrived and found him lying close to the bottom of the stairs. He was already dead."

Shocked, I hung up the phone. My friends stood huddled in a small group, unsure what to do or say.

"I need to go home," I choked out through a flood of tears. "My dad died today."

Before anyone in the cabin reacted, I muttered that I needed to be alone and slipped outside. I took off down the road and into the woods. Running hard up one of the hills to my left, I broke into a clearing. I stopped and stared up at the endless star field above me.

"Why did he die?" I shouted to the sky. "I should have stayed with him! It's all my fault!" My voice echoed off the mountains. I collapsed in the meadow and stared at the heavens. My heart ached. Stretched out on the hillside I gazed up at the sky and bawled my eyes out.

I arrived back in San Francisco Monday afternoon for the wake that evening. The funeral was set for the following morning.

Anna and I went to Frankie and Lily's house to help them get ready for the wake. Slowly and carefully we climbed each step, quietly dreading the depth of sorrow we faced inside. It was hard enough to handle our own loss. We prepared ourselves to watch Frankie and Lily grieve the loss of their only child.

"For cryin' out loud, he was only fifty-one," Frankie cried as we entered the door. "The doctor said your father died of a broken heart."

That evening, I arrived early for the wake, wanting to see Dad alone. He lay in the coffin with his hands folded across his chest. Hesitantly, I made my way to the casket, my eyes fixed on his face. Standing over his body, I looked down at his hands—the hands I'd held a few days earlier. I wanted to reach into the casket and take his hands again, to remind him I loved him, but I was afraid to touch him. Instead, I slowly lifted my hand and with one finger gently touched him on the chest.

"I'm sorry, Dad," I whispered, weeping gently. "I shouldn't have left. I shouldn't have ever left you. I'm so sorry."

About fifty officers from the police station marched in to open the wake ceremony officially. Attired in full-dress uniforms, they draped an American flag on the casket.

Mom arrived and proceeded down the center aisle, wailing as she walked toward the casket. Like a desperate grieving widow on the verge of fainting, she flung herself in the arms of the nearest police officer.

"Why is she here?" Anna hissed, rolling her eyes in disgust. "She hated him! She only wants his pension."

All five of us kids were in the front row. We followed Anna's lead and glared at Mom in disgust.

"For cryin' out loud," Gino seethed as he leaned close to me. "She needs to get her head out of the sand and realize this is not about her. Is she ever going to see how what we have gone through has affected us?"

It seemed to the five of us that Mom always wanted the spotlight to be on her. We didn't want the spotlight on us; we wanted to turn it off. We wanted the curtain drawn. We wanted the show to be over.

The following morning, at the conclusion of the funeral, the five kids climbed into the shiny, jet-black hearse to accompany Dad's body to the grave site. The last time we'd gathered together was when we huddled on the cold bathroom floor that memorable Christmas Day years earlier. Now each sibling faced the finality of Dad's death with different expressions of grief. Some secretly sighed with a sense of relief. Others felt a measure of regret for what never would be.

Me? I had sensed Dad was drowning. I was the one who was supposed to keep him afloat. But I let go . . .

And he died.

CHAPTER 13

ride your wave

The next few years I juggled taking more courses with taking mission trips to the Philippines. Whenever I returned home from another long trip, I went straight to my grandparents' house.

"Where've you been—China?" Frankie would beam as he peeked over Lily's shoulder.

"Why didn't you tell us you arrived back from your travels?" Lily said as her trembling hands excitedly opened the gate. Grabbing my arm, she gently pulled me into the house.

"I just got back yesterday morning. It all happened so fast," I said excitedly. "It's good to see you!"

"We got all your letters," Lily said, pulling me close to her side. "Frankie said you promised him you'd always come back."

Looking into Frankie's eyes, I smiled. He nodded his head and smiled back. Lily pulled me into the kitchen as Frankie followed close behind. "Sit down here at the table. You look too skinny. I'll make you some raviolis." She pulled the ingredients from the refrigerator and then asked, "What did you like the most about this trip?"

"I think what I liked most is what I learned about myself. I really love to help children. It made me feel so good to be able to give my

life away for others and feel that appreciation back. It's like that is what I was born to do with my life."

"Where are you going to go now?" Frankie asked.

"I don't know. I'd love to go back to the Philippines and start an orphanage for all the kids who don't have anyone to take care of them. But for now I'm thinking about finishing my college degree. No matter what, I'm staying around for Anna's wedding."

Anna had been dating Brett since her first year at college, and they had finally decided to get married. Brett was a well-known major-league baseball player, and life seemed to be looking up for Anna.

Frankie walked down the hall to his closet, pulled out his blue suede jacket, and proudly put it on over his brown polyester shirt and white suspenders. "I'm going to wear my new coat when I walk Anna down the aisle."

"You're going to wear that jacket, Frankie? Does Anna know?"

"She asked me to walk her down the aisle. She didn't say nothing about what jacket to wear. I've got a closet full of clothes. I don't need anyone telling me what I'm going to wear. Anna likes this jacket," Frankie insisted. "She told me so."

"Frankie," Lily interrupted, "go to the garage and get me some bags of ice."

"Yeah, yeah, yeah. I'll be right there," Frankie said as he headed for the door.

I followed him down the steep steps to the backyard and into the musty garage. As soon as I walked in I noticed a clothes rack to my left jammed full of coats, pants, shirts, and sweaters.

As I neared the clothing, Dad's scent washed over me. The Hawaiian shirt Anna had sewn stuck out from the others. Reaching to untangle a web of jumbled-up hangers, I pulled the shirt close to my face and closed my eyes. I got lost in the memories of Dad proudly slipping the shirt on as he got home from work, and tears began to pour down my cheeks. For a moment I heard his voice as he strutted through the neighborhood proudly telling everyone, "You like my new shirt? Anna made it for me." I sensed his hand holding on to my arm as he whispered in my ear, "You're the only one who knows how much it hurts your dad, my Christina. You'll never hurt your daddy, will you, Bella?"

I quickly opened my eyes and shoved the shirt deep in the middle of all the other clothes. Stepping from the musty garage into the sunlit yard, I reminded myself that through the constant cycle of change I needed to keep looking up and moving forward. *Don't stop to sit down. Don't question. Sometimes there aren't any answers.* Turning my attention to things present, I went to find Frankie.

"Frankie, let me take you for a ride," I offered as he emerged from the wine cellar.

"No, Lily needs me here. I don't want to go nowhere," he said as we walked back up the stairs to the kitchen. "Where do you want to take me anyway?"

"Oh, Frankie, you know. The beach!"

"The beach! For cryin' out loud, I'm not going to the beach right now. It's only fifty degrees out there. The sand's going to be blowing like a tornado." Sitting back down at the table, he poured some coffee.

"Oh, go on," Lily prodded him. "For Pete's sake. You're getting to be an old man. Go with her."

"Yeah, Frankie, you're eighty-three years old. Life's too short to sit around here every day. When's the last time you saw the ocean? C'mon, you're coming with me," I said, pulling his arm.

"All right, all right, all right, I'll go," he said grudgingly as he stood up.

When we arrived at the beach, Frankie got out of the car and stood in awe as he looked out over the water. He took his shoes off, rolled up the bottom of his polyester pants, and let the waves gently roll over his aging bare feet. His dark brown eyes followed me as I took off running along the water's edge and back again.

Taking a deep breath, I let the ocean breeze blow over me. I was home. Seeing Frankie standing at the water's edge made me smile. I liked that I was special to him, and he to me.

* * *

After several weeks of visiting with friends, I focused my attention on Anna's upcoming wedding.

The morning before the big day I joined Anna downtown to

purchase flowers for the tables at the reception. We stopped for an ice cream cone. A young girl at a corner table caught our attention. The child's long black hair hung in her face as she licked her cone.

"Use your napkin!" her mother snapped. "You're being a slob."

The little girl didn't pay attention. Instead, she stood up and walked over to look through the glass at all the different kinds of ice cream.

"Sit down!" the mother scolded as she stomped over, roughly pulling on the girl's arm. "Can't you stay still for five minutes? Eat your ice cream, or I'll never get you another one."

"Someone needs to lock that woman up," I whispered.

Anna didn't hear a word I said. Her eyes were focused on the scene.

The girl sat still now, trying to obey. Her delicate feet dangled from the chair as she obediently licked her cone. Moments later her white napkin slipped off her lap and fluttered to the ground. As she leaned down to pick it up, the scoop of chocolate ice cream suddenly plopped onto the dirty floor. The little girl's face instantly clouded over with fear. Before she sat up her mother grabbed her arm and dragged her toward the bathroom.

Anna stood up in a flash. I followed her to the bathroom. As Anna opened the door, the mother gripped the girl by the shoulders, repeatedly shaking her body. The frightened girl desperately pleaded, "Please stop, Mommy! It hurts!"

"Why can't you behave?" the mother scolded.

Anna got right in front of the woman's face, like the mother had been doing to her child, and angrily shouted, "What gives you the right to hit a child? I should slam your head against the wall so you know what it feels like."

Afraid Anna was going to deck her, the mother let go of the child.

Anna remained controlled and immediately called the police. They arrived moments later. One policeman took the mother aside for questioning as a female officer made sure the little girl calmed down.

"The poor kid was simply trying to eat an ice cream cone. Can you imagine what it's like when they're at home?" Anna asked.

We locked eyes, both knowing and remembering.

"Yeah, I can," I quietly admitted. Memories of my mom's angry face filled my mind. We tried to focus on the last-minute wedding purchases, but it was hard to shake off the melancholy mood that had swept over us.

Finally the big day arrived, and Anna took Frankie's arm for her walk down the aisle. Frankie insisted on wearing the blue suede jacket. Anna wanted him in a tuxedo, but she didn't press the issue. Watching Frankie walk her down the aisle, I suddenly felt old. *Time passes so quickly. It seems like yesterday we were all kids.*

After the wedding ceremony Gino and I hung out together most of the evening listening to the music and stuffing ourselves at the Italian buffet. As we watched Anna and her husband dance, we agreed she had picked the perfect guy for herself. Brett was dependable, funny, calm, steady, and handsome. He was easygoing, and she was type A. They offered a good balance for each other.

* * *

After Anna's wedding, my attention quickly returned to college and finishing my degree. On the day final exams began, an announcement came over the loudspeaker: "Attention students: You must pay your bills in full before your exam grades will be posted."

Immediately I checked with the business office. "Has my grant come through yet?" I asked.

"Sorry, Christina, we still haven't heard anything."

I only had about 30 percent of the money I needed to pay my bill, and I had no idea what I'd do if the grant didn't come through. My friend Amie and I climbed one of the big oak trees on campus and prayed together that God would help. Just as we walked in the front door I heard my name being called over the loudspeaker. "Christina DiMari, please come to the dean's office."

I sighed. It had been a long time since I heard those familiar words. A knot in my stomach tightened. I prepared myself to hear that I couldn't take my final exams.

"There you are," the dean said. "We've been looking for you.

I need you to come with me. The president of the college wants to talk with you."

We walked through the main lobby past a crowd of students. Fidgeting with the books in my arms, I prepared to enter Dr. Lee's office.

"Come on in," said a cheery voice.

As I entered, he stood up behind his desk and extended his hand, motioning for me to sit down. He looked as jolly as he sounded with his Irish brogue. White hair surrounded a bald spot on the back of his head. The green sport jacket he wore barely closed around his waist.

"Some of your professors told me about your desire to help abandoned children," he began. "I admire your courage and enthusiasm. What are your plans now?"

"I plan to finish my studies and get my degree," I began. "But I also want to go back to the Philippines to help the street children."

"Let me tell you a story," Dr. Lee began. "There once was a woodcutter who wanted more than anything to cut trees for the king. One day the king gave the woodcutter a beautiful shiny ax and told him to go to a certain forest and cut down as many trees as he could. The woodcutter was thrilled to get this opportunity. He went straight to the forest and with great enthusiasm and dedication began to chop down tree after tree. He worked diligently year after year, cutting down more trees than anyone ever expected. One day the king sent for him and said, 'You are doing a fine job! You have done what I asked of you. There are many more trees to be cut, but if you are going to be most effective in cutting them all, I need you now to take a rest and allow me to sharpen your ax. When you are rested and your ax is sharpened, then it will be time to go again into the forest.'

"Christina," Dr. Lee continued, "you are the woodcutter in this story. You worked hard in helping the children and teaching others. Now it is time to sharpen your ax by furthering your education."

"Dr. Lee, I don't—"

"About fifteen minutes ago," he interrupted, "I received a phone call from a businessman who graduated from our school some time back. Someone gave this man financial assistance during his college days. This businessman wants to pass on that same gift to a student who needs some help. He specifically mentioned he wants his gift to go to a student who studies hard and who has a heart to help less fortunate children. I told this gentleman I would do some checking and get right back to him. I walked straight to Dr. Albright's office to ask him if he knew anyone who met these requirements. [Dr. Albright was the professor who taught many of my classes at the time.] Dr. Albright smiled and pointed out the window. 'See that girl up in the tree? I believe that's your girl!' Christina, although you have a gift in working with children, I think you're making a good choice to finish your degree." Looking at his watch, Dr. Lee smiled warmly. "Looks like you better go take your finals!"

"Wow, thank you so much!"

As I turned to walk out the door, he stopped me. "Oh, Christina, one more thing. You do your best to keep up your grades and stay focused on finishing your degree. This gift today will get you through this semester, and I am personally going to make sure the rest of your bills are paid from here on."

Racing down the hallway, I grabbed Amie's arm and pulled her outside to tell her what happened. Amie stood speechless as I finished recounting the meeting with Dr. Lee. "Can you believe that?" I shouted. "I'm going to remember this day forever!"

With the question of how I would pay for school answered, I increased my commitment of volunteering for an organization in San Francisco that helped out with at-risk kids in the inner city. I worked with up to fifty kids every week, but I handpicked about seven girls and spent time with them in a smaller group every Friday after school. We met at the beach, where I led them in spiritual application lessons incorporated with basic life coaching. I was riding my wave, feeling good about life.

I continued to maintain a 4.0 grade point average, an educational first for me, and graduated from college with honors. The second commencement day in my life proved as unforgettable as the first.

One of the professors handed out the diplomas as the students walked across the stage. I took my place near the end of the long procession line, feeling extremely proud. My turn came, and I headed toward the professor, anxious to receive my diploma. As

I approached him, he smiled at me, then stepped out of the way as Dr. Lee walked forward from the back of the stage. Dr. Lee took the diploma from the professor's hands and, with a big jolly smile on his face, handed it to me.

"You have done well," he said as he shook my hand. "Your ax has been sharpened. May God guide you from here."

"Thank you so much!"

Descending the steps, I glanced inside the cover. The diploma was there! I smiled as I looked over to where Frankie sat and caught him winking at me.

This was the end of an important era in my journey. I didn't realize at the time how singing the hymns every morning in chapel and listening to my teachers tell stories of their own journey with God would influence me. Without my even knowing it, they were instrumental in building a foundation under the new life God promised he would give me if I would only keep my eyes fixed on him.

Anna sent a card of congratulations. The note simply read, "Way to go! You proved her wrong!"

I smiled, knowing what she meant, but I shook my head slightly as I thought to myself, *Maybe more than proving Mom wrong, I proved to myself I could do it.*

Anna had also sent a small gift box. Opening the present from Anna, I pulled out keys to a car! Even though it was a used car, I knew it was a huge sacrifice for her to spend that much money on me.

While I had been in school, I had visited several different churches, hoping to find some connection with people who wanted to help others. It was a big awakening to realize that there were so many different denominations. Eventually I found one with people who believed as I did—not people who were trying to live in an unrealistic box with a perfect set of rules, just real people trying to live a life of faith and shine their light for others who needed help.

My pastor and his wife, Jim and Betsey, knew I needed time after graduation to sort through my plans for the next phase of my life.

"Why don't you take a month and think through all of your options?" Pastor Jim suggested. "We're going to Jackson Hole,

Wyoming, for two weeks to visit our son. I want you to come with us. You'll love it there. Awesome mountains, water-skiing, hiking, mountain climbing, kayaking, white-water rafting on the Snake River, and pretty much whatever else you want to do in the outdoors." Jim encouraged me to be patient as I waited for God to show me where to take my next step.

"Remember, when God seems silent, make sure you are really listening. You may not hear his answer because he may not be answering the way you anticipated. If you are confident that you are listening for God and still there is no answer, then keep on doing what he last told you to do. God will let you know what he is doing in your life in his timing, which is often different from yours. Stay open. Your answer may come in the next song you hear, the next book you read, or through someone you meet."

I continued to listen and hoped to have clear direction soon. I also agreed to join Jim and Betsey and their children in Jackson Hole, not knowing how such a seemingly small decision would forever change the course of my life.

CHAPTER 14

parade of lights

The aroma of my hot coffee blended with the scent of pine as I quietly slipped out the cabin door into the early morning stillness. The sunrise gave promise to the spectacular June day awaiting me in the mountains. Pulling my sweater around my shoulders, I headed down the winding dirt path through the towering pine and aspen trees standing like silent sentinels along my journey. The fresh mountain air and the peaceful sound of the river in the distance beckoned me onward. Rounding a sharp bend in the path, I stopped midstride as a clearing opened before me, unveiling the majestic Snake River.

Unspeakable beauty surrounded me on every side. The mountain range stood in awesome grandeur, filling the skyline in the distance. Though summer had arrived in the valley, snow still clung in the high mountain crevices, daring the sun to find its hiding place. An eagle circled overhead, searching the rushing waters for a tasty fish for its breakfast. I sat down on the remnants of a fallen tree and soaked in the stunning surroundings. Deep thankfulness filled my heart as I enjoyed the solitude and magnificent beauty before me.

The next ten days consisted of quiet morning walks and invigorating afternoon mountain adventures. In the evenings, Jim and

Betsey and I spent time with Don and Jo Moore, who owned the land where we were staying. Sitting around the campfire, we shared stories and sang songs while roasting marshmallows.

The last day of our mountain vacation came all too soon.

"Let's do something fun on our last day," I suggested to Betsey and Jim, "like finding the hot springs we heard about from the rafting guide."

"No, I think we're going to go to town and shop some," Betsey replied.

Lacing up my hiking boots, I looked up at her in dismay. "Shop? You can shop anywhere. What a waste of a day! C'mon, we need to do something today we've never done before."

Jim and Betsey's son, Steve, interrupted. "If you drive me to work at the golf course you can take my car all day to do whatever you want. Just come back and get me at eight o'clock tonight. You won't get my mom to hike up to the hot springs. If you want to go on your own, we'd better get going."

By midmorning I found myself deep in the wilderness as I made my way up the steep, twisting trail through the mountains. To my right a bull moose buried his head in a pond, digging up grass to eat. Deer and elk meandered through the trees seemingly unaware of my presence. Two hours later I found the steaming water at the natural hot springs. By late afternoon I knew I must extract myself to head back down the trail if I hoped to make it to the golf course by eight.

I arrived a little early, and while waiting for Steve to get off work, I noticed two preppy golfers coming off the course. Knowing they didn't see me in the car and being in a rather playful mood, I waited for them to walk right in front of the car. Then I blasted the horn with full force.

"Wow, do you always honk your horn at people you don't know? You scared the daylights out of me," one of the guys said, smiling. "I'm Joel. This is my brother, Michael. We're trying to find a phone to call for a ride down to our condo in the village."

"Get in. I'll take you down there," I offered. "I still have a half hour before Steve gets off work."

Joel sat in front with me while Michael jumped in the back. Joel reminded me of Kevin Costner. Michael's light blond hair and blue eyes contrasted with his brother's darker features.

"Are you guys on vacation?" I casually inquired.

"Well, kind of. We work here most of the summer in a music festival," Joel offered.

"What do you do at the festival?"

"I play the viola, and Michael plays the violin."

"Where are you from?" I asked, looking in the rearview mirror at Michael.

"We're from Alabama, but we live in Kentucky. What about you?"

"I'm from California," I stated proudly. "Do you guys have any other roommates?"

"Yeah, I've got a good one, my wife," Joel said with a laugh. "She is an interior decorator."

"What does your wife do?" I asked, making eye contact again with Michael.

"I don't know." Michael blushed.

"What do you mean you don't know?"

"He's not married." Joel chuckled, exposing Michael's bluff. "Our good friend, Pete, stays with us. We doubt he's home to come pick us up, so it's a good thing we ran into you. Pete has lived an exciting life. He even grew up in the Philippines."

"What? I've spent time in the Philippines too," I said, startled by the coincidence.

Pulling up to their condo, I got out of the car to help them get their bags out of the trunk. Being Southern gentlemen, they insisted on opening the trunk and lifting the clubs out themselves.

I stood there unsure what to do with myself. "What's the big deal with me lifting a couple of golf bags?" I asked, as Joel slammed the trunk. The two of them smiled and assured me they didn't want me lifting anything as we said a polite good-bye. I watched them walk up the stairs to their condo. They both appeared unusually nice. As I drove away, I couldn't shake the feeling that I'd clearly missed something that was supposed to happen.

Back at the Teton Pine's golf course nestled under the Grand Teton mountain range, I drove a golf cart around while I waited for Steve to close up the pro shop. Rounding the clubhouse, I heard someone call out my name. I drove back to the car to find Michael and Joel's wife, Joan, waiting for me. They invited me to join them

for dinner and a movie back at their condo. I told Steve of my plans, and we took off.

* * *

"Kamusta ka?" I said, greeting Pete in Tagalog, the main Philippine language.

"Mabute' at ikow?" he replied, asking me how I was doing in return.

We talked to each other in Tagalog while the others stared at us in amazement. Pete had spent time in the Philippines because his parents were missionaries.

"So who is your favorite missions author?" Pete queried.

"Definitely Elisabeth Elliot," I answered without hesitation. I had read every book she'd written up to that point. I went on and on, telling them all about her life and how her books inspired me to help the orphans in the Philippines.

Over an hour later Pete finally interrupted me. "I bet there's one book she wrote you haven't read. It's called *The Mark of a Man*."

"Well, actually I did read that," I said with a smile. "In college, if a guy wanted to date me I gave him that book. All the guys in school joked about it. If someone took me out, the next day the other guys would ask, 'Did she give you the book yet?'"

Pete, Joel, and Michael all laughed.

Caught off guard because someone actually knew of the book without my bringing it up, I looked at them curiously.

"How did you know about that book?" I asked.

"Today must be your lucky day," Pete replied, pointing across the room at Michael. "Not only do we know of the book, but Michael has already read it!"

I looked over at Michael, who was sitting in a chair on the other side of the room, and said suspiciously, "You're kidding! Have you really?"

"Yes, I have," Michael quietly admitted. "I read it when I was in college."

"If you know that book so well, I ought to look familiar to you," Pete hinted.

"Familiar?"

"Think about the book. Who is on the front cover?" Pete asked, smiling.

"Her nephew, Pete . . . No way! Are you that Pete?"

"That's me."

I couldn't believe he let me talk so long about his aunt Elisabeth. We all enjoyed a good laugh and continued our conversation late into the night. At 3:00 a.m. we decided to call it a night. Michael, though quite reserved, offered to drive me home. Making our way back to Jim and Betsey's cabin, we noticed the sky lit up with a spectacular meteor shower. Falling stars streaked across the sky like a parade of dancing lights.

Michael pulled the car over to the side of the road. We got out and sat on top of the hood of the car, tilting our heads back to watch the amazing light show.

The same feeling I'd sensed when I dropped off Michael and Joel earlier now intensified.

I hadn't really noticed Michael all night since he was so quiet. Now that it was just the two of us, I began to appreciate who he was. As we watched the stars, we asked each other questions and started to get to know one another. He seemed genuine, like the kind of guy you could count on. When he began to share about his faith walk with Jesus, that's when I really connected with him. It was like something inside our souls had been where the other had been, even though our worlds and experiences had been so drastically different. He told me about growing up in a Christian home and how that had played a huge role in shaping who he was. When he asked me about my life, I told him about my sister. I didn't even want to begin trying to explain my growing-up years to him. I kept everything focused on where I was then.

Meeting Michael felt meant to be. I could almost grab the moment and hold it in my hand. He felt the same way. Unfortunately, I planned to leave the next morning to go back to California, and Michael was going back to Kentucky in a few weeks.

When we arrived at my cabin, I tried to get him to drop me off far enough away that I could sneak in without anyone knowing. Being a Southern gentleman, he planned to walk me to the door.

The headlights were aimed straight at the cabin, bright enough to wake up anyone inside. As I was about to hop out and say a quick good-bye, Michael opened his door, motioning he planned to walk me to the cabin.

"No, I'm fine," I insisted. "I'd better hurry before I wake anyone up."

Michael would not take no for an answer.

As we said good-bye to each other I knew I would see him again.

I went back to California the next morning as planned. Michael called me that night, and we began a long-distance courtship. In the past, my dating relationships had never lasted long. Either the guys got too clingy and I ditched them, or I didn't trust them. As soon as a guy started to sink his claws into my space, I ran—and quickly.

Michael's Christian upbringing provided a sort of stability. I admired his personality—it was strong, stable, secure, faithful, dependable, and gentle. He was handsome, clean-cut, and athletic. He pretty much had all the qualities I was attracted to in a guy.

He enjoyed all sports, loved to fly-fish, and enjoyed being in the mountains, which assured us some commonalities from the get-go.

Two months later, Michael arranged for me to fly to Kentucky to visit him and his brother, the same one I had met while in Jackson Hole.

During my stay, I decided to find out more about this man's occupation. "So what do you do with the violin anyway?" I asked one afternoon. "Do you, like, stroll in restaurants or something? It seems like more of a side-gig type deal than a real job."

"You'll see," he said, laughing. "Tonight we're going to one of my concerts."

"Great, I can't wait to watch you play."

That evening, Michael led me to my seat in a large music hall filled with about two thousand people.

"Look for me onstage," he whispered, turning to leave.

What a trip! I thought to myself, looking at the now completely full house. *I wish Katie and Elena were here. They would totally crack up seeing me sitting in a concert hall.*

A short time later, all the musicians took their places on the stage—everyone except Michael. The lights started to dim. I wanted

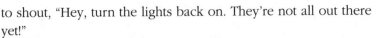

to shout, "Hey, turn the lights back on. They're not all out there yet!"

I leaned over and nudged the guy next to me. "I came with this guy who said he would be up there somewhere. Do some of them play in a different part?"

He shrugged his shoulders and probably thought I got stood up by my date.

The gigantic hall turned dark and completely quiet. Suddenly, a single spotlight drew our attention to the side of the stage and followed one musician out to the center.

I elbowed the guy next to me again. "Hey, there he is!"

"He's who brought you here?"

"Yeah, that's him," I said, pointing to Michael.

Leaning over, he whispered, "That's the concert violinist. He's the main guy."

Well, I thought, *that sure beats strolling in restaurants.*

CHAPTER 15

wild stallion

My relationship with Michael continued to grow in the following months. We talked on the phone every night for hours and visited each other frequently. My childhood friends, Katie and Elena, watched curiously, especially when we were still dating after the first month, then the second, then the third. The long-distance nature of our relationship really helped me at this point because I didn't feel smothered.

About six months after we met, Michael paid me a special visit in California. One evening while we were watching a movie, he suddenly got up and stopped the video. He walked back to where I sat, got on his knees, and gave me a small box.

Oh, how nice, he's giving me earrings, I thought. I slowly opened the box, prepared to look surprised. Instead, I saw an engagement ring. *Ahhh! I don't want to get married!* I thought. *Why did he do this?*

I sat frozen, staring at the ring. I finally opened my mouth to form my response. "Oh, I wasn't quite thinking of that yet."

Michael went back to Kentucky with the engagement ring in tow, deeply disappointed. I went to my church to tell Jim and Betsey. They both looked at me and laughed.

"I knew this was coming," Pastor Jim remarked.

"Well, I'm glad you did, because I didn't."

"What makes you uneasy about it?"

"Everything!" I quickly responded. "I'm freaked out at the thought of marrying anyone. I know Michael and I get along great. I totally imagine us being great friends, but the whole marriage thing is so iffy. What if he is this way now, then he turns weird on me after we're married?"

"Christina," Betsey interrupted, "you've always wanted to get married one day and have children."

"Yeah, one day, but not right now!"

"He seems to have the qualities you like."

"He does. I determined a long time ago that I wouldn't date anyone who had a bad temper, gambled, or struggled with alcohol and drugs. He doesn't do any of the obvious things I worry about. He is the nicest, most honest, hardworking guy I've ever met. But what if he is really not as good as he comes across? What if there's some secret weird thing that will come out later?"

"Do you love him?" Jim asked.

"I can't get married to him anyway. I'm going back to the Philippines to start an orphanage!"

"Christina, do you love him?" Jim asked again.

I looked at him, utterly flustered. "I don't know. I'm not even sure I know what love is! I just need space. The whole idea of marriage makes me feel trapped."

I called Anna and asked her what I should do.

"Michael wants to get married!" I began. "Gino wants me to go to Italy with him for two months, and I want to go back to the Philippines to start the orphanage. Marriage freaks me out. When it comes down to it, I don't know if I can ever trust anyone enough to marry him. I don't want to get stuck with the wrong person. What if he ends up trying to tell me how to live my life? What if he turns out to be a total control freak like Dad?"

"Well, he is totally different than you are. But you both get along really well. Just do it! If it doesn't work out, get a divorce!"

That's weird for her to say, I thought as I hung up the phone. *I don't want to get a divorce.* She understood I didn't want to feel

trapped, but I wanted the kind of relationship that survived the trials of time and could go the distance. If I couldn't have that, I didn't want to get married at all. I knew that's what Anna really wanted for me as well.

Pastor Jim understood some of my fears.

Michael was caught off guard. He thought everything was fine between us. The ring for him was the next step. I had been trying to tell him about my upbringing one piece at a time, but he didn't have any idea that marriage was such a big issue for me. He loved me. For Michael, that was enough to move forward.

Pastor Jim suggested Michael and I do some premarital counseling, and we agreed. For the next three months, Michael flew out from Kentucky to California every few weeks for long counseling sessions. In the first session, Jim told me that at any time during the three months I could give an answer to Michael, either yes or no. But I must give my final answer by the last session.

For our first session, we were assigned to watch the movie *The Man from Snowy River*, the story of a young mountain man in Australia who tamed a legendary wild stallion and won the heart of the only daughter of a wealthy rancher in the valley.

"Christina," Jim said as we prepared to leave his office, "when you're watching the movie think about how you're like the wild stallion, and Michael is like the rancher who wants to put the saddle on the horse."

Wrinkling my nose, I looked at him like he was crazy. "You're kidding, right?" Pastor Jim doubled over with laughter in his chair. *It's not funny,* I thought to myself.

That evening, Michael and I popped in the video and settled back for our first counseling assignment. Not only was the movie entertaining, it opened up a new territory of discussion between us.

"Pastor Jim is right about that horse," Michael shared. "You are like that—free-spirited, independent, full of life, and free of restraints. But that's what I love about you."

"Really? Are you sure you're not going to want me to be different after we're married?"

"No. We'll both have adjustments to make, but I don't want you to feel stifled."

"Good. I worked my whole life to be free. The last thing I want now is to feel trapped," I said, relieved.

"I don't want that either. We're both independent. We both need to give each other freedom. Yet we can come together in a partnership as friends in marriage. We can make it work well for both of us."

Our next assignment was to make one list of the things we wanted out of marriage and another list of our concerns. Pastor Jim talked about our lists in the remaining counseling sessions. He pointed out our strengths and also talked about looking out for upcoming obstacles we might trip over. Our stark differences brought the balance we both desired. I liked Michael's stability; he liked my adventurous spirit. I liked his steadfastness; he liked my energy. The biggest hurdle I saw was living far away from the ocean and my girlfriends. The ocean had been my home since I was a child; my soul was connected to it in ways that were so deep I couldn't find words to explain it to Michael. He saw things very logically and assured me I could come home whenever I wanted. I saw things intuitively and was worried that something deep inside me might shrivel up and die if I couldn't be near the water.

* * *

The three-month deadline was up as we walked into the last counseling session with Pastor Jim. Gripping the door handle, I turned to Michael and announced, "Yes, I will marry you!"

Pastor Jim married us exactly five months later in the fall of 1988. Although I preferred a small celebration with my close friends on the beach, Anna talked me into a more traditional wedding.

Frankie insisted on wearing his blue suede jacket to walk me down the aisle.

"Frankie, I want you to wear the tuxedo I rented for you. You'll look awesome in it."

"Forget about it! I'm not wearing no tuxedo! You can put it on me when I'm dead, but I'm not going to put it on while I'm breathing."

"Frankie, you have to!" I insisted.

Defiantly he walked away from me to sit in his chair.

"Why are you grinding your feet into the ground over such a simple matter? What's the big deal over wearing what I want you to wear for one day? For cryin' out loud, you can take it off as soon as the ceremony ends."

Frankie stuck to his plan.

The morning of the wedding came. Disappointed, I watched Frankie walk into the church dressed in his brown polyester pants and blue suede jacket. Fully dressed in my wedding gown I peeked out of the dressing room and motioned for Frankie to come to the door.

"Frankie, Gino has the tuxedo in your dressing room. You have to put it on!"

"I'm not wearing no tuxedo!" Wrinkling up his nose and shaking his head, he stated adamantly, "I look good in this." He proudly patted his chest. "Nobody's going to make me change my clothes."

Rolling my eyes, I leaned up and kissed him on the cheek. "Oh, Frankie, you do look great, but this is a special day. This moment will never come again. I thought it would be so cool for me in my pretty dress and you in your Mafia tux to walk down the aisle arm in arm. Oh well, I've got to finish getting ready. I'll see you in about twenty minutes."

With ten minutes to go, I peeked once more through the door. Frankie wouldn't budge. "Gino, go make him put that tux on!"

"What's the big deal? He's not going to change his mind. Let it go."

"What's the big deal with wearing what I want him to wear? Go make him put it on. This is the one day in my life when I'm supposed to have things go the way I want. Already it's turning out to be what everyone else wants. Angela and Anna didn't want to wear the dresses I picked out for the bridesmaids, so I had to change all the dresses, and now I hate them. I should have gotten married at the beach, barefoot in the sand with a simple satin white dress like I wanted to."

Then I thought about Michael. I guess it didn't matter that everything seemed to be going wrong. Marrying him was what this whole day was all about anyway. Realizing I was losing sight of the main thing, I focused on Michael and the family we were going to create together. This day was going to usher me into a new season in my life, one that I was eager to embrace.

Ten minutes later Elena, Katie, and Tashina ran into the dressing room in their bridesmaid dresses.

"It's time!" they burst out in unison.

I sat in front of the mirror, looking at myself all dressed up with a strand of pearls around my neck. "Do you guys think these look real?"

"No," Elena said without hesitation, "but it's your wedding day, and you can wear whatever you want."

"What are you thinking?" Katie asked, seeing I was lost in thought.

"Oh, I don't know where this weird feeling came from, but this morning I realized I didn't own a fancy necklace to wear. Then I started crying for no reason at all. My mind suddenly told me this is the kind of thing a mother is supposed to be helping me with. So many other girls I know who have gotten married received a genuine strand of pearls from their mothers on their wedding day.

"I don't have any pearls, and I don't have a mother I would even want them from. I tried to shake the feeling off, and I went through all my drawers to find something meaningful. That's when I found these. Lily bought them at the five-and-dime store and gave them to me when I was a child. I've saved them all these years. They're cheap, but it's the only necklace I own that has meaning."

"I know what to do," Elena said excitedly as she unhooked the strand of pearls from around my neck. She double-looped the pearls around my ankle. "There, now you can wear the meaningful pearls, and no one will see that they're cheap."

Our laughter filled the room as Elena straightened my dress.

Without hesitation Tashina took off the pearl necklace her mother had given to her and placed it carefully around my neck. "Here, Christina, I want you to wear this."

Silence filled the room. The four of us quietly faced the mirror, staring at the necklace. I sat up straight, feeling much more beautiful.

"Really, Tashina, are you sure?"

"Definitely. But don't go running off to Hawaii with it! You have to give it back after the ceremony or my mother will freak!"

Katie wiped a tear from her eye as Elena shouted a high-pitched California girl roundup call. "Okay, are you ready now? It's time to get married!"

The four of us walked out into the foyer. Karen, a family friend, arranged the girls in the order that they should walk in, with me at the end of the line.

"Someone go get Frankie. He needs to be out here now!" I frantically ordered, realizing it was time to walk down the aisle.

Gino swung open the men's dressing-room door. There stood Frankie, fully dressed in his sharp black tuxedo with his hair slicked back with gel. Covering my hand over my mouth in disbelief, I burst out, "Frankie, you are so hot!"

"I never knew I was so good-looking," he said, walking over to take my arm in his.

"Yeah, Frankie." I winked at him. "I've been trying to tell you there's so much more out there. Sometimes all it takes is a change of clothes."

Frankie walked me down the aisle to "O Mio Babbino Caro," the same Italian opera song I used to sing in the kitchen with him as he made his spaghetti sauce many years before. Halfway down the aisle, my mind wandered to Dad, wishing he could have been there.

Pastor Jim stood delighted beside Michael at the end of the aisle. Tears started to well up within me. Anna, standing at the altar as my matron of honor, caught my eye and started making comical faces to get me to stop crying. I swiftly shifted from tears to laughter as Frankie tightened his grip on my arm, determined to complete his role of escorting me down the aisle.

I took my place next to Michael. Pastor Jim, Michael, Anna, and I all breathed a deep sigh of relief. While Tashina sang a song, I struggled to contain the fluctuating emotions continually pulling me from laughter to tears.

"Who gives this woman to be married to this man?" Pastor Jim asked, fixing his eyes on Frankie beside me.

Frankie, now eighty-eight years old and hard of hearing, didn't answer.

Leaning over and whispering in his ear, I coached him, "Say, 'I do.'"

Looking at me warmly, he smiled.

I looked at Pastor Jim, not knowing what to do.

"Who gives this woman to be married to this man?" Pastor Jim repeated.

No answer.

Leaning over again I spoke more loudly into Frankie's ear, "Say, 'I do.'"

He looked at me, innocently smiling, and said, "What do you want, Christina?"

I started laughing again. For the third time, I leaned up into his ear and said louder, "Say, 'I do!'"

Frankie put a smug look on his face and looked blankly at Pastor Jim.

Anna and I could barely contain our laughter. For the fourth time, and this time loud enough for the entire church to hear, I shouted, "Frankie, say, 'I do.'"

He smiled from ear to ear. Then with his classic look, he spoke loudly, "Yeah, yeah, whatever you want."

Laughter filled the church. I looked at Pastor Jim and hoped it passed. His smile told me it did.

"Thanks, Frankie." I kissed him on one cheek and then the other.

Frankie left my side to take his seat next to Lily in the front row. Right before sitting down, he turned and slowly walked back toward me. Standing boldly in front of Pastor Jim, Frankie faced our guests. I wasn't sure what he was doing. Gently taking my hands in his, he looked Michael straight in the eye. "You take good care of my girl. She has waited a long time for this. You treat her good. You got that? See? Look at her now. She's already crying. Whatever you do, don't make her cry."

Kissing me on the forehead, he spoke loud enough for all to hear, "You look pretty today." Nothing in the rest of the one-hour ceremony topped that moment.

Good friends and relatives dancing to Italian street music set a charmed tone at the reception afterward. During the meal we played a movie we'd put together of Michael's and my growing-up years. Everyone found their seats and quieted down. The fifteen-minute presentation opened with some of my favorite photos of

Dad and me while the song "Daddy's Little Girl" played in the background. Within seconds, Angela stood up and walked out. Without hesitation, several relatives followed, making their way through the crowd. One after another, family members stood and left the room.

"Look at all of them," I said angrily to Anna. "They've got some nerve walking out like that! What are they all leaving for?"

During the movie, I found myself getting more and more upset at them for hating Dad. As soon as the video ended, I walked out of the reception hall to find a place to be alone.

"Are you okay?" Anna asked a few minutes later, intruding upon my solitude.

"No, I'm not! Dad's no longer here. I merely wanted him to be part of it in some small way through the video. Why did they all make such a big scene and get up and leave? What's the matter with all of them anyway?"

Gino popped his head around the corner. "I've been looking all over for you. Hurry up! The girls are ready to start their special dance."

I decided to put my anger aside and not let it ruin my special day.

Elena, Katie, and Tashina had written a song about our friendship entitled, "You'll Always Be a California Girl!" The lead singer of the band sang as the girls showed off some of their best-choreographed moves. We all doubled over laughing at the smooth dance routines. Our laughter suddenly turned to tears and hugs at the realization I was leaving California for good.

Michael took my hand and led me to the dance floor as the band began to play a slow song. As we danced together, I looked over at my girlfriends all sitting together watching us. Tears streamed down our cheeks, as we were all keenly aware of the life passage this day meant. I don't know if any of us could put into words what we were feeling, but nonetheless, we knew we were all in the same place. When I looked at my friends sitting there, I didn't just see the three girls sitting there. In them, I saw my whole life up to that point. I had made it to this place because I'd had them with me. My friends, my sister, and my ocean.

As Michael and I danced, I wished I could have it all. I wished we could just live in California. I wished I didn't have to move clear to the other side of the country where I didn't have the things that made me feel safe and at home.

Although I felt as if I was leaving a huge part of myself behind, I prayed that God would help me to trust in him through this life transition. It seemed he was stretching me to let go of some things I held dear in order to embrace something new that I couldn't yet see.

CHAPTER 16

breaking the cycle

"This is awesome!" I shouted. Extending my arms, I tipped my head back, allowing the rain to pour on my face.

"Run!" Michael shouted back, taking hold of one of my arms. "Hurry! Let's get under that tree."

A tropical downpour had interrupted our Hawaiian honeymoon and trapped us on Kampala Golf Course, which Michael, an avid golfer, couldn't resist playing. The eighteenth green stretched like a peninsula down to a rocky cliff overlooking the beach below. We found ourselves huddled under a palm tree over a mile's walk from our rental car.

"It better stop raining soon so I can go get the car, or we'll be late for our dinner reservations," Michael said, looking at his watch.

Taking a quick look around, I decided it was not going to stop raining anytime soon. "Here, give me the keys," I said, forming a plan of escape. "I'll go get the car."

"I'm not letting you go get the car. We're going to stay here until it stops. Then I'll go get the car," Michael insisted. "Sit tight. It'll stop pretty soon," he assured me as his hands disappeared into his jacket pocket to hold on to the keys.

"That's ridiculous! I'm not standing here all night. I'm going to get the car."

"No, you're not."

Reaching my hands into his coat pocket I vigorously attempted to loosen his hands from the keys. In a tug-of-war he wrapped his hands tighter, and I pulled harder as our struggle intensified. Moments later we stopped, looked at each other, and broke into laughter. Seeing my opportunity, I grabbed the keys from his momentarily weakened grasp and took off running down the fairway through the rain. Climbing down the rugged cliffs to the beach, I ran about a mile until I reached the parking lot where we'd left the car. Five minutes later, I pulled to a stop as close to Michael as possible and hopped out to run back to meet him.

"Christina, is that you?" a voice called out from my left.

Looking closely, I saw a man and woman huddled together under a tree on the seventeenth green. I stared at the couple with a blank look on my face.

"Christina? It's John and Nancy."

"What a trip! What are you guys doing here?" I shouted, recognizing some friends from San Francisco.

"We've been under this tree waiting for it to stop raining so we can finish our game," John said, smiling. "I heard you came to Hawaii for your honeymoon, but I never thought I'd run into you in the rain on a golf course. Look at you! You're drenched. Where is Michael?"

I pointed down the hill. "He's under that tree, trying not to get wet."

As the three of us approached Michael, John called out, "What in the world are you doing under the tree down here by yourself?"

Shaking his head, Michael surrendered. "I was trying to protect her, but she won't let me."

I was twenty-seven years old when Michael and I began our journey of discovery together. Our separate worlds had been enormously different. It was our differences, however, where we continued to find our balance. We each tried focus on what we liked about the other, especially when we got on each other's nerves.

Early in our marriage, I knew it was time to reevaluate where to place the relationships in my life. My girlfriends and I had always said we were like a dolphin pod. We traveled through life together and took care of each other. Keeping my pod small had provided safe boundaries for me. I envisioned a ripple of circles surrounding my pod, and I defined other relationships and their importance to me by placing them inside one of these circles. Anyone who was critical, manipulative, or controlling was put "out to sea" beyond the farthest circle.

In addition to my girlfriends, Anna, Gino, and my grandparents continued to travel with me in my inner circle. I kept Michael one circle out as we began our journey together. These other relationships had been tested in the fire of life. Ours was just beginning. I welcomed the new phase but embraced it with a certain amount of hesitation, still wondering how he would be once we got married.

Kentucky, with its lush bluegrass, horse farms, and rolling country hills, was a stark contrast to San Francisco and the siren call of the Pacific Ocean. It wasn't long before I made some good friendships. I worked hard to make it my new home, but I felt like a misplaced mermaid. As I watched some of my new girlfriends ride their horses, I longed for my surfboard and a good wave.

Since Michael had to travel a good bit for performances, we decided I wouldn't get a job right away so that I could travel with him. Frequent trips to San Francisco provided a saving grace for me during our first years of marriage. The ocean, familiar surroundings, and friends rejuvenated me. Frankie seemed lonely since I moved away, and he especially enjoyed my visits.

Besides going to California, the highlight of my year was summertime. Each year I looked forward to spending several weeks in Jackson Hole—the same place where Michael and I first met. Most of all I loved being in the mountains. The cabin where we stayed sat fifty feet from the banks of the Snake River. Immersed in the outdoors, we hiked, swam, and went white-water rafting. We also hung out at pristine mountain lakes and fly-fished the days away.

The first week of the summer of 1990, we hiked three miles to a mountain lake fed by melted snow water. Once at the top, I was overcome with a wave of nausea that worsened as the hike progressed.

"Maybe you didn't drink enough water," Michael offered.

"I drank the whole hike. It's something else. Everything's spinning," I said, lifting my pack onto my back. "We better get back before I get too sick."

For the next week I collapsed on the couch. Feeling no better, I finally called Anna. "I can't stop getting sick. What can I take to make this go away?"

"Have you checked to see if you're pregnant?"

"Pregnant?" Could I be pregnant? I always knew that when I was ready I wanted to have children. Ever since I was young I looked forward to the time when I could be the mom and do it right—be a good and loving mother. "I'd love to be pregnant," I told Anna. "But this better not be how I'm going to feel. There's no way I'm pregnant! I'm only sick. I feel like I have a bad case of the flu and someone put me on a boat in the middle of the ocean in a hurricane."

"Christina, you better go see a doctor to make sure. Call me as soon as you know something. I'll bet you anything you're pregnant."

* * *

"Well, sweetie, you are indeed pregnant," the doctor announced as he entered the room. "Looks like you're going to need to hang on tight. You've got a bad case of hyperemesis."

"Hyper what?" I asked. "Well, really, I don't care what it is. I only want to know how long it's going to last. I can't stand feeling like this!"

Handing Michael some papers, the doctor shrugged his shoulders, saying, "Sometimes it lasts a couple of weeks, sometimes a couple of months, but most women are over the worst of it by three months. This will be a good time to have your mother around. You're going to need the support."

My face turned red for a moment while I suddenly remembered the letter my mother had recently written to all of us, politely excusing herself from her role of being our mother. As if she ever really was. Goose bumps froze my arms and sent chills up my back. Even though there were other people in the room, I felt like I was all alone. The faraway gaze in my eyes told the doctor I was momentarily not quite with him.

"Make her drink as much as she can, even if she thinks she can't keep it down," the doctor ordered, shaking Michael's hand. "And try to blend some food in the blender and let her eat it like soup. If she doesn't keep something down in the next few days I'm going to have to admit her to the hospital."

Three weeks later, with two hospital stays to get rehydrated, I called Anna. "This is such a drag!" I protested. "I thought it was going to be fun being pregnant. Now I'm in the middle of the mountains, and I'm stuck lying on a couch while the room around me spins in slow motion. I try to drink or eat Jell-O, crackers, watermelon, or soup. I can't keep anything down."

"It will probably end at three months. Hang in there."

I just need to make it to the end of the summer, I coached myself.

Michael sat with me playing Yahtzee for hours on end trying to keep my mind occupied on anything other than how nauseated I felt. Together we dreamed of what it was going to be like starting our family. "I'm going to do my best to do it right," I said. "I'm going to make sure our children know I love them. And I'm going to do fun stuff with them, like teach them how to ski, surf, and play baseball."

Although we'd been married for two years at this point, Michael still didn't really understand my background since I *never* talked about it. I figured the only way to deal with my past was to block it out. I continued to tune out all the bad memories and looked forward to creating new ones with Michael and our baby.

"I want to do everything together as a family," Michael added. "We'll take family hikes, fly-fishing trips—everything we do here in Jackson Hole, we'll all do together."

"I'm going to find out what our kids are good at and buy whatever they need to practice and develop their skills," I added, shaking the dice in the Yahtzee cup. "I'm going to tell them every day I'm proud of them. I'm going to dream with them about their futures and encourage them to go after their dreams. If they're not good at something, I'll make sure they don't feel stupid, but I'll help them learn if they want to."

Two months later my condition showed no improvement. I was only 120 pounds when I started the pregnancy and dropped weight fast. The doctor in Jackson Hole suggested I fly home to Kentucky to see my doctor there. I was admitted to the hospital for observation and to get some IV fluids. The sickness didn't go away at three months. It didn't go away at four months. It didn't go away at five months. After six months of alternating weeks between the hospital and home, Anna called.

I clung to her words: "Be tough! There are only three more months to go. And for cryin' out loud, make yourself eat!"

During this time, I struggled to fight the thoughts that accused me, telling me I must have done something wrong and God was punishing me. I knew that wasn't the kind of thing the God I believed in did, but when every ounce of strength was being stripped from my body, my mind became a battleground of accusations that I was too weak to fight off.

Over the months, several different people had offered their solutions as to why I was so sick. Their words became harder to tune out. One said, "You are just sick because you harbor unforgiveness in your heart." Another offered, "You're so sick because you were rebellious against God and he is refining you." And another told me, "You're being tested. Hang in there! People are watching you to see how you handle this." I wanted to scream. Didn't people have something better to do with their lives than try to make me feel worse than I already did? That's one thing I dislike: when people feel as if they have to offer simple one-liners.

I continued to tune out negative words that didn't offer any support or understanding and focused my eyes on the God I had come to know—a God who is kind and compassionate and who desires to walk with me through whatever situation I find myself in here on earth. I imagined God sending me an angel to sit on my bed so I wouldn't feel alone.

The pastor of the church Michael and I attended called to see what we needed. That afternoon he sent a member of our church to visit me in the hospital. When the man got up to leave, he offered a prayer for us and read a verse that would become my lifeline for months to come: "Though [you] stumble, [you] will not fall, for the LORD upholds [you] with his hand" (Psalm 37:24).

I felt as if I were falling, and the image of being held by anything at this point, even if only on a spiritual level, was helpful.

The doctor who oversaw my condition was at a loss as to why I wasn't getting better. "This is becoming a whole other issue now," he said, trying to hide his growing irritation with me. He held my chart in his hand and looked at me. I knew he thought I was some nutcase he was tired of trying to figure out. "You should be getting better by now, not worse. I'm going to send in someone to talk to you. I wonder if maybe you have a deeper issue here about being a mother. Are you afraid of being a mother?"

"No!" I said. "I want to be a mother. That is not why I'm sick!"

"The baby has been taking from you to get what it needs, and now you don't have any more to give. We are no longer simply worried about the baby. I'm also going to send in a surgeon to talk to you about putting in a main line so we can feed you. The IV fluids are not enough anymore."

Michael sat quietly in the chair in the corner, unsure what to do.

I picked up the phone and dialed Anna. "The doctor doesn't know what's wrong with me! He wants to send in a shrink to talk to me to see if I have an issue with being a mother."

"What? Just because he doesn't know what to do to help you get better he's trying to put it all on you. What a jerk. Don't tell him anything about Mom! He'll for sure assume that's your problem."

I hung up the phone and stared at the ceiling. *Please, God, I need you to help me.*

About fifteen minutes later a doctor who worked with high-risk pregnancies walked in. "Hello, I'm Dr. Keating."

Oh no, I thought, *another doctor who wants to tell me she doesn't know why I'm so sick.*

She walked to my side, sat beside me on my bed, and took my hands in hers. I had just met her, but I felt like I'd known her forever. I knew she was going to help. "I hear you're having some problems keeping things down," she said gently.

"The other doctor doesn't understand why I'm so sick. What does he think? That I love throwing up?"

"Just because you're sick doesn't necessarily mean you have other issues."

I really didn't know why I was so sick, but I was growing very frustrated with the whole thing. My own mom might not have been there for me, but more than anything *I* wanted to be a mother. "I want this baby," I told Dr. Keating.

"Let's go ahead and try some different medications and see if we can prolong putting the feeding tube in. You keep on trying to drink."

As Dr. Keating got up to leave, I stopped her. "Is there any way you could be my doctor?"

"I think we can work that out," she said, smiling as she slipped out the door.

Over the next few months, I feared I didn't have the strength and endurance to make it to the finish line. The intense nausea made me feel as if I were being tossed around in huge waves until I couldn't do anything but crawl under my sheets and hope I didn't die. Dr. Keating helped me through the process. She offered kindness and support when I felt completely alone and helpless.

After nine months of sickness, IVs, and hospital stays, I finally delivered a healthy six-pound baby boy. Nothing in the entire world compared to that moment.

Michael and I took turns holding Jake. Although I was exhausted, all I wanted to do was hold him and look at every little detail about him. A good feeling filled my heart when I looked at Michael bonding with his son. It wasn't something I could explain in words, just a strong knowing that he was going to be the kind of dad I wanted for my son.

After Jake was born, Anna flew in from California with her oldest daughter, four-year-old Jamie. "You're the first one to have a boy!" Anna announced as she entered my room, loaded with gifts for the baby and me.

She reached down and picked Jake up. "You look like your mother," she cooed, holding him close to her face. Jake's bright eyes stared back at Anna while she talked to him. "Can you believe you finally made it to the end? That was intense!"

"You got that right. But look at him. He's so cute!" I said, beaming. "Every second of the last nine months was worth it."

Holding Jake in my arms signified to me that I had won another battle. My dream of becoming a mom transpired. I embraced my opportunity to break the cycle of an uncaring mother living in a dysfunctional family.

Nuzzled against me lay the unwritten pages of my little boy's life. I studied his face, fingers, and toes. I held my breath as he cried and hoped I'd know what to do. I couldn't get my fill of gazing into his big blue eyes. Stroking his soft face, I picked up a book called *The Runaway Bunny* that Anna had given me and began reading to Jake.

> Once there was a little bunny who wanted to run away. So he said to his mother, "I am running away."
>
> "If you run away," said his mother, "I will run after you. For you are my little bunny. . . ."
>
> "If you run after me," said the little bunny, "I will become a fish in a trout stream and I will run away from you. . . . If you become a fisherman, I will become a rock on a mountain, high above you."
>
> "If you become a rock on the mountain high above me," said his mother, "I will be a mountain climber, and I will climb to where you are."
>
> "I will become a little sailboat, and I will sail away from you."
>
> "If you become a sailboat and sail away from me," said his mother, "I will become the wind and blow you where I want you to go."[2]

I put the book down. I looked into Jake's blue eyes. It was settled. That was the kind of mom I planned to be.

CHAPTER 17

cut off

"Frankie, Jake just turned six months old. I want you to see him before he gets any bigger. I'm bringing him home next week," I announced eagerly.

"You're going to put the baby on the airplane? Yeah, yeah, that's good. That'll make Lily so happy! You want me to come get you at the airport?"

"Are you kidding? You're going to get thrown in jail one of these days if the cops catch you driving. Anyway, I already arranged for my girlfriends to pick me up. They're excited to see Jake too."

As I walked into the baggage claim, Elena reached for Jake, lifting him high into the air. "What a trip!" Katie shouted. "This is so cool that you're a mom."

"How's it feel?" Elena asked, nudging my arm.

"It's the best," I said with a smile. "A warm feeling washes over me every time I look at him or touch him or hear his cry. It's the best thing that's ever happened to me." As we walked out of the terminal, my friends and I looked at each other and then at Jake. We knew time had taken us to a new place. "I'm so glad we're always going to be friends," I said, wrapping my arms around their shoulders. "It means a lot to share this with you guys. It's times like this

when I realize how much more than friends we are. You are my family."

As Elena wiped her eyes, I knew she understood. "I wouldn't miss this for anything!" she said, nudging me in the side.

"I know what we're going to do now," Katie said, eyeing me up and down. "We're going to pig out! You're too skinny! It's a wonder you didn't float away."

"I sure felt like I was going to. Honestly, some days I was afraid to close my eyes. If I did, I thought I would float right out of my body. Having Jake was a piece of work for sure. It took all my determination to stay grounded and focused. But it's over now. Look at him. I still can't believe I have a baby!"

Pulling up to Frankie and Lily's house, Elena wildly honked the horn. Frankie stood at the window smiling. By the time I managed to get Jake out of the car seat, Frankie and Lily had scurried down the steps I used to run up as a kid. I hesitated placing Jake into Frankie's arms as he and Lily both reached out for him. Frankie was ninety-one and not as steady as he once was. I couldn't miss the moment though. Frankie tenderly reached his hands under Jake's arms and lifted him in the air. My heart beat faster as I stepped closer, ready to catch Jake just in case.

"Baby, baby, baby," Frankie cooed, not taking his gaze off his only great-grandson. "My little Jake." Frankie beamed with pride as he cuddled my son.

* * *

Although I dreaded the thought of going through another pregnancy, I wanted more children. I knew much of what I had learned in life came from my siblings. I had learned to be courageous from Anna and the importance of sticking together from Gino. They are part of my past and, in essence, part of me. I was more than willing to endure another nine months of illness to give Jake a lifetime companion.

On Jake's first birthday, Michael and I discovered we were having our second child. I desperately hoped my pregnancy would be different this time. It wasn't. Within the first week Dr. Keating set me

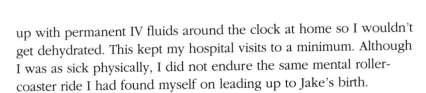

up with permanent IV fluids around the clock at home so I wouldn't get dehydrated. This kept my hospital visits to a minimum. Although I was as sick physically, I did not endure the same mental roller-coaster ride I had found myself on leading up to Jake's birth.

Jake was eighteen months old when I gave birth to Trevor, a few days before Christmas 1992. My dream of a brother for Jake was realized.

Jake provided nonstop entertainment for Trevor, even stopping to lean over and clap Trevor's tiny hands when his entertaining shows ended.

Trevor was a joy to care for. He went to bed without fussing, ate what I fed him, smiled all day, and provided company for Jake. I looked forward to many more children, but not to the sickness accompanying the pregnancy. Since the pregnancies were so difficult, and we had two healthy boys, Michael and I decided not to have any more children.

With my attention on my two young sons, I made no trips home to San Francisco the following year.

Lily was diagnosed as entering the first stages of Alzheimer's. Her condition deteriorated quickly, and Anna decided to place her in a nursing home. Shortly thereafter, Frankie prepared to join her. Anna was given the task of reviewing Frankie and Lily's finances to arrange payment for their care.

"Frankie, where in the world did you get all this money?" Anna said, shock evident in her voice and face.

"What are you talking about?" Frankie replied, irritated. "Rotten family. That's nothing. There should be a lot more than that."

Shuffling through the papers, Anna threw her hands in the air. "We had no idea you stashed all this money! Frankie, how do you want this divided up in your will? Do you want me to separate it in five equal shares amongst the grandkids?"

Jerking the papers out of Anna's hands, he looked at them one by one. Then he threw them on the table in front of Anna and shouted, "That's life for ya. You live your whole life, and then you have to leave it all to everyone else. And where is everyone now? Your father's dead! Lily's lost her mind. You're trying to tell me I have to move into that nursing home. And Christina?"

Pointing to the chair I had often occupied next to him by the front window, he hollered, "She promised me no matter where she went, she'd come back. She's not coming back. Now what am I supposed to do?" He waved his hand in the air and barked, "Forget about it! Christina, she doesn't care about me anymore. Take her out of the will!"

I didn't know of Frankie's decision at the time, but several months later I was in San Francisco for my younger sister Carrie's wedding. I noticed something was eating at Anna. She was unusually quiet as she rushed around the house picking things up, putting things away, and fiddling in the kitchen. She wasn't the type to hold anything back. I poured my coffee, sat down on the couch, and began to flip through a magazine.

Finally Anna stopped what she was doing and looked at me. "Christina, I need to tell you something. Before I put Frankie in the nursing home, I helped him get his money in order, including his will and how he wanted everything divided."

I immediately knew what was wrong and interrupted her. "No way. Did he leave Angela out?" Frankie was known for making irrational decisions depending upon his mood.

She looked at the ground, then looked at me and shook her head no.

"Gino? He left Gino out? He is going to totally freak out!" I exclaimed.

Anna's face was still solemn.

"Well, what, Anna?" I pleaded for an answer. "What did Frankie do?"

She banged her hand firmly on the table. "It's you, Christina! He left you out!"

"Me?" I questioned, slapping my hand across my heart. "No way! Why did he leave me out?"

I knew I was going to start crying. I got up and walked out of the house in shock and sat on the front porch.

Why did he do that? My mind continued to spin. *Where did that decision come from?*

Anna came out and sat down next to me, not knowing what to say.

"Why? Why did he do that to me? I knew I was special to Dad, yet I couldn't fully appreciate it because it was mixed with so much anguish. Frankie was different. I was special to Frankie with no strings attached. I knew Frankie loved me. Why would he reject me?"

"You've got to try not to take it personally. He freaked out at having to go live in the nursing home. He felt like you deserted him. He wasn't thinking straight."

Placing my hands over my ears like I wasn't hearing what she said, I tried to comprehend it all. "This is insane! I don't understand. I don't under . . ."

"I dreaded telling you. I'm so sorry."

I stood up and began to walk down the street.

"You going to be okay?" Anna cautiously asked.

I nodded my head, trying to hold back a flood of tears. "Yeah," I mocked. "I'm okay. I am always okay. No matter how much life changes, no matter how confusing our whole family is, I will always be okay!"

Walking down the street, I turned around one last time and shouted, "But sometimes I am not okay! Sometimes I just want to scream, 'No, I am not okay!'"

After a long walk I came back and asked Anna, "Am I so totally dense I actually thought Frankie loved me? Sometimes our family is so confusing I don't know what's real and what's not."

"I think Frankie felt you betrayed him when you married Michael and moved to Kentucky. He planned on you staying around. Whenever you left on trips before, even long ones, he looked forward to you coming back. I guess when you left after you got married, even though you came back for visits, he felt like he lost you."

"Lost me?" I asked, throwing myself on the couch. "How can he lose me? I'm not something he can misplace. I'm a person! I call him all the time! I write him letters and send him pictures. I come out to visit as much as I can. What can he possibly be thinking? How can he take what we've shared together since I was a kid and one day decide to throw me out the window as if I don't exist anymore?"

"Don't worry about it. I'm going to talk to the lawyer about it," Anna encouraged.

"Oh, Anna, you know as much as I do that this is not about the money! This has everything to do with my relationship with Frankie. This is his way of cutting me off, telling me I no longer belong to him. He might as well put it in writing: Christina is no longer part of my family. She's done. Finito! Just like that. In one rash moment of anger, I no longer exist. He ended up like everyone else! I thought he was one of the few things I could count on in life. Of all people, why did he cut *me* off?"

After surfing with friends in San Diego, I spent some time reflecting on where I was in my life and what would become of me if I acted like Frankie and dissociated myself from him. I wrote in my journal how I was feeling and prayed that God would help me let it go. That afternoon I was out on my board in the middle of some calm baby waves, letting the rhythm of the water help me catch my balance.

Not far from me another surfer hollered in my direction, "Dolphin in the roll wave!"

Adrenaline burst through my veins. I had never been in the water with a dolphin before. I wasn't sure if I should start paddling toward shore or stay where I was. I stayed.

The dolphin was alone, like me. It surfed the roll waves close to my board for over an hour; then, just as quickly as it came, it disappeared under the water and swam out to sea.

I knew my answer.

I wanted to be like the dolphin—supportive. If I reacted in anger or bitterness I could become more like a shark. I didn't want to become something I hated in others.

I would not let Frankie's bitterness and anger toward me draw me into acting the same way toward him. He wanted to throw my chair out the window. I wasn't going to let him. If he wanted to throw chairs, then he would have to throw his own chair out the window because I wasn't going anywhere. I wasn't going to shut him out as if he didn't exist. He was one of the good things in my life I wanted to keep.

I still didn't know how I could have read him wrong. *Is that what life is all about?* I wondered. *People you count on letting you down? Does it all go back to me? I can't change others. I can only*

change me. But sometimes I want people to be what they're supposed to be—steady and dependable.

Then I thought about God. Over the years, I'd learned bit by bit that he possessed those qualities I needed. I continued to look to God, who assured me in his Word that I belonged to him, that he would fill my empty places, and that he would guard my heart with peace. I decided I wouldn't put my hope in any person anymore. I continued to explore how God is unchanging, dependable, and consistent. When the rug was pulled out from under me, it wasn't his doing. He was there when I fell. He helped me get back up, brush myself off, and learn how to be a better person for my own children and grandchildren.

CHAPTER 18

saying good-bye

Hot gingerbread cookies and warm apple cider simmering on the stove became a Christmas tradition as we opened the boxes of ornaments and decorated our family tree. Michael carefully unpacked the lights, gently untangled the knots, and began to wind them around the tree. As I turned up the holiday music, the boys and I started to decorate. Michael patiently put together the train set that circled the tree. As soon as the first whistle blew, the boys shouted and jumped up and down with joy. Jake, a curious five-year-old, knelt down and leaned over, resting his elbows on the floor. Trevor, who had turned four the day before, imitated his brother and knelt down beside him. Together, in pure childlike wonder, they watched the train go round and round the tree.

What an awesome thing to experience Christmas the way it was meant to be, I thought silently as I watched my family.

Celebrating the holidays brought as much joy to me as it did to Michael and the boys. By giving them the memories I wished for, I was able to replace my own.

The weekend after Christmas I left for San Francisco to visit friends. I made plans to see Frankie and Lily while I was there. My first stop was Lily's nursing home. She was so far along

in the progression of Alzheimer's, I wasn't sure she knew who I was.

I then drove the short distance to the nursing home Frankie now lived in. This was my first visit with him since Anna told me he had disinherited me. I steeled myself to face the betrayal I was sure I would find in his face.

As soon as I walked into his room, Frankie smiled. "Christina! Where've you been—China?"

"No, Frankie, not China. I haven't been to China. I have never been to China, and I will probably never go to China. I've only been in Kentucky. I would rather be here, Frankie. I would rather be here with you. I would rather be here where my ocean is. I would rather be here where Anna and Gino and my friends are."

He straightened up in his bed and shouted, "Good! That does it. You come back here. This is where you belong!"

Belong? One day you belong and the next day you don't. So many conditions, yet I didn't know what they all were. After a long pause I sat next to Frankie. "No, Frankie. I don't belong here. I belong with my husband and children. I wish we lived here, but since we live in Kentucky, that is where I belong."

Frankie's eyes studied my face. Turning slightly, he stared out the window. Time passed in uncomfortable silence. "Have you seen Lily?" he asked, breaking the stillness.

"Yeah, I did. I saw her earlier this morning. She looks really good, Frankie. I think she's eating better."

"They won't let me see her!" Frankie wailed. "We've been together our whole lives, and now they're going to make us die apart. I can't stand it any longer. I want to be where she is."

"Frankie, you know Anna did everything possible to keep you two together, but when you kept throwing silverware at the nurses every time they went near Lily, I think that pretty much did you in."

After he stopped crying, Frankie looked at me with that look he had when he knew I was looking at him.

I wanted to ask him, "So are you going to put me back in the will, or what?" But I said nothing. *I love that old grumpy Italian man,* I thought to myself, smiling. *I don't know if I'll ever understand why you took me out of your will, but I'm not going to stop loving you.*

After a while, I leaned forward, kissing him on each cheek. "Frankie, I've got to go. I'll send pictures of the kids when I get home."

A few months later, on August 25, 1996, I received a call from Gino. Lily had died. When I arrived in San Francisco, Anna doled out my responsibilities. "Go down to the nursing home and gather Lily's things. Then I want you to be the one to tell Frankie. We'll all go down and get him later this afternoon for the funeral. Make sure he understands she died. He has to understand that before he sees her."

A knot in my stomach tightened. "Why me?"

"You know how to handle Frankie."

I wanted to refuse my assignment, but I knew I was the one who should break the news to my grandfather. Perhaps picking up Lily's things would help prepare me for the task at hand. A few hours later, I solemnly walked into Lily's empty room. A photo of us five kids dressed in our Easter outfits was proudly displayed on her bed-side table. Her rings, rosary beads, and some personal items covered the rest of the small tabletop. Opening the top drawer, I reached in and picked up Dad's police badge. His name and badge number glistened in the subdued light streaming in the window.

Sitting on the bed, I gazed at the badge. *How did I get to be thirty-five years old?* I wondered, my mind churning. *Memories from long ago still seem like yesterday.*

A smile spread across my face as I thought of the many streetcar rides Lily and I took downtown to celebrate my birthdays. During my college days she was sure to slip me some cash and say, "This is in case you need a little something." Her home was a safe harbor when the storms darkened the sky and scattered the puzzle pieces of our fractured childhood. I stood up to leave, filled with so many memories. "How do you tell someone that his wife of seventy-three years is gone forever?" I asked the empty room.

Ten minutes later I pulled into the parking lot of Frankie's nursing home.

Frankie appeared to be asleep as I walked quietly into his room. "Hey, Frankie! How are you doing?"

"Christina! What are you doing here?" he slurred as he slowly opened his eyes.

"I came home for a visit, Frankie." Shutting the door behind me to assure privacy, I walked to the side of his bed and pulled up a chair. I held his aging hand gently in mine. Frankie's eyes assured me he didn't know what I had prepared to say. So old, so frail. And now so great a loss to bear.

"Frankie, Lily is not doing well."

"What did you say, Christina?"

"Lily, she's not doing so well," I said louder.

"You went to see Lily today? That's good. Can you take me to see her?" he asked, leaning forward to make sure I heard him.

I took my hands from his and struggled to find the right words. Seconds ticked by. "Frankie, she's not doing good," I repeated, louder, as I leaned closer.

"Lily's not doing good?"

"Yeah, Frankie, it's Lily," I said, relieved he finally understood.

"Yeah, no one's doing good anymore. We're all old." He chuckled. "I think Lily's starting to forget things, like she doesn't know who everyone is. Did she know you, Christina? Did she know it was you?"

I shook my head and took a deep breath. "No, Frankie. She didn't know it was me this time." I stared out the window, searching for the right words, the right way, the right time. I couldn't find them. Perhaps there wasn't a right way to do this.

I took Frankie's hands in mine once again. "Frankie, Lily died. She went to sleep last night and never woke up again. She is gone. Finito. Dead."

"Someone died? Who? Who died?" He threw his hand forward as if shooing everyone out of his personal space. He started shouting, "They're all dead! All of them! Vince's dead! Johnny's dead! Leo's dead! Corina's dead! Rita's dead! Lucia's dead! Your father's dead! And Gino, your brother, he never comes to see me anymore. He's dead too!"

Who's he talking about? I don't know any of those people. Maybe those are all friends he grew up with. "Frankie, come on. Gino's not dead. He comes to see you."

With a disgusted look on his face and a quick wave of his arm again he screamed, "Ah, everyone's dead! I'm the only one left! I'm

going to die here on this bed I'm lying on. I'm going to die right here, alone!"

Oh, great, I thought to myself. *Now he's all worked up, and I don't even know if he gets it that Lily died.* "Frankie, do you understand that Lily died too?"

He looked at me as if he didn't understand what I'd said. Then he shook his head as he always did when he copped a bad attitude.

"Do you understand, Frankie?"

He shook his head and said, "No."

I leaned all the way up to his face, and this time uncomfortably shouted, "Lily is dead!"

"What's all the shouting about in here?" the nurse asked as she peeked in the door.

Leaning back in the chair, I let out a deep breath. "I'm trying to tell my grandfather that his wife died yesterday," I said, trying to hold back the tears. "We're going to pick him up this afternoon to take him to the service. I have to make sure he understands now so he doesn't freak out when he gets there."

The nurse got right in Frankie's face and shouted louder than I did, "Frankie, do you understand what your granddaughter is telling you? Lily died. The kids are picking you up later today to take you to see her. Do you understand?"

Frankie didn't say anything.

Moments later he looked directly at me. Defiantly he nodded his head as if to say he understood. Then he started rambling, "The poor kid. Why didn't anybody tell me? Everyone's dead now. They're all dead. That's okay. I'm just going to stay here until I die. I can't move or walk or hear anything. All I do is sit here and stare at the ceiling all day."

He cupped his hands in mine. We ignored the nurse as she placed an extra cover over his feet.

No more words came for either of us. We sat silently, our thoughts drifting, not unlike the many afternoons we had spent sitting in our chairs . . . silence our companion, each of us lost in our own thoughts, in our own worlds. Though this day, Frankie's face betrayed him. A slight smile convinced me the memories playing in his distant eyes were fond ones. Was he remembering what he first loved about Lily, or what she looked like on their wedding day? Did he recall the good times in their family when Dad was only a kid running around the house playing cops and robbers?

Occasionally Frankie turned to study my face as well. Perhaps he remembered me careening down the hill on my banana-seat bike trying to fly like an eagle, or how he made the best sauce and the biggest mess in the kitchen while I danced to Italian music that filled the house.

His smile turned to a tear, then two, then three. Reaching for a tissue, I leaned over and dabbed them gently. Frankie had seen so much change in his life. Was he able to make sense of it all? Or any of it? Perhaps he wondered why I grew up and moved away, or how he got old so fast. Or perhaps simply why his son and his wife died before he did.

Later that day, Gino pushed Frankie's wheelchair slowly toward Lily's coffin.

"This can't be real," Anna said with a sigh. "Look at us! It's us five kids again, together, with no one else in sight. We buried Dad. Now we're going to bury Lily."

All five of us stood around Frankie as Gino and Anna lifted him out of his chair. Frankie leaned on the casket looking solemnly at Lily. I leaned over and whispered into my little sister's ear, "That's what you're going to look like when you're old and dead."

Carrie started to laugh but her sobbing burst forth as she fought to catch her breath. Moments later Angela lost her battle to hold back her tears as well. Anna's eyes welled up, but she managed to maintain control. Gino stood solemnly beside his grandfather, biting his lip. My tears came next as I watched Frankie reach his hand forward, caressing Lily's peaceful face, her hair, and then her hands.

"It doesn't look like her," Frankie whispered as he carefully looked her over. "Her hair was blond; now it's all white. She was fat! Why is she so skinny? But that is her favorite dress she has on, so I guess that is her." He reached for her cold hands. "Good-bye, Lily. I won't see you anymore."

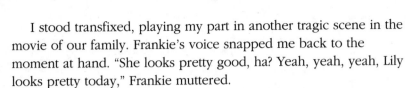

I stood transfixed, playing my part in another tragic scene in the movie of our family. Frankie's voice snapped me back to the moment at hand. "She looks pretty good, ha? Yeah, yeah, yeah, Lily looks pretty today," Frankie muttered.

We buried Lily the following day in the plot next to Dad and said good-bye.

CHAPTER 19

turning the tide

True to form, we all went our separate ways after the funeral. Gino, in charge of cleaning out Frankie and Lily's house, decided to hold a citywide garage sale without thinking to mention it to his sisters first. In one windy weekend, everything in the house was sold. The antique Italian furniture, the two chairs by the window, all the dishes, all the silver, and all the photos—gone. I felt like my memories had been sold for ten cents on the dollar.

The garage sale uncovered another mystery. When Gino cleaned up after the house was cleared out, he found envelopes in holes in the wall, behind pictures, and under the flooring. They contained thousands of dollars. Thousands of dollars in secret money. Why didn't Frankie ever tell us about it?

We never found out. Six months later Frankie died. Anna and Gino dressed him in his blue suede jacket. Still trying to come to terms with the fact that he'd cut me out of his will, I stood beside the casket looking at Frankie.

You crazy old man, how could you possibly think I would abandon you? Didn't you know I understood too well how that felt, that I wouldn't do that? Was I supposed to stay next to you looking out the window for the rest of your life? I didn't know that was our

arrangement. I thought maybe you cared about me. How silly of me to think that! No one ever cares about the children.

"Christina!" Gino said, startling me out of my thoughts. "Put your face next to Frankie! See, you have his same profile! The same nose! The same eyes! You're exactly like him!"

Angela, Anna, and Carrie all doubled over in laughter as I leaned over and placed my head alongside Frankie's. Gaining my composure after a good laugh I shrugged my shoulders. "There was a time I would've taken that as a compliment. But everything's changing. I don't want to be like Frankie anymore."

"Is this where they put Frankie?" a gruff voice hollered from the doorway in the back of the room.

"Yeah! Come on in," Gino instructed as he walked to greet the stranger. "How do you know Frankie?"

"I've known Frankie since he was a kid, just coming over from Sicily," he answered in an Italian accent as strong as Frankie's. "I used to hang out with Frankie and all his brothers and sisters. His sister Josie, she was a beauty! Where is everyone?" he hollered, looking around the room. "Where are Joey, Johnny, Leo, Corina, Rita, Josie, Lucia, and the rest of them? What's the matter with them after all these years? They can't come and see Frankie even in death?"

All of us kids looked at each other like this guy was either disoriented or in the wrong room.

"Who are you talking about?" Gino questioned.

"I think you have the wrong Frankie," I said putting my hand on the man's shoulder. "Here, let me help you find who you're looking for. This isn't your guy. Frankie's an only child. He doesn't have any brothers or sisters."

"That is Frankie DiMari," he insisted, peering past me at the casket. "I'm positive that's him."

Right then Lily's only living sister, Ginger, arrived accompanied by her son, Ricky.

Gino wrapped his right arm around Ricky, pulling him into the conversation. "Hey, do you know this guy? He's rambling on about Frankie having a bunch of brothers and sisters."

Shaking the old man's hand, Ricky probed, "What is it you're telling the kids?"

My mind went back to the nursing home, remembering what Frankie hollered: *They're all dead! All of them! Vince's dead! Johnny's dead! Leo's dead! Corina's dead! Rita's dead! Lucia's dead! Your father's dead!*

"I know this is Frankie DiMari! I knew Frankie like I knew the rest of them. I knew your dad, Agostino. I knew them all!" the man insisted as we crowded around him.

Standing at the edge of the casket, I looked down at Frankie. *What's the deal with all these people? Who are they? What are you holding out on?* I stared at him lying there, tight-lipped in life, tight-lipped in death.

"This doesn't make any sense!" Gino argued. "If this is really your guy, why didn't we know he had any brothers and sisters?"

All eyes stared at the unknown visitor, waiting impatiently for an answer.

"Everything got all messed up when Frankie got burned in that fire," he hesitantly began. "All you kids were young then. Frankie's father ran one of the big mob rings in the city. Everyone knew Giuiseppe. When he died, he left millions of dollars behind to his wife and kids. Frankie's mother was old-fashioned. She put all of the money in Frankie's name since he was the oldest son. Well, that didn't go over so well with the rest of the kids. They didn't trust Frankie to share it equally."

Shocked, we encircled the stranger as secrets from years gone by tumbled easily from his lips.

"Their mother was ill and on her last leg when Frankie got burned in that fire down on the Embarcadero in downtown San Francisco. That's when Vince and Johnny went to see their mother. They all went in there crying like babies, telling their mother the burns were so severe that Frankie's whole body was traumatized, and he died. Their mother went ballistic! Then they moved in with the pen and convinced her to rewrite the will, taking Frankie out of it completely and leaving the money divided amongst the other kids."

"That's why we didn't know any of them," I gasped. "Frankie hated them. That's why he was silent. The bitterness he swallowed by not being able to forgive them ate at him for the rest of his life!"

"Shhhhh! Let him continue!" Anna ordered.

"She left Lily a house and a good bit of money so she and your father would be taken care of, but that was it. Frankie survived his injuries, as he was expected to. He was in the dark about all this until his mother died a few months later and the will was unsealed. Frankie hit the roof! He refused to speak to any of his siblings ever again. He separated himself from the whole lot of them and pretended they didn't exist. They died as far as he was concerned."

"Ricky, did you know about this?" I asked.

"Yeah. You kids weren't supposed to find all this stuff out. The relatives figured the less you knew the better," Ricky confessed.

Wiping his brow the man continued, "I thought after all these years they would have made some peace with it all. Frankie felt betrayed by his siblings. He cut himself off from every one of them. He tried to make a new start with your father, but then—"

"Frankie loved you kids," Ricky firmly interrupted, as if he didn't want us to hear any more. "This has nothing to do with you. He loved when your dad brought you kids around. That's the only time I ever saw Frankie smile."

Shaking his head, the man sighed. "I don't know. It's a mad world we live in. Brother turning against brother. They didn't only mess up Frankie's life, they messed up their own lives as well. The whole bunch of them did nothing but fight and argue over all the money for the rest of their lives."

We all stared at each other in amazement. Some of the pieces began to make sense to me. I'd had strong suspicions there was something behind Frankie's silence. His passing exposed the secrets he'd managed to keep hidden in life.

"Are any of them still alive? Do they live around here?" Gino queried.

"For cryin' out loud!" the man shrieked. "The whole bunch of them lived within fifteen miles of each other their whole lives. I can't believe you kids never knew! I know for sure Joey's still alive. I see him every once in a while. I don't know about the others. Joey can tell you. He and Rebecca live over by Sloat Boulevard."

"Joey and Rebecca," I contemplated. "Hey, wait a minute! Is that the Joey and Rebecca who are my godparents? They disappeared when I was about six years old?"

Anna quickly joined in, "Now it makes sense. Joey is Frankie's little brother!"

"Yeah, they used to send me a hundred-dollar bill in my birthday card," I said, dredging up more memories.

Interrupting what had become a full-blown inquisition, the mortician announced it was time to go to the gravesite. Anna and I squeezed each other's arms tightly as the mortician slowly closed the casket lid for the final time, shutting Frankie's body inside his final resting place.

When afternoon came we placed Frankie's body in the ground next to Lily and my dad in a plot overlooking the southern rolling hills of San Francisco. As the casket was lowered into the ground I wiped my eyes and turned to look at each one of my siblings. We were all that was left of the family we had known.

Anna quietly stood at my side. Gino took the crucifix from the casket in his hands like it held special power or meaning. It was his reminder of Frankie. Carrie and Angela hung their heads as they slowly and solemnly walked to the car. I couldn't leave. Gino stood silently beside me.

"Here, this should be yours. I don't need it," Gino managed to choke out, handing me the crucifix.

"I don't want it, Gino. You keep it," I insisted, wiping my eyes with a tissue.

Shoving it into my hand, Gino persisted, "I don't want it. Take it. That's the end of it. It's yours."

Before I could pass it back, I felt a hand on my shoulder. It was Ricky. "Christina, you've always been special to me. Things were tough on you kids growing up. If you ever want to talk, please call me anytime."

I didn't want anyone telling me I was special. I didn't want to be special to anyone in this family.

Ricky took his mother by the arm, and they slowly walked away. Ginger's raspy voice mourned, "That's probably the last time I'll ever see those kids."

I stood on the hill looking down at the gravesite of Dad, Frankie, and Lily. The sun blazed brightly. The sky gleamed brilliant blue. The day looked happy, but it was not. Deep inside my soul I felt

heavy and all alone. A gentle breeze blew my hair. It was all over. They were all gone.

Closing my eyes I took a deep breath and tried to connect to the core of who I was. I thought about how easy it had been to let other people define who I was by their impressions of me or by the way they treated me. I didn't want my life defined by anyone else, most especially those who hurt me.

I imagined Frankie's betrayal going down to the grave with him. I was not going to walk away from that moment carrying the sting of his rejection with me. Somehow, understanding that he didn't know how to break the patterns of what happened to him enabled me to let it go without much struggle. His taste of betrayal linked him to a past he couldn't escape, no matter how deeply he shrouded himself in silence. I wasn't going to pick up that torch and continue the legacy of bitterness, silence, and isolation. I chose peace over bitterness and forgave Frankie.

In my mind's eye I held the torch of the legacy that had been passed from who knows where through the hands of Giuseppe to Frankie to Dad. I took the torch from their hands and with one big breath blew hard. The flame went out. It was up to me to turn the tide.

PART III

hold on tight!

GOD REWROTE THE
TEXT OF MY
LIFE WHEN
I OPENED
THE BOOK
OF MY HEART
TO HIS EYES.

Psalm 18:24 (The Message)

in one moment

The next couple of years passed quickly as Michael and I focused on raising our children. Although I still missed living in California, I settled into creating a strong sense of family for my husband and children in Kentucky.

It wasn't long into our marriage before I realized I didn't have to brace myself in the fear that Michael would turn out to be like my dad.

I admired Michael for being gentle, kind, and loyal. Though it wasn't always easy, we continued to work on creating a balance in our marriage, allowing us to fulfill our vow of joining paths without destroying our unique individuality. We encouraged each other to go after our dreams and gave each other space to make them come true.

We approached parenting in much the same way. What Michael saw modeled in his parents gave him a good frame of reference in raising our boys. Raising children as modeled by my parents would be nothing short of a disaster, so I was prepared to do just about everything differently. Most of the time we didn't know what we were doing or how to do it, but we gave it our best shot. We relied on our intuition and a lot of trial and error. I also watched people. I

saw what I liked and what I didn't like, and then I tried to let my observations shape the kind of mom I would be. I told my kids from the get-go there were a couple of things they could count on from me as their mother. I wouldn't always be a perfect mom, but I would always love them. I wouldn't always know how to handle something, but I would do my best.

I often reflected on something my friend's mom told me when I asked her for advice: "The best thing I can tell you is not to get overly hung up about the details of raising your children and instead think about what you want them to remember once they are grown. Then live your life keeping those goals as a priority."

That advice helped me more than any of the books I read. Together, Michael and I thoroughly enjoyed developing a parental relationship with our sons, growing spiritually, and spending tons of time together as a family.

Every June meant sunshine, surfing, spending time with friends, and having fun in California. Michael worked out of town for a few weeks, so that was my chance to take the boys back to my stomping grounds. It thrilled me year after year to see the connection they both shared with the water, even though they didn't grow up by it. Somehow, it got passed from my soul into theirs.

In the summer of 1998, Jake had just turned eight and Trevor was six and a half. One day during our vacation in California, I spread our towels out on the beach and made a picnic with my friends. The boys, whom I had signed up for a surf camp, met with their group in the roll waves close to shore.

I smiled as I watched them paddling out into the waves, maneuvering their boards against the current, and popping up to catch a ride. Several people walking the beach stopped to watch them.

Elena, Katie, and a few of their friends and children met us for the afternoon. Leaning back on the hot sand, I reached for a book to read to two of the little girls while my boys were finishing their lesson. The book, *Are You My Mother?* was a favorite of my boys but not mine. Nonetheless, that was the one the girls wanted to hear.

In it, the mother bird leaves the nest to go find food for her baby, who is about to be born. While she is hunting worms, the egg

cracks and out pops the baby bird. Tired of waiting around, the baby bird goes in search of her and asks everything he sees, "Are you my mother?" Near the end of the book, I often got completely frustrated with the bird and felt like shouting, "Forget about it, bird, your mother's not coming back. Get over it, and go find your own worms!" But I didn't want the children to hear that. I wanted them to know they could count on their mother coming back. So I continued reading until the bird finally finds his mother and they live happily ever after.

Turning to watch my boys ride their last wave in to shore, I thought about how I had always said I didn't need a mother. *Who needs a mother like the one I had? Not me.* As I thought about how deep and broad my love for my kids was, I was knocked over momentarily by something I wished I could have experienced.

Beside me a little girl let out the string of her kite. Five different-colored diamond shapes were strung together and held on one string. Tilting my head upward to the sky, I watched the five diamonds dance in the wind with perfect rhythm. A breeze from a whole other world—the world of my past life—washed over me. All of a sudden I felt a strong sensation of the connection, the rhythm of mothering, I had missed.

I closed my eyes and reached out my hand to feel it, but there was nothing to touch. There was no one there. Only emptiness. Only momentary illusions of what could have been.

I brushed it off. I wouldn't let something out of my control govern my emotions. I shook my arms until the feeling went out of my hands. I coached myself, *Don't want something you'll never have. What I can control is me, who I am, and what I have to give to my own kids who need me.*

Trevor broke my thoughts as he kicked sand all over the towel and shouted, "Look, Mom! I found a shell that's alive!"

"What a trip!" I said excitedly. "That's an ocean star! Hardly anyone ever gets to see one alive. You must be having a lucky day. Hurry, we better get it back into the water!"

Trevor and I ran to the shore. He held the ocean star under the water, letting the waves wash the sand off. Jake came running to see what Trevor had found.

"Can I touch it?" Jake asked as he pulled at part of it.

"Be careful!" I warned. "Whatever you do, don't break it."

"Why?" Jake asked. "It's just a starfish."

"No, it's not," I said, shaking my head as if he should know all about it. "It's really a star!"

"It is not!" Jake insisted.

"Can I keep it?" Trevor asked.

"No. It will die if it's not in the water. Here, give it to me. I'll throw it back. You two better get going. Your instructor is ready for another round of waves."

I held the ocean star in my hand as I watched my boys run to meet up with their group. The memory of my dad's voice echoed from a place far away in my distant past as I recalled him telling me the story. Water washed over my feet as my mind swarmed with thoughts and memories from scores of different directions.

Elena didn't say anything when she sat down next to me.

"This is really trippy, isn't it?" I asked Elena, still looking intently at the ocean star. "I haven't seen one of these since we were in high school. I can still see Ripple trotting past us with the starfish hanging out of his mouth. Look at us, we're in our thirties, and it feels like it could have been yesterday."

"Remember what Chip told us?" Elena asked as she reached her hands into the water. "As long as the ocean star is connected to its source of life, it will grow back all the missing pieces that got injured along its journey."

"Yeah, I can still hear his voice," I said.

"I wonder if we'll ever feel all put back together while we're here on this earth," Elena said as she buried her feet in the sand.

The ocean breeze blew Elena's dark black hair over her eyes. I reached to pull it back and tucked it behind her ear. The world around us went still as we looked out over the water. In the silence, we understood more about each other than anyone else on the face of the earth.

"There's something else I'll always remember," I said as I tossed the ocean star back into the roll wave. "The day Rosie died, I promised her that if I ever figured out how to put the broken pieces of my star back together again, I'd be a light that would shine for

others. I told her I'd do it for both of us. Only problem is, I still haven't figured out how to do it."

That night while we watched the sunset, I whispered a prayer to God: "If you will help me figure out how to put the pieces of the ocean star back together again, I will in turn help others find their way home too."

* * *

Within a month of that prayer I found myself lying on a cold hospital bed ready to be wheeled in for surgery.

This is not a big deal. Women go through this all the time. Alone in the hospital room, I repeated the kind of "self-talk" that had served me so well in my thirty-eight years of life.

But other thoughts filled my mind as well. *I wish Anna and my girlfriends didn't live clear on the other side of the country.*

A nurse came in to prep me for surgery. "Is your mom going to be here to help you?" she asked, making small talk. I shook my head no. The nurse chattered on, asking me questions about where I grew up and about my family. I wanted her to stop talking to me. I tried to tune her out by using more self-talk. *You're fine! Be tough. You don't need anyone. You can take care of yourself.*

My thoughts were again interrupted as Dr. Keating walked in. "How are you doing?" she asked with a warm smile.

Hoping she wouldn't sense my nervousness, I smiled back and told her, "I'm okay."

"I'll be back after I get ready," she said as she patted my leg on her way out the door. "Don't worry about anything. There's no need to be nervous."

I felt reassured knowing my doctor, who had helped me through my pregnancies, would be performing the surgery.

The anesthesia began to work. I felt as if I was awake yet in a dream at the same time. The nurse's words continued to echo in my mind, "Is your mom coming to help you?"

No! She is not coming to help me.

My mother was merely one of many questions about my past shrouded in a mysterious veil of secrecy. My childhood still felt like puzzle pieces that lay scattered in some closed corridor of my memory. I hoped that one day I'd be able to put them together. Try as I might, I couldn't figure out which piece went where.

The anesthesia continued to pull me toward unconsciousness. As I drifted further from reality, I saw a deep pit before me. It was filled with the darkness of my past.

What is in there? Why does it seem locked away in a different time, yet always lurking behind me? I sensed I was being pressed to give my answer before the anesthesia completely won its battle with my conscious mind.

A knot inside my stomach tightened as unpleasant memories bubbled to the surface. *Why am I thinking about that mess at a time like this?* I felt like a little girl again. I wanted my sister to be with me in the operating room, telling me everything would be all right.

I realized Dr. Keating was standing next to me. She gently reached down and took my hands in hers. Her comforting touch washed over me. In that moment, I felt as if she held my entire life in her hands. Her eyes seemed to penetrate my skin and see into my soul. She had no idea what I had been through, and yet it felt as if she knew all about my past and was telling me that everything was going to be okay.

"Christina," she said gently, "everything is going to be all right."

Those simple words spoke to a part of me buried deep within the wreckage of my past. I was enveloped in something from another time, another place, a distant memory. Her words somehow seeped through the protective walls around my heart. Somehow I believed her—I believed that everything was going to be all right.

The funny thing was, she was only talking about the surgery. But for one brief moment, I thought she was talking about my life.

* * *

"Christina, you made it," my friend Ellie whispered as she gently dropped ice chips into my mouth.

"I feel really strange," I slurred, barely able to open my eyes. "This medicine has me totally wigged out."

Sitting next to me in the recovery room Ellie continued to talk to me as I slowly came out of the anesthesia. "I told you having a hysterectomy wasn't going to be easy. When I had one, I felt like someone sent me to Mars for weeks, and I couldn't get my feet back on the ground."

Later Dr. Keating came in to check on me. Her kind voice reassured me, "You'll feel more like yourself once the medicine wears off. Remember, it may take some time for your body to balance back out. Get some rest, and I'll be back to check on you later in the afternoon."

"She's so nice!" Ellie said.

"I know. I'm so lucky."

Thinking back to before the surgery, I asked, "Do you think everyone has strange thoughts from anesthesia?"

"What are you talking about?"

"While the nurse was prepping me, she innocently asked if my mom was coming to help me. As I was rolled into surgery I found myself drifting into the recesses of my mind, wondering what really happened back when I was a kid. Then I saw this pit. . . ."

"Those must have been some heavy-duty drugs they gave you!"

Though my head was still swimming, we broke out laughing.

A few days later I was released from the hospital to go home. Three days of pain, no sleep, and feeling out of sorts was making me long for my own bed.

"I get to go home," I announced as Michael walked in the hospital room.

"I can't take you home right now," Michael said. "My rehearsal starts in an hour. I'll come get you at lunch when it's over."

"Look, this is not a time to be practical. I feel horrible, and I want to get in my own bed!"

Though not the timing he chose, Michael rushed to get the car. The nurse wrapped me in a white blanket and wheeled me down to meet him. Michael put the car in high gear and raced out of the parking garage. I was aggravated he thought it such an inconvenience to his schedule to take me home. He wasn't even planning to stay around to help. Since he wasn't, I was determined not to let him even if he did come to his senses. He was furious that I couldn't wait until noon to go home.

We didn't say a word to each other the entire drive. The tension grew thicker and thicker as each of us stubbornly held our positions. I finally broke the silence. "Would it be too much of an inconvenience for you to stop and get my medicine? Since I'm going to be home alone it would be nice to know I won't be dying in pain."

He swerved into Walgreens drive-through service and waited in the left line. A red van pulled up next to us in the right lane. I glanced over. It was Misty, one of the mothers I knew from school. Her eyes widened as she saw me bundled in my white blanket with a scowl on my face.

"Christina, are you okay?" she asked, sincerely concerned. "You look horrible!"

Looking out my window I shook my head no.

Misty leaned out her window and shouted to Michael, "Is she okay?"

Michael rolled down my window and leaned past me, assuring her, "Yes, she's fine. She just had surgery, and I'm taking her home. She's okay."

I rolled my eyes.

Misty started laughing. If I'd had my wits about me I would have gotten out of my car and into hers right then and there.

Irritated with my attitude, Michael dropped me off at home and sped off so as not to be late for his rehearsal.

Gingerly walking up the stairs I crawled under my sheets and called Elena. "Can you believe I just had surgery, I can barely walk, and he drops me off without even offering to help me?"

"I feel bad I wasn't with you. I would have taken you home and made you some yummy soup."

"I know. Oh well, I'm sure I'll be fine once I get some rest. I'll call you in the next few days to let you know if I've survived."

"Don't be too hard on Michael. Guys don't get important stuff sometimes."

"Whatever."

After picking the kids up from school, Michael arrived back home with bags of groceries. "What do you feel like eating? I'll make you whatever you want," he offered in a gesture of peace.

"I don't need anything."

After two days of refusing any help from him, I finally lashed out. "If you ask me one more time if I want some crackers or Sprite, I am going to freak! I do not want *you* to get me anything. If I want something, I'll get it myself! Stop asking me!"

Something deep inside started to crack. If I hadn't felt so sick and angry, I would have used every ounce of energy to shut the gate threatening to open and expose my past. But I was too physically weak and too emotionally drained. Something was crumbling inside me, and I couldn't stop it.

"I don't know why you couldn't see with your two eyes I needed you to help me!" I said, directing my frustration with full force at Michael. "I needed you to take me home and be with me! Do I have to get my head run over by a car before you realize I need a little help? Of all people, I should be able to count on you. But all you could do is think of yourself."

"I'm not used to you needing me like that. You're always so tough. I figured you'd be fine by yourself."

"I know. I've never needed anyone to take care of me. I don't know where this is coming from—although it's not like I just fell and skinned my knee. For cryin' out loud, I just had major surgery!"

"Christina, don't feel bad about it. I'd like it once in a while if you were more like this. I just wasn't prepared for it."

"Oh, that sounds like a cop-out. You need to know there might be once or twice in my entire life that I need you to help me and that was one of them. Isn't there ever going to be a time in my life when I don't have to be so tough?" A lifetime of confusion welled up inside me. "For once in my life, I want someone to take care of me. Is that too much to ask?"

Resting my head on Michael's shoulder, I bawled my eyes out. "I'm sorry I got so mad at you. Something is happening inside of me. I don't know what it is. I feel like something cracked open, and all the pain I buried growing up is coming to the surface. I want to make it go away, but I can't figure out how."

"You've always focused on the positives that shaped you from living through all those years. I don't know—maybe you should let yourself look at the stuff that was a bummer," Michael suggested.

My mind drifted back. "I can make myself look at it. But what I'm most afraid of is having to feel it. I hated those feelings. There's nothing good back there. To feel anything good at all I have to go all the way back to when I was a child with Dad. Other than that there's only confusion and memories of how I couldn't trust anyone."

"It might be good for you to talk to Anna about it."

"Anna will think my hormones are whacked out. Our whole lives, it never mattered how we felt. Our feelings couldn't change anything. We had to keep on moving. Stay focused. Be tough. To talk about it, we'd have to break our number one rule: 'Whatever you do, don't look back.'"

CHAPTER 21

riptide

After several weeks of hashing over these thoughts, I finally called Anna. "Do you ever think about stuff that happened when we were kids?"

"Yeah, sometimes I do," she said hesitantly, "especially as we've all gotten older. I can see each of us affected in different ways. Really, we all have stuff that still bothers us."

"I thought once Frankie died I'd be able to let go and start over," I admitted. "I just want to be able to figure out why it was so bad."

"All I know is I wanted to get as far away from it all as I could," Anna said with a sigh. "It's like we survived a war or something."

"I know. That's exactly what it feels like to me too. But somehow in the midst of it you took over before you were even in first grade. Thank you for everything you did for me—for us. I don't know what we would have done without you."

"I felt like someone would take us all away if I didn't take care of you guys."

"You made me believe everything was going to be all right, even when it wasn't all right at all."

"The only thing I ever wanted for you guys was for you to believe someday everything was going to be okay. I will say this—

the longer I'm a mom, the more I realize we missed out on something major. I'm not saying it's bad, because I think we trained ourselves at such a young age to handle whatever came our way. But some of the basic needs we had as children got buried somewhere."

"Maybe that's what's happening to me. All of a sudden, whatever got buried in the past is poking its way into my present."

"You know what you need to do?"

"Yeah. I need to get in the ocean! That's what I hate about living here. Whenever I need to figure something out, or I feel out of sorts, I have nowhere to go. I just want to get on my surfboard so bad and get in the water! I don't know why I had to move so far away from the ocean. I feel so far from home sometimes," I said, getting all choked up. "I don't know why I'm having a meltdown. I just want to come home."

Anna started to laugh on the other end of the phone.

"Whatever you do, don't tell me to be tough," I said. "I'm sick and tired of having to be tough all the time. I am going to sit down right here on this path and I'm not moving. I don't care what you say."

A week later I received a letter from Anna. Inside the envelope was a drawing her girls had made of the ocean with a free-spirited girl surfing the swells. Also enclosed was a plane ticket and a gift certificate to one of my favorite surf shops. A note at the bottom read, "Get packing! I arranged with Michael to send you home to surf for as long as you can handle being away from your family. I already talked to Elena and Katie, and they are planning on taking time off work to join you. I'm going to meet you up in San Francisco for the weekend. Gino can't wait to see us! He insists we stay at his house."

* * *

Two weeks before my trip to San Francisco, I went for a long walk in the woods by my house at dusk. I had just started a Bible study by Beth Moore called *Breaking Free*, and I wanted to go to a quiet place to think about the lesson I was working on. Soon the clear sky was lit up with bright shining stars. A familiar song about God

played on my Walkman—"You Are All I Need." Gazing up at the stars, I sang the lyrics over and over again until all of a sudden I realized I didn't like the song.

"You want to know the honest truth about how I feel right now?" I prayed out loud. "I hesitate even saying it, but you are *not* all I need! When everyone else walked away, you have stayed by my side. I wouldn't have made it if it weren't for the way you guided me, but sometimes I just want someone human to talk to, someone I can actually see with my own eyes and touch with my hands."

In most situations if I needed to talk to someone I could talk to my girlfriends or my sister, and if it wasn't something I needed a girl's brain for, I could talk to my husband. But this feeling I was experiencing was something totally different than anything I had ever felt before. It wasn't something my girlfriends had experienced. My sister would either tell me to get over it and stop dwelling on things I couldn't change or she'd try to give me a solution to fix it. I knew Michael would probably just look at me with that blank look that told me he was trying to get what I was saying but didn't. I didn't want someone to solve my situation; I just wanted to talk to someone who would listen and possibly understand how I was feeling.

Over the years I had talked with God so much that I had learned to hear the way he talked back. It was like a whisper in my heart.

As I gazed up at the nighttime sky, one radiant shining star stood out from among the others. I fixed my eyes on it.

Make a wish.

I stared at the star and began to form my thoughts. "Starlight, star bright, the first star I see tonight. I wish I may, I wish I might, have this wish I wish tonight. I wish for . . ."

I struggled. To wish for what I wanted would mean breaking my lifelong rule of not wanting something I didn't have. I also wasn't stupid; I wasn't going to waste a wish. I didn't want anything different about my past. I wanted something different about my present.

What do you want?

"What do I want?" I gazed long and steadily at the brightly lit star. "Sometimes I wish I had someone a little older than me to talk

to. I don't want someone who thinks I'm nuts just because I've hit a bump in the road or feels the need to tell me what I should or shouldn't do. I just want someone I can talk with, who I can relate to, and who will understand what I'm feeling. I don't know, God, it would be nice to have someone to talk to about basic life stuff, like how to handle different situations that come up with the boys or sharing something great that happens, like an 'older friend.' That's what I wish for."

As I walked back home I kept feeling as if I was hearing, *Surrender your wish*.

"Surrender it? That fast? Why is your answer no? Do you want me to want only you? That would be fine if I lived in heaven. But I live on earth. Don't you think it would be a good idea for me to feel a little support down here where I actually live? Sometimes I just want to hold something in my own two hands instead of having everything be in the realm where I can't touch it."

The following day my girlfriend Ellie called. I explained to her what I had experienced the night before. She had some insight.

"I just read this story I thought you would like to hear. This little girl had dime-store pearls she cherished more than anything else. One day her father asked her to give him the pearls. Over and over again she said no, you can take anything but the pearls. All along the girl's father had a beautiful strand of genuine pearls in his pocket to give her in exchange for her dime-store set. The moral of the story is that when we are asked to surrender something, it often is because God has plans to replace it with something much better."

"That makes me think of the pearls my grandmother gave me," I said. "Ever since I wore them on my wedding day, they've been a symbol for me, representing what I missed by not having a mother in my life."

"I've learned so many times that when I feel prompted to surrender something, it's usually for my own good," said Ellie. "It's a positive way for me to lay down all my hopes and dreams of how my wish could be answered. It moves my wish into a realm where God can answer it in the 'above and beyond all I can ask or imagine' territory."

Once we finished our conversation, I knew what to do. Digging out my special brown wooden box, I opened the lid and looked at the few items I'd saved since my childhood. Inside was a green bandana tied to a weathered rope used for Ripple's collar, a letter Dad wrote to me before he died, and the golden surfboard necklace Gino gave me for Christmas the day we thought Dad was going to kill all of us. Underneath was the program from my wedding day and the set of pearls Lily gave me when I was six.

I lifted out my pearls, wrapped them in a golden box with a pink bow, and performed a little ritual of surrendering my wish.

Somewhere deep in my thoughts I heard some words of hope. *I'm not going to send you one "older friend." I'm going to send you many. They will all be different and unique. Keep your eyes open. I'm going to have so much fun sending them to you. Enjoy!*

In the following days I kept my eyes open to those around me whom I could learn from, and I continued to explore how God could provide what I was lacking by not having a mother and father in my life.

Through the years I had learned to track my journey through drawings, art, photography, and journaling. In my own journal, I drew symbols from a verse that read, "The LORD God is a sun and shield; the LORD will give grace and glory; no good thing will He withhold from those who walk uprightly" (Psalm 84:11, NKJV). A sun, illustrated like a shining pearl, was my symbol of how God would provide for me in motherly ways through his creation; a purple shield was my symbol of how God would provide for me in fatherly ways through the guidance of his Word.

Then I began asking questions. *What about you, God? Did you know what went on during my childhood? Why is it all bothering me so much now?*

A passage came to my mind: "The truth will set you free" (John 8:32).

I felt free before that nurse started asking me if my mom was going to help me after surgery. What else do I need to be free from?

In my mind, I saw a lid being lifted off a deep dark pit—the same pit I saw before I had surgery. I felt compelled to look in, yet scared to death to go into that darkness.

I saw an image of Jesus going down into the pit. Halfway down, he turned and asked me to follow him.

"In there? I don't think so," I said. "I've followed you many places, but I'm not going in there."

Time seemed to stand still. Nothing in the image moved, as if he was just giving me more time to think about it.

"Are you sure I need to do this? It was really a mess in there!"

Trust me.

"I really don't want to go in there."

I know. Don't worry, I'm going with you.

Reluctantly, I took a deep breath and stretched my hand forward to grab hold of his hand.

"Okay, I'll go. But whatever you do, don't leave for even one tiny second."

I will never leave you or forsake you. Even when you feel like you're alone, remember, because I am at your right hand, you will not be shaken.

Later that day, my friend Ellie came for a visit. Since we were close in age, we often talked about raising our children and the different stages of spiritual growth we found ourselves in. As we sat in the white wooden rockers on my front porch, I flipped through a magazine while she thumbed through gardening books, deciding how she was going to design her new garden. A quote in the magazine jumped off the page at me: "A journey of a thousand miles begins with a single step."

Looking out over the rolling hills and towering cedar trees, I pondered the sentence for a few minutes. Interrupting Ellie's focus on gardening, I read her the quote. "How do you know what the next step is?"

Laying her magazine down, she leaned back in the rocker and looked out over the horizon with me in silence for several minutes. "I think you'll have a tug-of-war over wanting to run from these emotions and wanting to face them," she began. "The first step is to decide you're not going to run."

Blocking the sun with my hand, I looked toward her. "You know what? It's kind of like being pulled into a riptide. Riptides pull you away from shore. If you fight one you only get carried out farther and

farther. When you know the pattern, you can swim parallel to get out of its pull until you're free. Then you can swim safely to shore."

"So what do you think that means to you now?"

"It's all about control. All my life I fought to keep control. All the memories I didn't know what to do with I shoved somewhere. By letting them out and looking at them, I'm going to need to trust that God has my life in his hands. Then I can surrender to the riptide and know that when I'm done figuring it out I will find my way back to shore. Somehow I know once I surrender, I'll be swept into that pit I keep seeing."

"We all want to leave our past behind us, but when it won't stay back there, we need to figure out what's still bothering us. You can't change what happened, but you can change what you're doing with it. I think it was good you ran when you were younger, but now you're in a safe place in your life. I think you're ready to look at what you ran from."

"Maybe there's more I need to know about Frankie and his family," I thought out loud. "Maybe Frankie's past has something to do with Dad. If it does, maybe I can find answers to some of the questions I have about my family."

Ellie sat up straight. "That's it! You need to go back and talk to someone! Who's still living who knew Frankie? You've got to find out. Maybe you can talk to someone while you're out in California surfing next week."

"Actually, maybe Joey, Frankie's youngest brother, is still alive," I said, my interest growing at the thought of unraveling the secrets of our family. "Maybe he will talk to me! He was my godfather."

"That's a good place to start. It's been my experience that when we're turned around, it's usually because a shift is taking place inside us. The lessons you need to learn will begin to present themselves, but you need to watch what's going on around you."

Before leaving for California, I tracked down Joey's phone number. Sitting at my desk, I took a deep breath. *I am thirty-eight years old. Why am I trying to reach someone I haven't heard from since I was seven?*

Picking up the phone, I dialed the number. "Hello," a man with a rough Italian voice answered.

Caught off guard at the quick answer, I fidgeted with the papers on my desk and responded, "Is this Joey DiMari?"

"Yeah, that's me. What are you going to do about it?"

I started to laugh, thinking, *This guy sounds just like Frankie.*

"This is Christina, Frankie's granddaughter."

"Yeah? What do you want to talk to me for?" he asked in a harsh tone.

"For one, you are my godfather! I'm not trying to make you feel guilty or anything, but I'd like to know who you are, what you look like, where you live—stuff like that."

"Oh, so you want my money! Is that it?"

"I don't care about your money! I only want to take you out to lunch and meet you."

"Yeah, that's fine. You call me sometime. I've got to go now."

"Hey, I can't simply call you sometime. I've got to plan it. How is Friday afternoon?"

"No, I don't want to go out to lunch. Forget about the lunch."

"Oh, come on, Joey. I'll take you somewhere nice."

"No, I don't eat! Forget about the lunch!" he demanded.

"Okay, forget about me taking you out. I will bring you lunch. What do you like?"

"I don't like nothing. I got to go!" he hollered as he threatened to hang up again.

"Okay, okay, forget about the lunch. How about just a visit?"

"Oh, I don't know. I have so much to do. I've got to go to the doctor's for my eye. I can hardly drive anymore. I have to go downtown to see my friend who is a painter. He has a condition no one knows about but me. He may show up dead one day, and I will be the only one to find him."

"Look, Joey, it seems like you're a really busy guy. If you have all that stuff to do, then surely you must keep some kind of a calendar. Why don't you go check your calendar and let me know if you have next Friday, July 15, free?"

"Yeah, yeah, sure." I heard him drop the phone and fuss with some stuff on his desk, making sure I could hear him going through a bunch of papers. After a long pause, he came back to the phone and said, "Yeah, sure, Friday looks good. It looks like most of that

stuff I got to do doesn't happen until November."

"Great, I will be there at noon," I assured him as I hung up the phone.

A few days before leaving for the West Coast, I stopped by Dr. Keating's office for a postsurgery checkup.

"I'm going to California in a couple of days, and I'm planning on surfing some. Do you think I'm okay to exercise now?"

"You're fine to go. What else are you planning to do while you're there?"

"I can't believe I'm going to do this, but I'm going to talk to my godfather whom I haven't seen since I was a kid. It's a complicated story. . . ."

"You can tell me how it went when you get back. I'll want to see you for one more visit in two weeks. Have a great time!"

I wanted to have a great time, but my intuition told me there was a lot of work ahead. My heart pounded with excitement mixed with a touch of uneasiness. Hidden mysteries waited to be uncovered. The real story of my childhood seemed just beyond my grasp.

CHAPTER 22

secrets

"When's dinner going to be ready? Hup two, let's go!" Gino huffed to his new wife. "And don't forget to put some fresh basil in the sauce."

"I'm out of fresh basil," Renata shot back as she stirred the sauce.

"Well, go get some!" Gino ordered.

"You go get it if you want it so bad!"

Anna and I listened intently to my brother and his wife bicker at one another. I stood in the doorway with my hands on my hips, surveying the all-too-familiar scene.

Gino leaned over Renata's shoulder to make sure she cut the onions to his standards. "What else you got to throw in there? How about some mushrooms? Here, put the broccoli in there too. Cut the stems off before you sauté it, and soak the vegetables in cold water first! Stop, you forgot to put the garlic—"

"Take a break and sit down!" I interrupted, walking into the kitchen.

Gino chuckled. Pouring a glass of wine, he sat down to enjoy his drink. "Oh, the portabella!" he shouted, leaping to his feet. "You need to add the portabella!"

"Gino, there is no portabella!" Renata snapped.

"Forget about the whole thing. It won't taste like Lily's without

the portabella!" Gino shouted, setting his now-empty wineglass firmly on the table.

"Look!" I insisted, my face inches from Gino's. "If you want the portabella, get out of here and go get it yourself!"

"This is none of your business!" Gino warned in a husky voice.

"I've been standing here for ten minutes listening to you talk to Renata just like Dad used to talk to Mom. I can't stand it any longer. What's the matter with you? Is that what you want? Did you want to become Dad? I liked you better when you were Gino!"

"I'm not Dad!" Gino yelled. "He was fifty-one when he died. I'm only forty-one. I have nine more years to prove I'm not him!"

Seeing the anger rise in his eyes, I quickly backed up, putting a few feet between my now enraged brother and myself.

"Don't tell me you don't want me to act like Dad, Christina. You were the only one who liked Dad. You stood up for him when he did nothing but trash everyone. You are so blind!"

"I am not!"

"You are too!"

"If you didn't like Dad, then why are you acting like him? Why are you drinking so much?"

I realized I had pushed Gino past his limit. As he lunged for me, Anna stepped directly in front of me. Gino had to go through her to get to me.

"You need to chill out, Gino," Anna warned.

Shaking, I stormed off to my room.

Anna took Gino to the opposite end of the house to cool down. They talked for hours into the night.

The following morning Gino awakened me. Walking into my room, he shook me playfully. "Hey, what's the matter with you for screaming at me like that?" he teased. "You scared the living day-lights out of me last night."

"Me? Screaming at you? You started it!" I snapped, sitting up in bed.

"Ah, forget about it. I'm not talking about it no more," he mumbled as he turned to walk away.

"What was that? Was that a measly attempt to maybe say you're sorry? C'mon, say it! Say, 'I am sorry.'"

Coming back to sit next to me on the bed, Gino pleaded, "C'mon, brown eyes, forget about it. It's all my fault."

"Gino, it's really hard to watch you raise your voice to Renata. It sends me right back to our own kitchen. I see Dad. I hear Dad. Then I look and realize it's you. You're running right into what you wanted to run from. Gino, you're not Dad. You're nothing like Dad," I said hitting him affectionately in the arm. "Somehow, you forgot who you are."

With a sad puppy-dog face Gino looked down at the floor. "Blasted man!" he mumbled. "Dad chased me then, and he chases me now. I can't get away from him." Looking at me, Gino verbalized the question we all wondered. "What was really going on back then anyway?"

"I don't know, Gino, but I do know one thing. I'm going to figure out why we have run our whole lives and why we still can't outrun the shadow of our past. I can't ever figure it out because I don't have all the pieces of the puzzle. Every time I try to sort it out I can't make sense of any of it."

"Hey, Christina, why don't you get up and get ready? We're going for a drive."

Half an hour later I slammed the car door shut. "Where are we going?"

"You'll see," Gino said with a smug look as he pulled out of the driveway.

After about fifteen minutes, Gino pulled the car up to the curve outside our childhood home. We sat in eerie silence, staring blankly at the house. Minutes ticked by as we studied every window, remembering what took place behind the closed curtains. The alley alongside our house appeared narrower. Sheer curtains billowed in the breeze as warm air swept through the upstairs window of our bathroom hideout.

My relationship with Gino and my sisters had taken on deeper meaning as I became older, since they were able to validate my history simply by existing. In one another we remembered where we'd been and who we'd become. Looking at Gino staring blankly at our childhood home, I saw my ten-year-old brother, not a forty-one-year-old man.

"I still hear their voices like it was yesterday," Gino said as he put his arm around my shoulder. "Why was everything such a mess?"

"I don't know, but whatever it was, I am glad it's over."

"No. It's not over. It will never be over."

"Gino, there's got to be a way. It's bizarre I'm even thinking this, but it's like Mom always said to us: 'You're going to need to figure it out for yourselves.' That's exactly what we need to do. We need to be willing to take a good look at all of this and do the work to put the pieces together. Maybe that will allow us to be free from this place once and for all."

We walked around the corner to the park. Sitting down on a bench I felt like I was caught in a movie of our youth being played out in my mind's eye.

"Hey, look!" Gino said, pointing to a nearby tree. "There's the tree I stood by when Dad made that cop bust me for smoking pot." Gino shook his head. "It seems like it was just yesterday."

"That's what's weird, Gino. How does everything seem far away, yet right behind us? Never in all my wild imagination would I have thought we'd be sitting here twenty years later, freaking out over what was going on back in those days."

"I still hear his critical voice echo in my mind over and over again," Gino said with a sigh. "'You're nothing but a pothead. You're never going to amount to nothing.'" Standing up, he kicked the dirt. "I want to prove to him he's wrong. I want to do something so big it's smack in his face I'm a success!"

"Gino, it all depends how you measure success. You look at success as having a prestigious title, knowing all the high rollers of the city, and making a ton of money. I look at the quality of life people live—if they're kind, if they think of others more than themselves. Successful people are those who can get knocked down over and over again and still keep getting up, looking up, and striving to be the kind of people God designed them to be."

Gino ran his hands through his dark brown hair. I looked back at him, knowing he was all confused.

"I want to look at life all positive like you do, but sometimes it's too hard to get back up when you're down."

I understood what Gino was feeling. I wanted to help him realize that when he couldn't get up by himself, God would help him. But somehow the thoughts of God got all twisted up in his head. He struggled with projecting Dad's faults on God, as if God, not our father, had caused his heartache.

I understood those thoughts because I'd had my own webs to untangle. There's just something inside that thinks God should have done something to stop the craziness. He takes the heat for all types of things he had nothing to do with.

In my head I knew God gives people free choice and it was the poor choices people had made that caused our pain. But in my heart it was easy to think he should have stopped my parents or never let them have children in the first place.

We walked back toward the car.

"You know, Gino, I've tracked down Joey, Frankie's youngest brother. I'm going to see him tomorrow. Do you want to come with me? He might be able to fill us in on some of the missing pieces of our past."

"What?" Gino blurted out. "He's not going to be any help. He hated Frankie. What can he know about our family? You're wasting your time on him."

"Maybe I am, but I've got to start somewhere. It's worth a try. Anyway, even if he's got no scoop, I might get some information out of Lily's sister, Ginger. I plan to meet her for tea after I meet with Joey."

"I don't know. Let me think about it," Gino said hesitantly. "Hey, let's get out of here."

Trying to shake off our somber mood, Gino drove straight to the beach. Together we ran along the water's edge toward the Cliff House.

"Come on, Gino, smile!" I teased, splashing water at him.

"You're the same way you were when we were kids." Gino said, chuckling and shaking his head. "You always tried to shake things off by having fun."

* * *

The following morning Gino made it clear he wanted no part of my excursion. Instead Elena joined me on my quest for answers.

Calling ahead to make sure Joey didn't skip town on me, I prepared him for our arrival. Joey waited for us in his yard as we approached the house.

"So you're Frankie's grandkid, ha?" he said in a smug voice as he extended his hand to greet me while giving me a once-over. "You look a lot like Frankie—God rest his soul."

I chuckled silently, noting that although his appearance was different from Frankie's, his expression and tone of voice were similar.

"Yeah, that's what everyone says, Joey. I know you don't ever eat, but we brought you some tortellini anyway," I teased. "It's fresh, straight from North Beach."

Joey provided us with the mandatory tour of his house. "Rebecca used to cry herself to sleep every night worrying about you kids," he began. "Now she's dead too. I'm left all by myself in this big house. I want you to know I didn't know nothing about the will. I was just the baby. For cryin' out loud, it was all the older kids who turned on Frankie."

Sitting down at the kitchen table, I probed gently for further information. "Were you ever close to my grandfather?"

"Yeah, yeah, yeah. I knew Frankie, but he was much older than I was."

"Tell me about the other brothers and sisters."

"There's Vincie, Johnny, Leo, Corina, Rita, Lucia, Josie, and then I came along. They're all dead now, now Frankie's dead too! I guess I'm next."

"Did you want to see Frankie before he died?"

"No, I didn't want to see him. What would I want to see him for? He didn't want anything to do with any of us. I sent flowers to the grave. God rest his soul."

"Do you know if I ever knew any of the others? Did they ever wonder about Frankie's grandkids?"

"Yeah, they all knew you kids. But everything in the family got crazy over the money. Vincie lost his mind over the guilt he carried for destroying Frankie. The family fell to pieces. Frankie refused to talk to anyone! He cut us off as if we didn't exist. There was a lot of stuff coming down."

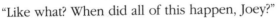
"Like what? When did all of this happen, Joey?"

Rubbing his head, he waved his hand in the air. "Oh, I don't know that. It was long ago. I'm old. How am I supposed to remember something like that? I've lived a long time. You know, when I was a kid the daily paper was only three cents. The Sunday paper was only fifteen cents."

Resting my arms on the table I leaned forward, determined to keep us on track. "Well, it must have been sometime when I was young."

"Yeah, maybe," he replied, now obviously deep in thought.

Sitting back in my chair I searched for questions that would take Joey further down the trail of bread crumbs I had stumbled upon.

"You know what? There's one thing I don't understand. Dad was totally loyal to Frankie. So if you and Frankie didn't get along, how did you and Rebecca end up being my godparents? You must have had a good relationship with Dad," I pointed out, confident I was on to something.

"Yeah, yeah. All this came down about the same time your father got into all that trouble!" he snarled, folding his hands across his chest.

"What trouble?" I asked, sitting up straight in my chair.

"It was all over the papers! No one knew what to do. I called to see if your dad needed any money. Frankie told me to leave him alone. He didn't want anyone talking."

"My father? What are you talking about? My father wasn't in any trouble!" I snapped defensively.

Taken off guard, my thoughts swirled. *I came here to find out about Frankie's silence. I'm not prepared to find out anything about Dad. What is he talking about? What kind of trouble was Dad in? What does he mean it was all over the papers?*

Not wanting to lose the momentum, I quickly leaned forward and asked, "What was Dad in the papers for? What did he do?"

Lighting up a cigarette, Joey began to stonewall. "I don't know. It was a long time ago. No one wanted to talk about it."

"Talk about what? What did he do?" I asked persistently.

"I don't know nothing! That was a long time ago. I'm tired.

I want to get some rest. You come again another time." Rising slowly from his place at the table, Joey showed us to the door.

"What is he talking about, Elena?" I asked, dismayed, as we pulled away from Joey's house. "Dad wasn't ever in trouble. Joey must be talking about some arrest or something Dad was involved in with the police department."

Driving to the other side of the city, I was confident Ginger, not one to be short on words, would be able to bring clarity to Joey's sketchy story about Dad.

Ginger greeted us at her door with a raspy voice, the result of years of chain-smoking. "Come on in, Christina. Who's this?"

"This is my friend Elena."

"Oh, what a beauty!" she said with a chuckle.

I scanned the familiar home I'd visited often as a child. Ginger's furniture was still arranged precisely. Her neat, orderly home gave the impression we'd walked into a museum full of antiques.

As we followed Ginger's tiny frame, fond memories filled my mind as we turned each corner. Ginger ran short of breath and sat down next to her oxygen machine. She quickly reached for the tubing attached to her nostrils and connected it to the machine. Making myself at home in the kitchen, I boiled water for tea to go with the fresh cookies I'd brought from an Italian bakery.

"Gee, I never thought I'd see you kids again after you all laid Frankie in the grave next to the others."

I smiled and continued to listen as I served her tea.

"How are the other kids? How's Gino?"

"You know Gino. He loves talking to everybody. There's no one in all of San Francisco who doesn't know him. He recently bought himself a brand-new, shiny black Mercedes convertible and drives around the city with his black sunglasses on like a big hotshot."

"Sounds like your father," Ginger added, as she sipped her tea. "What about the other girls?"

"Anna and Brett still live in San Diego. Their girls are growing up fast. Jamie is starting high school this year, and Jessie is going into fifth grade. Angela and Carrie live in Oregon."

"What about your mother? Has she done any better being a grandmother than she did being your mother?"

"No." I sighed. "It's like she's a computer that was made without the mother program. Being a mother or grandmother was never in her agenda. My kids don't even know who she is. That's okay though. I don't want them to have all that emotional garbage of wondering why they have a grandmother out there who doesn't even care that they exist."

"It's a wonder you all ended up okay after all that fighting going on in your house."

"You knew about that? That they didn't get along?"

"Didn't get along? That's putting it mildly. Mother Mary knows, your father tried. He gave her everything she wanted. Nothing made her happy. All she ever cared about were fashions, who she knew, and what party she was invited to."

"If they didn't get along, why did they ever get married?" I asked.

"They should have never gotten married. I knew way back then something was wrong. The whole picture of it all didn't sit right with me."

"Ginger, was Dad ever in any big trouble? We just saw Joey DiMari this morning, and he said Dad had gotten into trouble for something. He said he didn't remember when or what it was about. Do you know what he's talking about?"

"What are you snooping around talking to Joey for?" As she frantically motioned the sign of the cross with her thin, frail hands, Ginger's labored breathing worsened. "That man and the rest of them caused nothing but trouble for Frankie and Lily their whole lives. You better honor Frankie and stay away from him. Frankie would roll over ten times in his grave if he knew you were talking to Joey."

"Ginger! I'm not a kid anymore. If you know something about Dad, I want to know."

"Your father was a good man. Lily and Frankie raised him good. Frankie was rough with him at times, but he was a good father. What are you asking me this for, Christina? Of all of the kids, you know your dad. He had a big heart. He took good care of you. He brought you over here all the time. Joey doesn't know nothing! He didn't ever talk to anyone on our side of the family. He's crazy! The whole lot of them, they are all crazy!" Ginger hollered, working herself into a coughing fit.

"What do you mean, they should have never gotten married?" I probed, hoping to keep her talking.

Waving her hand wildly in the air like Frankie used to do, as if shooing every thought far away, she continued, "Your mother wasn't ready to get married, much less have children. I don't know. Something was wrong way back in the beginning with those two. Then all you kids started being born, all five of you, one after the other. Lily did so much for you kids. She knew that mother of yours was no good to you. Lily blamed your mother for everything. Not me! It wasn't all her. There was more going on Lily didn't know about."

"Like what, Ginger?" I probed, sliding to the edge of my chair. "Was Dad in trouble? Do you know something?"

Doubled over in a coughing fit, Ginger reached once more for her oxygen.

I wanted to grab her by the shoulders and scream, *C'mon, Ginger, if you know something, don't hold out on me! Don't be tight-lipped! So many secrets—why are there so many secrets?*

Composing herself she continued, "Your father got into trouble when you kids were young. It was all over the papers. It was horrible. No one knew what to do."

"What did he do?" I begged.

Studying my face, she realized I had no idea what she was talking about. Trying to take back her words, she fumbled, "Oh, nothing. Your father was never in trouble for nothing. Anyway, it was all a big hoax, a setup. He never did nothing!"

"Well, what was in the papers? What did the papers say?" I pleaded.

"What paper?" she stated with a blank look. "What are you talking about? There was nothing in the paper."

"Ginger, you have to tell me if Dad was in trouble. I've got to know! It might provide me with some answers I'm looking for."

"I didn't say nothing. What are you talking about? Paper? I never said nothing about a paper!"

Elena and I exchanged glances. Who was missing something here—us or her?

CHAPTER 23

tidal wave

My childhood friends met me in the morning. Katie listened intently as Elena and I filled her in on the previous day's visits with Joey and Ginger.

"I tossed and turned the whole night, racking my brain for clues as to why Dad could have been in trouble," I told them.

Wrapping her coat around her shoulders, Elena shivered from the cool ocean breeze blowing across our makeshift breakfast at the beach. "We always knew there was something wrong with your dad. Even before he moved out, he seemed really depressed," Elena reflected between sips of her hot coffee.

"Who knows, maybe whatever he was in trouble for explains why your mom detached herself from all of you," Katie thought aloud.

"No, she checked out long before Dad lost his balance. Who knows why all that stuff was the way it was."

"What do you think he did that landed him in the newspaper?" Katie asked.

"I'm sure it had something to do with that time his friend was killed at the station. That's the only thing I can think of that makes any sense. Soon after that is when he left the house for good.

Something must have come down that finally sent him over the edge."

"How are you going to figure it out?" Elena asked, burying her feet in the sand.

"I'm heading straight for the library to see if I can dig anything up."

"Are you sure you want to do this?" Katie asked. "Sometimes the mess of the past is so tangled up that it's easier to ignore it than it is to figure it out."

"I've been ignoring it my whole life, but it won't leave. It's like a shadow that I can't outrun. I'm tired of it following me. For the first time in my life I guess I'm ready to go there."

Taking the last sip of her coffee, Elena encouraged me. "Go for it, Christina! Call us as soon as you find something."

When I got to the parking lot I took one last look out over the ocean waters. I thought back to when Dad and I walked the beach looking for seashells and chasing the tide. *What could he possibly have done that was so bad it landed him in the paper?* I had to know.

I closed my eyes and a verse of Scripture I had memorized came to my mind: *Though he stumble, he will not fall, for the LORD upholds him with his hand* (Psalm 37:24). I imagined myself going into the pit. It was dark and spooky and slippery. Fear gripped me, and I opened my eyes. Taking a deep breath, I asked God for courage. Then I closed my eyes again, but this time I imagined myself in God's hand. I imagined myself falling—but even though it felt as if I were falling, I knew I really wasn't. Underneath it all I imagined God's sturdy hand holding me steady.

Twenty minutes later, I walked up the steps and through the front door of the library. Several floors of books, tapes, records, files, and magazines towered above me. I began my long and tedious search for anything mentioning my dad on the third floor. Several hours later I called Elena. "This is like searching for a needle in a haystack. It might take months before I uncover anything."

"Hey, did you think to call down to the police station to see if they stored any records on your dad?"

"Yeah, I did that today. I called several times, and each person says the same thing. 'All I am allowed to tell you is when your

father started at the police department and when he left.' For cryin' out loud, I know that much!" I said, the frustration growing in my voice. "Finally, someone gave me the name of a lieutenant who might be able to help. I left a message on his voice mail and begged him to call me back."

* * *

After another restless night I arrived early the following day at the library. Tenaciously flipping through file after file of old newspapers, I came up empty again. At three o'clock my cell phone rang.

"Hello, this is Lieutenant Conner. How can I help you?"

I explained my situation.

"I can tell you when your father started working in the San Francisco Police Department and when he ended. Will that help you?"

"No, I already know that. That's all anyone else at the station will tell me also. Surely there must be some way to get some information."

"The only one who has access to the records is the person himself."

"Well, that's impossible. He's dead!"

"I'm sorry. I cannot give out his file information."

"Who can? There has to be someone who can release it. Who else can I talk to?"

Silence.

"I can't promise you anything, but give me some time to look into it. I'll get back to you."

I pored over the endless microfiche files until the library closed.

The following morning, I was the first person through the library doors when they opened. I continued my search where I left off. Nothing. Not even a trace.

At noon I called Lieutenant Conner and left a message asking if he'd please call me back again.

Elena called. "Christina, I just told my dad everything you're doing. I think he knows stuff about what was going on. He wouldn't talk much about details, but when I told him you're trying to find something in the paper around the time we were in high school, he told me to tell you that you are in the wrong time zone. He said to look back, way back, before you were even born."

Chills ran up my spine. "What? What could he have done back then? That doesn't make any sense, Elena."

"I know. I'm starting to get a bad feeling."

With three hours left until the library closed, I felt as if I was racing against time. Frantically, I reached for another round of old newspaper files on microfiche. Alone at my cubicle I loaded the file into the computer. Scanning the pages feverishly I searched for clues. Two more hours flew by. I was nauseated from not eating, and my eyes ached from rapidly scrolling through hundreds of pages of newspaper articles. *It's time to call it a day,* I thought.

My cell phone rang.

"Hello, this is Lieutenant Conner."

"Thanks for calling back. I'm still at the library. I can't find anything!" Then without taking a breath, I pleaded my case. "Lieutenant, I don't know if you can imagine this, but I have three sisters and a brother. You knew my dad as a policeman, but we knew him as our father. Whatever he struggled with created havoc at our house. We survived that craziness, but the consequences of what we lived through still affect us today."

I didn't want to start crying, but I couldn't help it. Right there in front of strangers tears streamed down my face as my voice choked out the words, "If there is anything you know about my dad that can help us, I need to know. Yes, my dad is dead. But we are alive. We are left living with the effects of his mess. Please don't tell me you can't help me if you can!"

"Okay, listen to me carefully."

I listened. He told me the dates when Dad started with the police department and when he ended. It was the same story. Then he added one additional date—a date he believed would be an important clue in my search. The date was not when I was in high school as I had expected. The date was back—as Elena's father suggested—way back.

One last surge of determination welled up within me. I loaded yet another round of microfiche from the year Lieutenant Conner mentioned into the computer and began the endless task of scroll-

ing, scanning, and rapidly dissecting entire pages—searching for the mere mention of Dad's name.

The decades-old articles swept me away to another era of San Francisco. Photographs and enticing stories on fashion trends, local news, business endeavors, movie stars, politics, and accidents filled the pages.

Then with one click of my mouse, there he was. The time warp containing the stories of years gone by suddenly revealed the horrifying secret held captive within its pages.

The headline shouted at me across the years: "Cop Charged with Molesting Children."

The article began: "Police officer Agostino DiMari was arrested and suspended from the Force yesterday on a charge of molesting a young girl. DiMari, father of three young children, with his wife expecting their fourth, has been a member of the police force for . . ."

A prickling sensation spread up my back and gripped my neck.

What? Dad! Charged with what? This is sick! I was repulsed. *There is no way! Not Dad!*

My eyes focused on the text of the article. I didn't want to look at the large photo displayed under the headline. I knew those eyes. I knew that face. I knew that man. It *was* my father.

Wiping my eyes as if I must be seeing things, I strained to center my attention on the photograph for a second time.

His piercing eyes stared at me, revealing his secrets—his guilt—his darkness.

Covering my face with my hands, I pleaded to no one in particular, "Please, tell me this is not true!"

Struggling to gain focus, I attempted to read the words illuminating the details of Dad's long-hidden secret. There were several charges against him—made by neighborhood girls and relatives. It was a total overload of one pathetic story after another.

Scooting my chair back from the desk, I buried my head in my hands, willing myself not to throw up. *Because I am at your right hand, you will not be shaken,* echoed in my mind.

"Well, I am shaken!" I blurted aloud, drawing stares from a few fellow researchers. *Why do you want me to see this?*

Slowly standing up, I meandered toward the large window

overlooking the city. *Okay, you are at my right hand. I know you are with me. Please help me handle this.*

Replaying the article in my mind, I leaned against the window, hoping it would hold me. *Angela was only three. Anna was only two. Gino was only a baby. Carrie and I weren't even born. Did he do anything to us? Did he go to jail? Everyone in San Francisco had to know!*

Questions raced through my mind as I searched for how to process the truth lying exposed before me. Earthquakes that rocked this city seemed trivial compared to the shock now rocking my entire world. Explosions of disgust and anguish ripped through the protective crust the years had formed around my heart. I wanted to cry, but the tears did not come. I wanted more than anything to wake up and realize I had had a really bad dream.

I called Lieutenant Conner. He was sympathetic. He told me to meet him at the station first thing in the morning, explaining that he would arrange for me to talk to someone who specialized in cases like mine.

I printed out a couple of copies of the article, gathered my bag, and left the library. In a daze I called Katie and Elena and asked them to meet me at the beach. I headed toward Market Street in an attempt to find something to eat. Inside a convenience store I waited in line to buy a snack.

Studying the faces of the people in front of me, I wondered what they faced in their own lives. What were their stories? A middle-aged black man waited to buy a soda and a bag of chips. A bag lady with an old tattered blanket wrapped around her shoulders waited patiently to purchase a bottle of wine. She talked to herself, perhaps because no one else wanted to talk to her. I watched. I didn't want to talk to her either. A teenage girl dressed in black with heavy chains around her waist stood directly in front of me. Not one of them could possibly guess what I'd just found out. Not one could guess my whole world had just turned upside down.

Shaken to the core, I bought my yogurt and drove straight to my little cubbyhole at the beach. I needed some time to thaw out from the icy chill gripping my heart. A four-decade-old newspaper article had become the key piece to our family puzzle.

Questions flooded my mind. *What in the world am I going to do with all this new information? This changes everything.*

Elena and Katie arrived, and we talked until the sun sat right above the water. I was reminded again of the power and support of my dolphin pod. When I was disoriented, they came alongside and brought me up to the surface. They helped me catch my breath as my childhood memories of Dad crumbled like a sand castle at high tide.

I had fallen headfirst into the dark pit. The power of the riptide was pulling me out to sea, and I couldn't even begin to think about how to get back to shore. All I could see was the massive tidal wave about to crash upon me.

CHAPTER 24

do you know the way?

First thing in the morning, Elena and I went to the police station. We approached the information desk and asked to see Lieutenant Conner. As we exchanged some small talk with the receptionist, she looked at the paper I was holding, the date written in bold marker across the top.

"Wow, that's from a long time ago," she said, startled, glancing at the clipping. "Are you doing research for law school?"

I shook my head no. I couldn't get any words out.

Looking closer at the article, she persisted, "Who is this?"

I wanted to lie. I wanted to make up some story. Then the shocking words came out. "It's my dad," I stuttered, hardly able to admit it.

"Oh, I'm so sorry."

"Yeah, me too."

Lieutenant Conner greeted us, then brought us into a room where we met another policeman who specialized in helping families cope with situations like mine. They sat us down in some comfortable chairs, offered us doughnuts and coffee, and then brought out a huge case file with all of Dad's records. We discussed the charges made against my dad and how they were handled. Although he was charged with several counts, he somehow avoided ever serving time for his crime.

I read page after page of domestic violence calls, revealing all the times the police came to our house and found us kids hiding in the bathroom. I read the details of when a rebel group had opened fire in the police station, killing my dad's partner. Apparently, the bullet had been intended for Dad. When the rebels realized they didn't get him, they threatened to hunt him down. That's why the police were sent to our house to guard his children while my dad was in protection.

By the end of the day I understood so much more. It was all starting to make more sense.

"Christina, things were a lot different back then," Lieutenant Conner said, leaning back in his chair. "We didn't offer the kind of counseling and support that is available today—not to mention your father was extremely manipulative and had many people fooled. The best thing you can do now is try to find someone in your family who is willing to talk."

* * *

I told Anna about my discovery, and we decided to try to find out more before talking to our other siblings. Anna tracked down Karen, someone we felt would know a lot and not be biased either way. Karen had been our neighbor when we were growing up. She had been close to both of our parents and our extended family.

"Anna filled me in," Karen said quietly as our phone call began. "I'm sorry you girls found out about what happened."

"I don't understand how all of us lived our whole lives not knowing any of this," I said, still sipping my morning coffee. "Did you know it all?"

"Yes, I knew," Karen said quietly. "Everyone knew. Everyone but you five kids. We were all sworn to secrecy. No one wanted any of you kids to find out."

"Why did everyone hide all this from us?" Anna implored.

"I've got to put this puzzle together from the beginning," I said softly. "The first thing I want to know is why Mom and Dad ever got married in the first place."

"That's probably a good place to start," Karen agreed. "Your mother was different from most girls back in the early 1950s. She had no desire to get married and settle down. She was into fashion and modeling. She dated all types of boys, but none seriously. I only remembered seeing Agostino one or two times. The next thing I knew they planned to get married. I knew something was wrong.

"I didn't find out until a few years later. Your father was good-looking and a smooth talker. He dashed around in a smart-looking car and stylish clothes. Your mother relished the attention and the flashy, material side of your dad. Well, her mother and father found out somehow the two of them had had sex and made them get married. Your mother was not interested in getting married or having children. Not only that, by the time the wedding came around, she was on to the fact that your father had a horrible, perverted side to him.

"Your mother tried to call off the wedding, but he threatened to hurt her or others if she did. The marriage created a time bomb. From the day they got married, she hated your dad for ruining her life. She was pregnant with Angela within four months. Ten months after Angela was born, Anna came along. Then she delivered you last three soon after that."

"Do you remember when the article came out about Dad molesting the neighborhood girl?" I asked.

"Yes, clearly. No one believed he did it. We all believed he was innocent. Your mother called her father, Paul, that day, crying for someone to come bail Agostino out of jail. Paul was the first one there. He even beat Frankie down to the station. He posted bail, and your dad was able to go back home until the trial date."

"I just read through the transcript of that entire trial," I interrupted. "He was not convicted, based on insufficient evidence."

"Well, we really didn't believe he did it. We thought the girl's mother was jealous of your mom for some reason and made the whole thing up. No one ever believed Agostino would do such a thing until one of the children in the neighborhood and also a relative finally opened up about the details of what happened to them.

It took a long time for the kids to say something because they each thought they were alone in experiencing it. A tactic of many

predators is to make the kids feel like it's their fault or that something is terribly wrong with themselves. One child mustered enough courage to talk about it, and then it all started coming out. Agostino was messing with kids in the extended family. Your mother's parents called all of their children and family friends and told us to keep our children far away from him. Everyone agreed to protect the kids."

"Yeah, all the kids except the ones who lived with him!" Anna angrily added. "What about us? Why didn't anyone do anything to protect us?"

"No one knew what to do," Karen said, unable to conceal her regret.

"So many people had to have known!" I shouted in unbelief. "All of the relatives knew, our neighbors knew! Why didn't anyone do anything to help?"

"I feel most of the blame for the discombobulated lives you children had lies with your four grandparents. They knowingly left you kids in an ugly situation because they wanted to hide the truth from others. They cared more about what others would think than about doing the right thing."

"Well, maybe Mom's parents knew the truth," I said. "But even if Frankie and Lily knew, they would never have believed it was true."

"Seems to me they got it backward," Anna said. "The right thing was to do something to help, but our grandparents were more occupied with thinking the right thing was to stay in a marriage once you'd had sex. I can't even imagine leaving my daughter in a situation like that! Anyway, if the article was splashed around the papers, didn't people already think the worst?"

My thoughts drifted from the conversation as all of a sudden it dawned on me. "That's why you all got up and walked out at my wedding when I played the song 'Daddy's Little Girl.' As soon as pictures of Dad and me went up on the screen, several of Mom's relatives got up and walked out."

"And me. I left too!" Karen interrupted. "For those who knew the truth about your dad, it was too painful to watch."

"Why did Dad treat Christina differently from the rest of us kids?" Anna asked.

"I thought he would have favored Gino, being his only son in the midst of you four girls. He was hard on Gino though. I never understood why. Maybe Frankie was hard on him."

"Why? Why was I different?"

"I think it was because he had already lost one baby. He wasn't going to lose you too."

"What? What are you talking about?" I asked, frustration rising inside me. "Anna, do you know what she's talking about?"

"Yes," Anna said rather quietly. "Go ahead and explain it all to Christina, it might be good for her to know all this now."

"What?" I asked. "Know what?"

"The year before you were born, there was another baby. For years no one knew what happened," she said sadly, "but I knew something wasn't right. Your mother tried to hide the bruises. Something happened one night. They got into an argument. He pushed your mother, and she fell hard. It put her into early labor. The baby died. Your father went ballistic. He promised to get better. He promised to change. He promised to stop drinking. He worked hard, but he couldn't bring back the baby.

"Soon after that your mother announced she was pregnant again. The struggle was too great. Your father broke his promises and continued to drink. One night around Christmas, another fight broke out. Your dad shoved your mom, and she fell, causing her to have severe bleeding. They rushed her to the hospital. It was touch-and-go. No one expected you to survive, but you did.

"You were so little, and the doctors feared you might not make it. They didn't think your lungs were strong enough. Your mother had a complete meltdown. Your father sank into a deep depression. He was tormented with the thought of losing you. He had already lost one baby; he couldn't lose another. I think your mother saw this as her opportunity to get out. If you died, then everyone would know how your dad really treated your mom and she would have an excuse to leave.

"Your dad put on his best behavior. Everyone saw it. He went to the hospital every day while you were in the incubator. He sat there next to you and sobbed like a baby. He talked to you all day long.

He reached his finger in and touched your hand. I think he was hoping to give you the courage to survive.

"Every day we worried you would die. Instead, you continued to hang on. You got stronger. Everyone praised your father. They said he saved you. When the nurse told him he could take you home, he stood tall and proud, carrying you out of the hospital like he was some kind of hero. I really think he believed he saved your life. From that moment on, his relationship with you was different from that with the other children."

"Maybe somehow my survival eased his guilt," I added, trying to digest all I was hearing. "Perhaps I became a savior for him in the private hell he'd created for himself. I don't remember anything perverted, though I vividly remember the torment that raged within him."

"That explains why your mother checked out early on," Karen said. "One thing I do know—your mother thought she lost her chance to get out when you lived, Christina. As much as your dad looked at you as the one who saved him, I believe your mom blamed you for keeping her trapped in her own turmoil. You became the main target for all of her frustration. I watched the whole sad, horrible drama play out."

"I remember when Dad left our house for good, one of Mom's sisters warned Gino and me to stay away from Dad," I said. "It made me really mad at the time. I figured she didn't know what was really going on. How could she? Everything that went on behind closed doors was a secret. There is no way I would listen to her."

"You never listened to anyone, Christina!" Karen blurted out. "You always ran away. I knew all along you were not running from your dad. You were running from your mother."

"To survive in that kind of mess as a kid, I learned early on not to count on anyone but myself. When the people who are supposed to be taking care of you aren't, you learn really quickly not to trust anyone. But in reality, even when I looked rebellious on the outside, I was only running in hopes there was a way to be free from it all."

Anna and I looked at each other. As we tried to process what we were hearing, it felt as if we had traveled back in time.

"When you and Gino were left on your own through most of your high school years, none of us knew what to do."

"I feel so confused," I said. "Where does this leave me now? I see the pieces, but I still don't know what to do with them."

"You girls missed out on a lot, but what makes me the saddest is you missed out on having a mother. Your mother never had it in her to give you what a mother is supposed to give her kids. I feel bad. Every young girl deserves to have a mother."

"Mom's the one who lost out," Anna insisted. "We made it without her."

"Yeah, I didn't miss it. I never got along with her anyway," I said defensively.

"I look at life like an obstacle course," Anna added confidently. "It doesn't matter how the obstacles get there. It's up to me to get around them. Life comes down to what we do with what is thrown in our path."

"That's exactly what I'm talking about," Karen explained. "I feel bad that you kids had to look at life like one big obstacle course."

We talked for several hours. Afterward, I collapsed onto the sofa and called Elena. We planned to surf that afternoon. Nothing made me feel more safe and at home than being in the water and tasting the salt in the wind.

As Elena and I paddled out into the water, I relaxed into the waves' rhythms and let the sheer energy of the water wash away my confusion.

"The limitless horizon has always been a picture for me, assuring me that no matter how stuck I feel, there is always a way out," I said as we sat on our boards in the calm part of the waves. "God must have a bigger purpose for me to know about this—a reason that is beyond my ability to see at this time."

"Even though it's hard now, you'll be glad once you sort all this out. Maybe being able to understand what was really going on will help you separate yourself from it all."

"It's so overwhelming. It's like I don't know who I am or where I've been. I'm questioning all of my memories."

"Christina, don't let your parents' mess tangle up who you are. You have always been you, even in the middle of the chaos when we were kids. You have always been positive, fun, adventurous, honest (except when we stole those clothes!), daring, and

kindhearted. Don't question who you are. All this stuff you're finding out is not about you. You only need to look at it so you can see
how it affected you."

"Yeah, you're right. It's just easier said than done. I feel like I
landed in the bottom of Dad's turbulent soul. I'm holding the pieces
of his life in my hands, but now I don't want to. I don't know what
to do with it all. This is the kind of time in life when I wish I had
someone out there who could show me the way so I didn't have to
figure out everything on my own. What have I done, Elena? Why
did I get so nosy?"

"Maybe you've been led to all of this so you can finally get free
from that ring of guilt your dad put around your shoulders."

"You know what it's like? It's like our family was on this boat
that exploded far out at sea. Everyone took off for the nearest shore
except me. Dad couldn't swim, so I had to keep him afloat. Over
time I couldn't hold him up any longer. That's when I finally let go.
When I turned to swim toward shore, a weight of guilt heavier than
Dad himself tried to push me under with each stroke I took to distance myself from him. When I finally made it to the shore, I
climbed up on the sandy beach. The first thing I did was turn
around to check on him. When I looked back, I couldn't see him.
He had been holding on to anything he could find to stay above
water. But his grip weakened until finally he couldn't hold on anymore. Then he was gone. All I saw was a life preserver floating aimlessly in the middle of the ocean. I never could shake the feeling it
was my fault he died."

"He cast you into that role from the beginning! It's not your fault
he died. Now that you know all he was involved with, there's no
way you could have saved him."

"I feel like God is showing me this to lift the guilt from my
shoulders. But I hesitate even letting it go, because I feel like then
I'll have to watch him drown over and over again."

"This is a lot to handle all at once. Take it one piece at a time."

Back on the sand, we watched moonlight dance off the crest
of the waves as they ended their march to shore. The cool
ocean breeze blew on my face as I closed my eyes and talked
to God.

"Where are you?"

I'm here in the pit with you.

"What are you doing?"

I'm helping you clean it out. Where are you?

"I'm standing here completely overwhelmed."

Where do I say you are?

"Safe in your hands."

Even when you think you're falling, I've got you tight.

"Are you going to send someone to show me the way through this?"

Oh my dear child, keep your eyes fixed on me. I am the way.

CHAPTER 25

a pure-white promise

"I don't care about anything you're finding out," Gino declared as we sat at our favorite outdoor restaurant in San Francisco. "That's all in the past. What do you want to go digging around that pit for?"

"Gino, you said you wanted to—"

"I changed my mind!" he interrupted. "Whatever you find, I don't want to know nothing about it. You hear? Nothing!"

By the time we finished dinner and Gino drank a few more glasses of wine, his tone began to change. Deep in thought, he studied my face.

"Our parents were supposed to acknowledge and affirm who we are," he said, finally breaking the long silence. "They were supposed to fill us with nurturing guidance."

Gino paused, swirling the red wine in his glass, searching for his reflection. His eyes filled with tears as his gaze deepened. Swallowing hard he continued, "Our parents never did that. Some people feel like birds inside the shell. They see no hope so they're afraid to come out. We struggled to find the courage to come out into the world, relying only on our own strength. I came out. Yet sometimes everything still seems dark and empty."

Listening to Gino, I wished I could have been his mother. I wished I could have provided all those things he needed. I knew that while words have the power to destroy, they also have the power to build up, encourage, and offer healing. We needed to build each other up where our parents had tried to tear us down.

* * *

I woke the following morning knowing I had one day left before going back to Kentucky. Because of the nature of the news, I reluctantly decided to call my little sister, Carrie, to let her know what I had found out.

After a long silence on the phone I asked, "Carrie? Are you there?"

"I'm here," she whispered. "I already knew." She sobbed. "He did it to me too! I didn't tell you. No one ever believed me. I hated him! I hated him so much!"

"I had no idea, Carrie," I said, my voice cracking.

"When you and I shared a room he used to wait until you left. Then he came after me. I didn't know what to do. I had nowhere to go. One night I lay on your bed watching *The Brady Bunch*. He came in and locked the door behind him. He climbed onto the bed with his body behind me. He took my hand in his and made me touch him. I wanted to throw up! He forced me to kiss him. Then he . . ." Carrie paused, trying to compose herself. "I tried to disappear until it was over, but I couldn't. He forced himself against me telling me all the time how this was the only thing I was good at. I tried to wash my hands over and over again.

"The television was on the whole time he was in the room. I hated that show after that. I knew there was no such thing as the Brady Bunch. I hated our family! I hated Dad. I hated Mom," Carrie shouted through her uncontrollable sobs. "Why did Dad hate me so much? Why did Mom not want to be our mother?"

"I don't know. I don't know, Carrie," I said, trying to figure out what to say.

"I know you didn't know anything. You were always at the beach with your friends. When Dad left the house for good, I was

petrified he was going to sneak up behind me and kidnap me. Why didn't Mom protect us? Why did she act as if we didn't exist? Didn't she know what happened to us when she wasn't looking? She left us alone to figure everything out, and look at what happened to me."

"We need to put that on her gravestone: 'Figure it out yourself.' That sums up her philosophy of life."

"I kept thinking someone was going to come and save us. No one ever came. How could they all know what was going on and not do anything to help us?"

"I don't understand either. I'm sorry, Carrie. I'm so sorry he did that to you."

"I blame Mom. It's all her fault! She was the mother. We were only children. She only thought of herself and left us to be alone in the house with him. She needs to own up to the fact she blew it. Sometimes you can't sweep everything under the carpet and act as if nothing ever happened. You have to say something. You have to say you wish it didn't happen!" Carrie insisted, still weeping freely. "You have to say you're sorry! She's not sorry though. She doesn't even care.

"She never liked any of us, but she hated you the most, Christina. She always made fun of you, but I think she secretly resented your free spirit because she wasn't free. She tried to cut your wings, but no matter what she did or said, you continued to fly away."

Three hours later we ended our phone call. I promised Carrie I'd try to help her sort things out.

Sitting at Gino's kitchen table, I stared out the window in shock. *I wish someone had been brave enough to speak up—to do something,* I thought silently.

When I called Anna to tell her Carrie's story, she confirmed that she had talked to Angela.

Emotionally exhausted, I called home to fill my husband in on all the pieces I had uncovered. "I mainly want to know one thing. You are my husband, right? I do have two children, right?" I asked, half-joking. "Just making sure I'm not losing my mind. I'm wiped out. I need to come home and go to sleep for a month."

* * *

My first night back home, I lay in bed, flipping through the mental notes I made from my time in San Francisco. Finally drifting off to sleep, I began to dream.

> *The beach I stood on was exceptionally crowded. A tidal wave, towering far above me, suddenly came sweeping in from the ocean. Panic-stricken, people on the beach pushed and shoved each other out of their way as they ran frantically to higher ground. Should I run? No! I didn't have to run. I was through running.*
>
> *I knelt down with my face to the sand and asked God to protect me as the huge wave rolled in toward shore. I thought maybe my prayer would hold the wave back. I was wrong. I looked up the instant the giant wall of water surged over me, ready to break and crash down upon its target. All the desperate fears of life itself were wrapped up in one monstrous swell, calling out, "You are mine. You cannot run from me. I am greater than you." Without hesitation, the unrelenting wave hurled itself above me, determined to crush out my life. Then I saw Jesus standing in the midst of the storm. I knew his voice; it was calm.*
>
> Don't look at the tossing waves. Keep your eyes fixed on me.
> *"Calm the water, God, please. The waves are going to crush me."*
> No. If I calm the waters you will not learn your lesson. I will help you.
> *"How, God? How are you going to help me with this?"*
> Fix your eyes on me. Hold on tight!

I awoke the next morning still feeling the tidal wave towering over my head. "You're not going to get me!" I shouted out loud as I ground my coffee beans.

"Who are you talking to?" Michael asked from his study.

"The tidal wave that is threatening me," I answered, half laughing. I told Michael about my dream the night before.

Then I remembered something my friend Daize Shayne, a world-champion surfer, once told me: "When I'm surfing, I've noticed that the ocean stars that survive the pounding waves and don't get washed up on shore to die are the ones that attach themselves to the rocks and hold on tight!"

As I told Michael my thoughts, he immediately thought of the verse in Isaiah: "You will keep him in perfect peace, whose mind is stayed on You" (Isaiah 26:3, NKJV).

"I think the dream means that although the tidal wave I'm facing is scary right now and it threatens to crush me, if I keep focused on God I will make it through okay," I said.

"It's all about faith," Michael added. "Faith is all about believing what you can't imagine or see but trusting that God will do what he said he would. This may be hard for you for a little while, but you need to remember something—this is how you have lived your entire life. If anyone knows how to do this, you do. Don't forget that. Let me take you out to lunch today."

"No, I can't. Dr. Keating told me to come back for one more follow-up visit when I was back from San Francisco. I'm supposed to be there at ten o'clock."

"I'll go with you," he offered, throwing on his coat. "We can go out from there."

* * *

"Did you meet with your godfather in San Francisco?" Dr. Keating asked as she walked into the examining room.

"Yes. Everything went pretty well," I replied without even thinking.

"Did you find out anything you didn't already know?"

My mind flashed back to the computer screen and the startling headlines above Dad's photograph. "Yes, I did. I found out a lot I didn't know. Should I tell you? It may take a few minutes."

Pulling up a chair, she sat down in front of me. "Yes, go ahead and tell me." Her eyes looked straight into mine. I knew she was listening.

Ten minutes later I finished my quick summary.

We talked more about how Dad probably had some mental illness and what I was going to do with all this new information. As she stood up to attend to her next patient, she said, "You call me if you want to talk in any more detail. Maybe we can take a long walk out at my place sometime."

"A long walk? I would like that," I responded without hesitation. "I love to walk."

"I'm going to be gone for the next few weekends. Can you do it the first weekend in December?"

"Yes, I can do that," I agreed, intrigued by the idea. "It'll be starting to get cold by then. Maybe there'll be snow on the ground."

"That will be fun. I'll call you to confirm when it gets closer."

Joining Michael in the waiting room, an unusual feeling swept over me. "Dr. Keating invited me to come out to her place to walk and talk some more."

"I can't think of many people you would want to talk to about this," Michael noted. "You've always liked her. I think you should go for it."

"Definitely, I'm going to."

Over the next three weeks, I couldn't stop thinking about Dad.

Sitting down with some old photos, I carefully held each memory in my hands. I gazed at a picture of Dad as he pretended to be a horse giving me a ride across our front lawn. Another was of the two of us running along the water's edge. I flipped to a photo that showed Anna and me squeezed in a booth at the Italian café when we saw Dad for the first time after he left for good. I held my childhood photos in my left hand and the one in the café in my right. Back and forth I searched the photos, searching for who Dad really was. Somehow I remembered him wrong. Somehow I got it all mixed up. I thought he was good, but he wasn't good at all. He was all bad.

He was a piece of work in life. He was a piece of work in death. I was angry with Dad for being weak. I was disgusted with him for the choices he made and for hurting so many innocent people.

* * *

One morning after a long run, I jogged up through the woods by my house to a meadow nestled in the midst of the trees. Every once in a while, I had seen a deer grazing in the clearing. Full of anticipation, I quietly tiptoed to the edge of the bushes that lined the clearing and peered over the leaves. No deer were there. I sat down on a stump to listen to the sounds of the birds and other small critters rustling around in the trees.

I looked back over my shoulder one more time to see if maybe a deer had appeared. A voice spoke through my mind: *The deer are there. Whether they are in the bushes or in the meadow, they are there. Every once in a while you get to catch a glimpse of one, but even when they are not visible to your eye, they are still there. That's what it is like with me. I am always here with you. There are times I reveal myself to you, but whether you see me or not, I am still with you.*

The assurance of God's presence gave me a sense of peace and contentment. I realized that although I thought I needed answers to all my questions—and at times I had even told God he was not all I needed—he still chose to touch me just when I needed him most. In those times when I knew he was near, I would get brave again.

Over the following days I prepared a luncheon to celebrate Jake's decision to be baptized. While I was stirring the spaghetti sauce, the phone rang.

"It's Dr. Keating," Michael said, handing me the phone.

"How are you?" Alice Keating asked.

"I'm doing well. I'm actually cooking for a big celebration I'm having for Jake this weekend."

"That's great," Alice said. "I'm so proud of you."

I stumbled over my thoughts for a moment, yet managed to keep the conversation going. After talking, we confirmed our walk at her place for the following Saturday.

"Are you going to go?" Michael asked as I hung up the phone.

"Yes," I said, slowly sitting down at the table.

I must have had an unusual expression on my face because Michael asked, "What are you thinking?"

"I don't know. All I did was tell her I was cooking and she told me she was proud of me." Tears welled up in my eyes. "I don't think I've ever had someone say that to me before."

All I could do was sit for a moment. I had never felt like this before.

The following Saturday I was awakened by Jake and Trevor

throwing open our bedroom door and jumping on our bed. "It snowed last night!" they shouted. "Tons of it. Everything's white!"

Our walk that afternoon was surreal. Alice and I bundled up and walked together down winding paths through the towering trees while snow fell softly from the sky. Once under the trees we disappeared into four hundred acres that overnight had been transformed into a magical winter wonderland. A waterfall cascaded over large rocks, creating several pools of water on its journey to the river below. Old gray stone walls formed boundaries along the paths we walked, randomly veering off through the middle of the trees. Though there appeared to be no pattern, it was evident the time-tested walls had long ago served some purpose. Climbing down the wet, icy rocks along the waterfall, we followed a snow-covered path to the river. Large, fluffy snowflakes flecked the tree branches, covered our shoulders, and delicately touched the water's surface only to fade into nothingness as the stream silently absorbed winter's first offering.

For three hours I walked with Alice. We shared simple conversation as well as comfortable silence. I had a thousand questions to ask her, yet I couldn't seem to get them out of my mouth. *Have you ever felt like I'm feeling? If so, what did you do? How did you handle it? What do you do when you're used to being able to blow through obstacles and you hit one that's too big?*

I held most of my questions inside at first. It wasn't that I couldn't trust her. It's hard to know how much to share with someone without crossing a boundary.

We shared stories of each other's growing-up years. It was easy to relate to her since we had common interests. Then she began to tell me some of the things she had learned along her own journey. As I listened, I began to think about things I had never thought of before.

I gazed at the pure-white winter wonderland surrounding me. The scene seemed to promise that the time would come when the darkness I currently faced would be gone for good, completely washed away.

As we walked leisurely along the peaceful paths, the tidal wave that had threatened me in my mind over the last month began to lose its power. We walked out from under the shelter of the trees and up a long, winding path over an open hillside blanketed in white. I silently thought about the night I made my wish upon a star, when I asked God for someone older to walk with and talk to.

He granted my wish.

I looked at Alice and wondered if she knew what I felt, or if she felt anything at all.

Even though I stayed in my own space and my mind was alone with my questions, there was something about Alice's presence that assured me that my feelings of being overwhelmed were understandable. I appreciated the fact that she didn't offer simple solutions to complex situations. Even though she only knew a fraction of my story, she seemed to understand this was going to be a long process of putting the pieces together.

My thoughts were interrupted when Alice gently took hold of my arm. "Look in the meadow!" she said excitedly. Breaking into the clearing, six white-tailed deer pranced across the open field, disappearing into the mist of snow and trees.

CHAPTER 26

the iron gate

A few months later I felt I was ready to call the counselor rec-
ommended by Lieutenant Conner. The advice he gave me was
extremely helpful.

"By understanding your choices and how they've played out,
you can begin to change what doesn't work, generating new
response patterns that move you toward what you want. With fresh
insight, you can take actions that allow you to live in line with your
truest desires.

"Picture your father in front of you," he said. "A part of him is
dark and messed up. There is another part that loves you. Try to
keep with you the light you saw, which is the part of your dad that
made you feel his love, even if the memory is from your early childhood. A glimmer of light was in there. Sadly, it was buried in the
chaos he created around him. Your biggest challenge is going to be
not throwing away the good you remember with the bad you
recently discovered.

"I believe your dad made some really bad choices early on, leading to his downward spiral. Take his problems with drinking, gam-
bling, a violent temper, and abusive behavior and mix them up with
the fact that I believe his depths of depression and split personality

were linked to some mental illness. There's no doubt that any kind of darkness starts with one bad decision. He made one wrong move long ago, which led to another, and another. It caused a ripple effect. The saddest part of all is that it didn't affect only him, it hurt many in his path. Nothing breaks my heart more than seeing the innocence of children robbed at the hands that are meant to protect them! Not many people think of the effect their bad choices will have on others. They justify their actions. They keep going. They go too far and can't get back out."

What he said made sense to me. I could see how my father's decisions affected the lives of each of us kids, all in a different way.

"In every dysfunctional home, each person has a role to play. Each of your siblings will need to take a good look at how he or she was affected by living with your dad's torment as well as your mother's inability to connect with you. Each of you was treated differently and will need to process and heal differently.

"Again, Christina, I can't say this enough: Your father was a deeply troubled man, but after hearing your story I believe he truly loved you. Try to remember that as you process all you are now finding out about the tormented side of his soul."

Seeing how messed up my dad was helped me realize how ridiculous it was that I felt so responsible for him. With this new insight, in my mind's eye I watched myself take my hands off Dad's life preserver, knowing I never should have been given that role. This time when I watched Dad slip into the depths of the sea, I felt as if a huge band connected my heart to his. It stretched as he sank deeper and deeper. The tension pulled tighter until I felt as though my heart was going to rip right out of my chest and go down to the depths with him. But then suddenly a cord deep within my soul completely snapped in two, and it was as if I were being thrown backward in the sand. Dad and I were no longer connected. Finally, after all these years, I felt as though a thousand pounds had been lifted from my shoulders. He was no longer inside my head or my heart, or following close behind like a shadow that I could never outrun.

I continued to read many books, worked in my creative journal, and explored ways my life was affected by living in the mess of my past. I wanted to be willing to change what wasn't working for me and work on the parts of myself that needed adjusting.

One day a friend of mine looked at me and asked, "That's great you've been able to answer much of the mystery behind your dad. Now, how are you going to process your mom?"

"I don't need to process anything with her. I never had a relationship with her. There's nothing to process."

My friend stared at me. Her blank expression clearly told me she didn't understand my comment.

"There is no doubt I had major stuff to clear out with Dad. I carried him around with me my whole life. Not Mom. She is nonexistent to me."

"But don't you feel like you missed something?"

"No! I'm not like her. I like being a mom. I'm the total opposite of her."

My friend started to laugh. I felt frustrated because she thought there was a problem, so I called Anna and asked, "Do you think I have an issue with Mom?"

"You have a huge issue with Mom," she stated without hesitation.

"What? I do not!"

"Yes, you do!"

"I do not! Well, if I do, then you do too." We both broke into laughter. "Really, Anna? I don't see it."

"I think you resent the fact she was not the mother she was supposed to be. Deep down you wish you had a mother."

"That's not true," I snapped. "If I admitted that, it would change the essence of how I've lived my entire life. I would turn into that poor bird still looking for a mother who can't be found."

"See? That's your issue."

"That's no issue! I don't wish I had a mother. I don't wish it even in the most remote way. Do you?"

Anna hesitated. "I don't wish I had *her*. I do wish I had a mother who had loved us and taken care of us."

Oh great! My stomach began to churn.

Mom was nothing more than a faraway memory I couldn't get in focus. Even what I did remember was like an image I reached for but couldn't touch and didn't even want to. She was there, but not there at all. Detached. Unavailable. Empty.

Sitting on my front porch, I called Ellie. I'd heard Anna's words, but the picture Ellie presented made more sense to me. "It's like you were born into an Indian tribe at wartime. When you were a young child your mother left you unprotected. Your only options were to run and hide or to pick up the nearest tools to protect yourself. At that point you split yourself down the middle. The part of you that needed a mother ran and hid until the war was over. The other half of you was tough. You knew survival was entirely up to you. You did it. Now you need to go back and connect with the part of yourself that hid."

"How do I do that?" I asked.

"This will be a challenge for you because you'll have to admit you have a need. The strong part of you isn't going to want to admit you need anything from anyone."

"I know," I said. "To me, needing someone is the same as being a burden to him or her. Forget that. I don't want to be a burden to anyone. I do fine taking care of myself."

"See? That's what I mean. If your kids need you, does that mean they are a burden to you?"

"No way. They are supposed to need me. But that's different. I like being a mother."

"It's not about that for you. It's about letting God look at the wounds your mom caused so he can heal you. He wants to go there with you, but he won't until you let him. The ride is just beginning. You might have to journey to that place where you shoved all the ways your mother tried to destroy you and explore what's in there."

"What? I don't know where that is. When I think about it, all I see is nothing."

"That's because you built a thick, tall fortress to protect yourself. Don't get me wrong, I think it's amazing that you were able to do it. But from the stories you have shared with me, I believe all this is coming to the surface because it's time to deal with it."

"It's not inside me," I said. "I built that fortress and shoved it somewhere else, far away from me."

"Everything we shove away is really just shoved somewhere in us. You'll find it. Pray that God will show you a gate into that place. Stay in tune with what is happening around you."

The last thing I wanted was something hanging over my head all summer. Part of me tried to shrug off Ellie's words, hoping to enjoy the outdoor activities our family planned. The other part of me couldn't help thinking about what she had said. Ellie had been through a lot in her own life and had been willing to share some of her experiences with me. I wanted to learn from her, but at the same time, I didn't want to go to that place she talked about.

After spending June surfing with my boys in California and visiting Anna, we arrived home in Kentucky just in time to pack for our annual eight-week family adventure in Jackson Hole.

Squeezing in my yearly physical exam with Alice Keating, I talked to her about all that had happened since we walked in the snow the past December. The first thing she asked was, "How do you think you made it through that part of your life? Did you have a role model?"

"Yeah, my sister Anna. She followed a straight road. Really, I've found most of my role models in books and from watching other people."

"It sounds like you are good at being in tune with what is happening around you."

"I think that being intuitive is one of the gifts you get if you have to live in a dysfunctional family. When every time you walk in the front door you need to quickly assess where everyone is, what mood they're in, and who's been drinking, you can't help but get pretty good at reading situations."

"Would you like to walk again before you leave for Jackson Hole?" Alice asked.

"Sure, I'd love to."

We planned to meet at her house the following weekend.

Leaving the doctor's office, I began to think about role models.

People often don't even know when they are having an impact on someone else's life. Over the years I'd admired Alice for being confident and professional yet compassionate and kind to me. She was the type of woman I wanted to be.

I thought about Anna. She had taught me to take responsibility for my own life, work hard, and be tough. We didn't look down the roads of self-pity, self-absorption, or complaints. Somehow she knew early on that no one was coming to help us; she knew we'd have to save ourselves. In the hardest of times she taught me to look for things that would make me laugh and appreciate all the good around me. Her actions modeled how to turn my poison into medicine by turning around and helping others.

Meanwhile, my eyes were opening to see life through a new pair of lenses. Elena called the night before I planned to meet with Alice and read me something she had come across.

> Whenever something happens in our lives we don't want, we instinctively push it away. The more we resist, the more stuck we become. And what we refuse to feel never goes away. It takes courage, practice, and a willingness to be open where we're habitually closed. The initial step is to become aware of what we're resisting and decide whether we even want to let go. If we do, there are only two questions to ask. The first is "What is happening right now?" In asking, we pay specific attention to the sensations in our bodies and any emotions associated with them. Instead of looking for an answer, we allow what's there to make itself known. The second question is "Can I be with it?" To be with what's happening means embracing whatever we find with no agenda whatsoever. In the expansion that follows, what's been trapped is free to chart its own course.[3]

I lay in bed that night thinking about how these words perfectly described how I felt at that moment. When something happens to me and I don't know what to do, my first reaction is to push it away as if it never happened. If I didn't "feel the pain" then it wasn't there. The words about how it takes courage to face things reso-

nated deep within me, and I began to coach myself, "I am a coura-geous person. I like taking risks. I like adventure. So what am I afraid of?"

* * *

I had a feeling that this walk with Alice was timely. As we walked, I tried to be open to anything that might be significant to where I was on my journey.

The hot, humid Kentucky days of early July had turned the white, wintry landscape of last December into an Amazon-jungle scene. Following the same path, we often found ourselves standing still to admire the picture laid out before us. Countless layers of translucent green leaves filtered the sunlight. As we rounded the last bend, Alice led me toward an old wrought-iron gate that was fixed between walls of old, gray stone slabs. The gloomy, deserted gate looked like something out of the Civil War era. Weathered over the years, it was tarnished with streaks of rust. The bars looked as if they had been securely locked for hundreds of years.

I gently placed my finger on the wrought-iron bars. The gate opened slightly. I stepped back for a moment looking at it. *Did this have something to do with the gate Ellie was talking about?* I didn't want to walk through it. I followed Alice up stone steps and over the wall. As we walked up the hill I continued to look behind me at the gate until it was out of sight. There was something about that gate I didn't like, as though it was inviting me to come on a journey to explore something I wasn't sure I wanted to see. I felt compelled to keep a clear picture of it in my mind.

Back at Alice's, she poured us each a glass of ice water, and we sat on her porch and talked. I thought about Ellie telling me I needed to learn what I'd missed. In the midst of our conversation the realization of what could have been washed over me.

I thought about what it would have been like to have had some-one who was willing to spend time with me, helping me sort out what path to take when the options looked overwhelming. I thought about what it would have felt like to have someone tell me I was good at something, valued, and appreciated. I wondered what it would have been like to have had someone tell me she was proud of me for my accomplishments or give me a hug when I felt bummed out. I wondered how it would have felt for someone to talk to me using words that were kind, supportive, and encouraging. I wouldn't have had to figure out everything on my own because I would have had someone to help me.

I began to taste what it was I had missed. It felt good at first. Then the realization of what I'd missed began to sink in, and it didn't feel so good anymore.

CHAPTER 27

voyage of discovery

After spending sixteen summers in Jackson Hole at our cabin on the river, our family has developed a relaxed routine. Our rustic log cabin has no phone, no television, and nothing to do but enjoy each other and the great outdoors.

Grizzly bears roam the mountainside behind our cabin. To our right, wide-open spaces stretch for miles. A sense of timelessness permeates our mood and dictates our desire to be completely without any schedule. Michael guides the boys and me on all-day fly-fishing treks along the winding rivers. As a family, we hike up to snow-fed lakes and take the Snake River white-water rafting trip down the wild rapids.

Other couples from different parts of the world, mostly fifteen to twenty-five years older than Michael and I, also come to this hide-away each year. The cabins are spread out along the river with a lodge at the far end where we gather at times for special meals. I knew each of the women from the other cabins pretty well, but for many years I never joined them in their outings.

One day Michael took the boys fishing since I planned to go white-water rafting for the day. On the spur of the moment, I decided to curtail my plans. In light of all that had taken place in the past year, I found myself drawn to some of the older women. I wanted to find out if I could learn from them. Michael wasn't sure what to think when he came back at lunch and saw me sitting on the porch with two of the older ladies.

"What are you doing?" Michael asked with a completely shocked look on his face.

"Can't you tell? I'm cleaning huckleberries," I replied, trying not to laugh.

"Mom," Jake asked, "why aren't you on your rafting trip?"

"Greta and Jenny asked me if I wanted to go pick wildflowers and huckleberries with them. I've never done that before. Look, we picked tons of them. We're cleaning them in preparation for making jam. They know how to make all types of stuff out of these berries."

"Can I watch?" Jake asked.

"Sure you can," Greta said. "We'll call for you when we're ready."

I spent many lazy afternoons that summer pressing wildflowers, cleaning berries, and talking with the older ladies. I asked them questions about their lives, and they asked me questions about mine. I was open to learning, as I was when I walked with Alice. Although I didn't understand it, something inside me was changing. I was slowly rearranging old patterns and making room for something new. It seemed as soon as I started paying attention, women whom I could learn from and talk with were everywhere.

One morning Jake and I took off for our annual 5:00 a.m. wild-animal photography adventure. By lunchtime we noticed smoke billowing up from the foothills off in the distance. As we neared our cabin, we learned a forest fire was coming our way. We ran to our cabin while firefighting aircraft flew low overhead, spraying slurry over the hills. Grabbing a few items, we rushed to safer territory. The family I'd stayed with the first summer I came to Jackson Hole welcomed us into their home until the fire was contained. Every night we sat around the fireplace in their living room eating popcorn and watching old Western movies.

Although I had known Don and Jo Moore since Michael and I first met, I shared more of the details of my life with Jo. We enjoyed morning walks along the river and sipped tea in the afternoon. She doted on my boys as if they were her own grandchildren. I felt saturated in that homey atmosphere.

A week later, when it was safe to go back to our cabin, Jo wrapped her arms around me the same way she had for the past sixteen years and said, "I love you."

I immediately started crying. As I tried to explain myself through my tears, everyone thought something must be wrong. Walking toward the car I managed to get a few words out—"I'll call you later."

Once Michael began to drive off, I started to laugh through my tears. It seemed ridiculous, but it wasn't. There was that unusual feeling again—that feeling of what I had missed and now had found. My whole body felt it, from my heart all the way to my knees buckling underneath me. *Is this what women get to feel when they have a mother's love and support? A love so powerful it nearly knocks them over? I'll never take this feeling for granted when it comes to me. Always, I'll recognize what a wonderful gift it is.*

* * *

Throughout the rest of the summer and into the fall, the realization of what I had missed steadily grew. In my mind, the old, gloomy, deserted gate loomed before me. I still hadn't gone in. What was in there? Maybe it was time to find out.

"God," I began to pray, "if there is something you want to show me, I'm ready to learn what it is you want to teach me."

Do not be afraid. With awareness comes change. With change comes creation. Fix your eyes on me.

Determined to let the light vanquish the darkness, I decided to approach the place where I exiled my pain. In my mind's eye, I gently pushed open the gate. I remembered something that Ellie had said to me: "The hardest part is facing the pain. Until you do, you'll never be able to move past it. Yet those emotions will be your teacher. Feeling the pain helps you identify what it is that bothers you. Tuning your mother out worked great when you were young, but it isn't a successful coping skill as an adult. Negative emotions can sometimes bind you to a person more than positive ones."

I saw a picture in my mind of the gate opening. I braced myself, ready to feel my mother's detachment and negativity. Beyond the gate stretched an immense field of haunting memories. As I stepped in, the stench of loneliness hung heavy in the air. Somber, barren graveyards stretched endlessly to the horizon.

"Oh dear, I think I changed my mind. I don't like it here. Why do we have to do this?" I asked God.

There's an important piece of your star buried in this place. We're going back to get it. Don't worry. I'll help you.

I resolved to continue.

Smoke billowed out of the ground near several old stones. Each stone had a name inscribed on it. Abandonment. Silence. Rejection. Criticism. Shame. The words blazed with fire, burning deep, searing holes in the ground. Flashbacks filled my thoughts. Attacks I thought would kill my body. Words like poison arrows aimed to destroy my heart.

Yikes! I said to myself. *No wonder I shut this gate good and tight. It's creepy in here.*

Gazing through the foggy mist I saw gifts scattered throughout the land. I knew at one time they were meant to shine, but they were dark now. Gifts that were meant to be opened but never were. Some of them were smashed to pieces; others were half-buried in the slippery mud next to a murky stream.

I went back to look at each one of the burning holes. Fear coursed through my body as the image in my mind began to change. The holes now were burning inside a heart that lay shattered on the ground underneath the smoke.

Then I saw her angry face coming after me.

I wanted to cover my ears so I didn't have to hear her critical voice.

I turned to bolt out of that place. But Jesus stood in front of me, took me gently by the shoulders, and turned me around.

It's okay. You don't have to run anymore.

I braced myself to keep going. I made myself look. I made myself listen. The image that had always been so far away came closer and closer until I realized the image was not far away at all. It was inside me.

I looked at the scene before me that represented my mother.

I saw how I had gone on without her. If I had stayed and listened to her poisonous words it would have meant choosing my own death. I felt pretty good that I had figured out how to make it without her. I told myself I didn't need her and focused on what I did have. I didn't expect anyone to come help me; instead, I learned how to be independent, resourceful, strong, and intuitive. Not a bad trade-off.

I saw that as time passed, the scene continued to change as I changed. Each phase of the journey was important in tearing down the walls of the fortress. Like a deflating balloon, the pressure of built-up anger started to ease.

I was then ready to allow myself a season to look back and feel sadness over the support, understanding, encouragement, nurturing, and love that I had missed.

I asked God, "Is confronting the emptiness not enough for me? What could have been . . . must I also see that?"

I want you to know and feel what you missed, so you will be able to fully understand what you are giving to your own children. This work is important in breaking the cycle.

When my tears had fallen and there were no more, I looked up and realized I was moving toward the next step.

I had started at zero when it came to forgiving my mother. With a deeper understanding about her background, I moved to about 50 percent. But the other half—that was a different story. I didn't want to forgive her for that part. If I did, I was afraid that would mean what she did was not really bad, and it was.

Although the journey would not be easy, I decided that I needed to embrace it as an adventure. As I traveled, I found that if I kept my eyes open and looked for clues, wisdom for the next step was almost always on my front doorstep. These clues came from a montage of things—books, sermons, magazines, music, and simple conversations.

Months later, Alice and I planned another walk. It had been a full year since we walked the path that led to the gate. While we walked leisurely through the trees, the clouds overhead turned dark and the sky began to roll with thunder in preparation for a summer lightning storm.

"Well, here we are at the gate," Alice said. "Complete with sound effects."

She knew the gate was a symbol to me, but I hadn't told her any details yet. I looked at her and wondered how she always seemed to know about things I hadn't yet explained.

The dark gate to my left seemed to contain all the bad and dark emptiness of motherhood. To my right, Alice and all the other older women I had been learning from represented the goodness of motherhood.

I felt as if I were standing alone in the middle between the two gates. I knew I didn't belong behind the dark gate, but I somehow felt as if I had missed out on the rite of passage that would allow me to enter the good gate. I began to understand that these women were not only role models of the kind of woman I wanted to be, but they had been a mirror for me, reflecting the kind of woman I had become. I knew I belonged behind the gate they represented, but I didn't know how to get in there.

Interrupting my thoughts, the clouds in the sky parted, allowing the sun to peek through momentarily. Streams of light filtered through the trees, illuminating the green moss growing on top of the stone wall that ran alongside the gate.

"Wow, that's so beautiful!" I exclaimed.

We stood side by side in the wonder of the moment. The clouds shifted and allowed more light to pass through, causing it to travel down the wall. As we marveled at its beauty, suddenly we realized that from the angle where we stood, the wall actually formed the image of a cross.

I looked at the gate in front of me. It was wide-open.

I immediately thought of words my pastor had spoken the week before. He quoted Mother Teresa saying, "Forgiveness will set you free."

"When you forgive someone, you're not telling her what she did is not bad. It is bad. Forgiveness doesn't validate the wrong or wish for a reconciliation that cannot be," he had said. "By forgiving her, you're simply telling her you're not going to hold her to her failures anymore. You're going to release your right to retaliate and not hold her to the webs of her past."

I was tired of people telling me I needed to forgive, as if it were the easiest thing in the world to do. The truth of the matter is, it is the hardest thing in the world to do. Most people would rather die than forgive.

Later that day in prayer, I asked for supernatural assistance in reaching the point of forgiveness. As I prayed, I noticed a butterfly fluttering right outside my window. As I gazed at the beautiful vibrant colors of its wings, the butterfly suddenly froze in midflight. I rushed to the window to get a closer look. Its delicate wings had become entangled in a spiderweb. I rushed outside, grabbed a stick, and carefully set it free.

My neighbor was in her garden and watched my rescue effort. "Was that a butterfly?"

"Yes! Wasn't that amazing?"

Feeling pretty good about myself for helping the butterfly escape the sticky web, I returned to my desk in the study. Still caught up in the wonder of the moment, I heard a still small voice whisper in my heart, *That's what I want you to do with your mother.*

"Are you kidding? She's not a butterfly. You ask too much. This is not an easy thing to do."

Sometimes the hardest things you face reap the greatest rewards.

I went back to the image of the gloomy scene behind the gate. Revelation flooded my mind. Throughout my life, I had run from my mother, trying to escape her negativity. For the first time I saw that her mess was not about me at all. It was all about her. New insight enabled me to take her power to hurt me out of her hands. I held it tightly in mine. I was now one choice away from letting her go. It was the hardest thing I've ever done, but I forgave her, even though she wasn't asking for it, even though it wasn't easy. Then I said good-bye to what could have been . . . but never was.

In my mind's eye, I immediately saw billowing, translucent waves of light fill the deserted places beyond the gate.

Fire consumed the stones and dissolved them into ash and dust. A mighty hand reached into the meadow, swiftly picked up all the ash and dust, and held it out before me. With one breath God blew it all away, vanquishing it into thin air. I saw it in my mind. I felt it in my heart.

Cool streams, clear as crystal, flowed from the heart of God and saturated the space with shiny, refreshing, soothing water. Deep into the seared holes the water cooled the damaged places where my mother's painful words and emptiness had pierced my heart.

His pure light of living water filled me—a lasting, healing balm.

I stood there all alone—me, now a grown woman. The independent voice within me that determined "I can take care of myself" had weakened. I now heard another voice that had been silenced from the beginning of my journey. It lay buried under the wreckage—silent, waiting, hoping that one day I'd come back.

There before me in my mind's eye was the secret place that nobody knew about but me. I reached my hands to carefully peel away the seaweed that sealed the entrance to the hidden cave. Standing before me was the part of myself I had hidden so many years ago, the part of me that would have gotten eaten by a shark and surely died, the part that wouldn't have survived without a mother.

The little girl broke into a warm smile. "For cryin' out loud, it took you long enough to come back and get me!"

"Well, let me tell you, it was no easy journey back to this place."

"Is it safe now?" she asked, looking up at me as if I were everything she ever needed.

I looked at myself and realized she was right. I had become the woman, the mother I had hoped for growing up. The part of me that needed a mother could come out now.

"Yes," I said. "The battle's all over. You don't have to run away ever again. I'll take good care of you."

"I have something for you," the little girl said.

"You do? What is it?"

The little girl reached deep inside her heart and pulled out the only piece of my star that remained. "See? You didn't let her destroy you. You had this all along."

Tenderly reaching with her tiny fingers, she placed it over my heart.

Blazing light flowed from the sky and filled my soul with healing. For the first time in my life my star felt all put back together again.

I thought about something I read: "Ultimately, the abandoned daughter is never completely abandoned unless she, too, leaves herself behind."[4]

I smiled as I reached forward and picked up the little girl. "Are you ready?"

"Where are we going?"

"Home," I said. "We're going home."

I walked back toward the gate where I had entered. It was gone. There was no more need for a gate. There was nothing left to lock away.

I had to go through the process of being willing to set my mother free. I watched the butterfly fly up into the sky. A smile spread across my face as I suddenly realized . . . the butterfly wasn't my mother. It was me.

CHAPTER 28

waves of blessing

It seemed that the pit I had entered led to a mountain that was buried under the sea inside of me. When the tip of the mountain poked its way to the surface, it created a huge tidal wave. The waves eventually settled down, and I found myself feeling as if I were standing on shore looking out at the water. The mountain I had traveled was now in full view above the surface.

Do you want me to melt the mountain?

I smiled. "No. I'm okay with the mountain now. It doesn't have power over me anymore."

We're not done, you know.

"Oh, I really want to be done now. I need a break!"

Don't worry. This is the best part. Now that you've let me repair your heart, I'm going to restore it to my original design, which was to have it filled with a lavish distribution of gifts. Gifts that are open.

"You are? What are they?"

They are MY BLESSING to you. "Every good gift and every perfect gift is from above, and comes down from the Father of lights, with whom there is no variation or shadow of turning." (James 1:17, NKJV)

In my mind's eye I saw a treasure chest on the shore where I stood. I reached to open it and saw scores of golden gifts inside.

Out of each gift came words—God's words. His words are not empty, written on paper in hopes of bringing comfort or guidance. He backs up his words by clearing my path, always staying by my side, and showing me who I am and how I should live.

My words will continue to be a light to your path and a lamp to your feet.

I looked out at the sea. Many more gifts were rolling onto shore with the waves. "What are these?"

"Reckless words pierce like a sword, but the tongue of the wise brings healing." These are the gifts I'm going to give you that will first pass through someone else.

Be aware. Pay attention. These blessings are gifts that are going to flow out of the mouths of friends, off the pages of books you'll be reading, through songs you'll be listening to, through the hug of a stranger.

* * *

My first gift came from my sister Anna on my birthday. I opened the tiny box. From deep inside the blue tissue I lifted out a shimmering silver ocean star dangling from the end of a sterling silver chain. I reflected on the promise of words from so many years ago—that when the ocean star is connected to its source of life, it will mend the broken pieces that got messed up along its journey. I couldn't put the necklace on fast enough. Looking at myself in the mirror, I smiled, as I knew this would be a symbol of my life forever.

I continued to track my journey in my creative journal. I often do this to look back to see what I have learned, to look forward to see how I can grow, and most importantly to look around and see how I'm doing.

To illustrate how I felt at that moment, I drew a picture of an ocean star. I labeled each of its five rays: spiritual, intellectual, emotional, relational, and physical.

This picture represented what I had been learning about how all these pieces were important. What I had gone through as a young girl affected how I viewed and treated these pieces.

Children who can't talk about the madness of what's going on around them tend either to explode and act out or to implode. During my childhood I wasn't able to choose how I felt or what I thought; I just had to make it through alive. As an adult, allowing myself a season to explore what I'd buried was the greatest gift I could give to myself and to my children.

There are times to go into the pit and clean it out and other times when it's best just to move on and get over it. When we are led into the pit, there is no need to be afraid. When God's light is allowed to shine into our darkness, the darkness will not overcome the light. His truth tears down all the lies that have become strongholds and keep us chained to our past experiences. His light keeps shining into every dark corner until every part of us is set free—free to be who *he* wants us to be.

There's a fine line between remembering and forgetting. I've learned that any pain that isn't acknowledged takes up space inside of us. We need to process it if we want to be healed. On the other hand, when the memories are traumatic, they can send us over the edge. I felt tossed around by the waves at times. But I learned that how quickly we fix our eyes on God when the winds change and the huge waves tower over our heads is far more important than the adversity or challenging situation before us. Looking at the whole process as an invitation to learn and grow helped me keep my balance.

The next step I went through was to take a good look at each of the tools I'd crafted to make it in life—such as my refusal to look back and my extreme independence. If we use our tools in times of war, they are our friends, shielding us from the darts of the enemy. But if we use them in times of peace, they shield us from the love and support God wants to give us. We need to know when to use them and when to lay them down. One by one I asked myself if each tool I created was still working for me. If not, I asked myself what adjustments I could make. For example, all my life I had told myself, *Never look back.* But when you get to a safe place, it's okay to look back long enough to learn, understand, and heal. The other tool I had often used was the need to be independent and take care of everything myself. I wanted to adjust that so others could be supportive of me.

I believed that God would take the land of cursing and transform it into a land of blessing. I didn't want to be defined by anything that had happened to me on that mountain buried under the sea; I wanted to go forward being defined only by who God says I am.

I came to understand that the Spirit doesn't set out to tear down anything in our lives that he doesn't plan to rebuild. He gives us freedom, not just to survive but to create something totally new. As I laid down old patterns, habits, and tools, I picked up each piece of the armor of God as laid out in Ephesians 6:

> Be prepared. You're up against far more than you can handle on your own. Take all the help you can get, every weapon God has issued, so that when it's all over but the shouting you'll still be on your feet. Truth, righteousness, peace, faith, and salvation are more than words. Learn how to apply them. You'll need them throughout your life. God's Word is an indispensable weapon. In the same way, prayer is essential in this ongoing warfare. Pray hard and long. Pray for your brothers and sisters. Keep your eyes open. Keep each other's spirits up so that no one falls behind or drops out."
>
> (EPHESIANS 6:13-18, *The Message*).

The waves brought in another gift, this time a book from a friend. The front cover read: "No matter your age, the approval of your parents affects how you view yourself and your ability to pass that approval along to your children, spouse and friends. Many people spend a lifetime looking for this acceptance the Bible calls . . . the blessing."

I read it in a weekend but need to read it over and over again throughout the rest of my life. It helped me understand my own journey, but even more, it gave me tons of ideas to ensure I am passing on the blessing to my own children.

The authors use the analogy of flowers growing in a garden to help illustrate how the basic components of the blessing work together.

> A flower cannot grow unless it has the necessary elements of life. Every flower needs soil, air, water, light, and a secure place

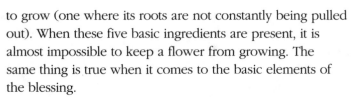

to grow (one where its roots are not constantly being pulled out). When these five basic ingredients are present, it is almost impossible to keep a flower from growing. The same thing is true when it comes to the basic elements of the blessing.

Like the basic needs a flower has, the blessing also has five key elements. These five elements, blended together, can cause personal acceptance to blossom and grow in our home today. Each individual part provides a unique contribution. Each is needed in giving the blessing.

A family blessing begins with meaningful touching. It continues with a spoken message of high value, a message that pictures a special future for the individual being blessed, and one that is based on an active commitment to see the blessing come to pass.[5]

Ever since my children were young, I have tried to be careful with my words, knowing they have the power to either destroy or build up. I focused on using my words to build my children up. In this way, I tried to pass on the blessing in their lives.

I pulled out the drawing of my starfish. With my art supplies spread out all over the table, I began to play around with what the symbol for the blessing should look like. Then it came to me— the sun over the ocean and the purple shield! My two symbols of God providing for me some of what I miss in not having a mother and father in my life. The symbols represent that I belong to him.

I began to draw the sun in the middle of the starfish, outlined with blue hues. Inside the circle I drew the purple shield. After blending the colors I leaned back and looked at my picture. It looked just like a sparkling diamond. I liked that. The diamond represents something of high value, something of great worth, something that sparkles and shines. Perfect. God in me adds all that to my star.

Then it all started to come together in my mind.

That's how we shine! When we allow God's blessing to be the center of our lives, our value and worth and ability to shine come not from ourselves but from God making his home inside of us. This was a whole new way of looking at life for me.

As I continued to explore what the blessing meant to me and how to apply it to my life, I kept running across another word.

Grace.

Blessing and grace go together.

I started to realize this after my husband told me about a conversation he'd had with his friend. When that friend came back from playing golf at Pebble Beach, Michael wanted to know how the game went. Of course his friend loved the golf, but what made the biggest impression on him was something that happened every night at dusk. A lone bagpiper dressed in a Scottish kilt strolled along the shoreline at Spanish Bay playing "Amazing Grace." Michael's friend is a pretty tough guy, and he said it brought him to tears.

Michael started playing around with his violin and, to the surprise of even himself, composed a rendition of "Amazing Grace" for solo violin that sounds just like the bagpipes!

George Beverly Shea and Cliff Barrows asked him to perform it at a Billy Graham Crusade. When the time came, Michael walked calmly out on the platform, his blond hair a contrast to his black suit. He tilted his head, rested the violin under his chin, and began to play.

The crowd stopped talking, stopped moving, stopped everything. You could have heard a pin drop. Over sixty-five thousand people were so moved by the music they stood to applaud before he even finished.

I understood why they wanted to stand and shout and clap and praise God. Grace says we don't deserve anything from God, but we're getting in on it anyway. Grace is receiving God's blessing, his unlimited supernatural favor. The beginning of the song says it all—"I once was lost, but now am found." I think something deep inside all of us wants to be found by God. What's so cool is that the Lord says, "If you seek me, you *will* find me" (see Jeremiah 29:13). The blessing means God is around, he can be found, we're special to him, he cares, and he'll help us. Sounds like what "home" should be.

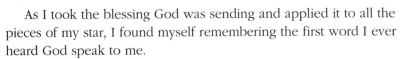

As I took the blessing God was sending and applied it to all the pieces of my star, I found myself remembering the first word I ever heard God speak to me.

Believe.

Believe what his Word says is true.

I am his child.

I am home in him. He wants to make his home in me.

His Word provides me with safe boundaries, clear direction, and a road map for successful living.

He is my authority. Some say authority is confining, stifling, and limiting to self-expression. But to me, God's boundaries are wide-open spaces where it's safe to explore who I am in him.

He sets me free. Not free to live a life of my choosing, but free to choose his best for my life.

He will never leave me nor forsake me. He is always with me.

The plans he has for me are good.

He is the same yesterday, today, and forever.

I can count on him.

He did not cause my broken heart but is committed to restoring it.

He doesn't promise to calm the storm, but he does promise to walk with me through anything I will ever have to encounter on this earth.

He loves me.

He will provide for me in both fatherly and motherly ways, either through others, his creation, or his words.

Yes, there are still times when the missing pieces present themselves. It's usually around the holidays when I pull the turkey out of the refrigerator and can never figure out which side is breast-up. Every single time I have to call my sister. Last year she sent me a whole set of Williams-Sonoma cookbooks for Christmas. But I don't want to read about it, I want someone to show me.

It hits me harder when it comes to events focused on my boys. When they have a school event and other grandparents are there. When they win their championship baseball game. When they get an A on a difficult assignment. There's no one I can call to brag about them. You can't overdo it with your friends. There are just certain things about your own kids that only your mom and dad would care about.

But I pay attention to those feelings when they come so I'll remember what to do and be when my boys have their own children. All those little things matter. A lot.

* * *

Throughout the following year many more gifts flowed in. Simple things people said or did. Passages I read. Things I heard. Random hugs. Words of encouragement. I looked up and noticed when they came.

My focus began to shift. Rather than just thinking about my life, I started looking at how I could take what I had learned and use it to help others.

While visiting my sister Anna in San Diego, I spent many hours walking the shoreline and dreaming of building an organization that would offer support and encouragement to young women.

Using the leg of a dried ocean star, I began to write inspirational words in the sand—words that I wanted to say to others.

Shine

Dream.

Believe.

Look Up.

Ride Your Wave.

Go the Distance.

I continued writing until the shoreline was covered with words. I placed the ocean star above the last word and then sat down next to it.

Within thirty minutes, the words had drawn more than one hundred visitors. They all stopped to read the inspirational sayings and ask me what they meant. As I explained my dream, an older woman looked me straight in the eye and said, "You need to make greeting cards of these sayings. You could sell them to spread the vision of your dream."

"Wow," I exclaimed, "what a great idea. I could do that."

I started that very day, and within a couple of months, I had launched my cards into the retail market, using the back of each card to share my dream.

Soon after that a few women I had gotten to know at my church encouraged me to go after the next phase of my dream, which was twofold. The first part was to create a fun, inspirational Web site where young women could be encouraged on their journeys through the sharing of stories and weekly life lessons. The second part was to host motivational workshops on beaches, in the mountains, and anywhere I could get the girls outside to experience the healing powers in nature.

God passed the next gift through one of those women.

It came the following winter, on my birthday. It was wrapped in a gold box with a pink bow, not unlike the box where two years earlier I had surrendered my dime-store pearls when I made my wish.

It was snowing the day this gift was randomly dropped off on my front porch.

A strong sensation surrounded me that God had something to do with this present. Deep in my heart I heard him whisper, *This is from me.*

I put the gift on my lap.

Time seemed to stand still as I reached inside the box.

First I lifted out a note that read, "These were designed and strung by a girl who lives in Hawaii. She reminds me so much of you. She is a part-time jewelry designer and spends the rest of her time surfing and traveling. I had so much fun buying them for you. Enjoy!"

I felt a wave of energy. My face got hot, my cheeks got all tingly, and then the sensation moved down my arms and out my hands. When you're in a moment like that, you know God is right there but you can't see him. You think you can reach out and touch him because he's right next to you, but all you feel is air.

The words themselves were the same words that God spoke to my heart when he said he was going to send me not one, but many older friends: *I'm going to have so much fun sending them to you. Enjoy!*

I lifted out a small blue-satin pouch, unzipped the top, and pulled out the most beautiful, unique set of pearls I'd ever seen.

"Whoa, what a trip!"

Tears welled up in my eyes.

Only God could have known about the gold box with a pink bow. Only he could have known about the fake pearls I had surrendered the night I made my wish upon the star.

I remembered what I had said to him the night he asked me to surrender something that represented my wish.

Do you want me to want only you? That would be fine if I lived in heaven. But I live on earth. Don't you think it would be a good idea for me to feel a little support down here where I actually live? Sometimes I just want to hold something in my own two hands instead of having everything be in the realm where I can't touch it.

Streams of tears began to flow down my face and onto the pearls I held in my hands.

They were genuine.

He was near.

I ran my fingers gently over each pearl, feeling its unique shape—a perfect circle, strung by a surfer girl.

Looking closer, I let out a shout. "There's a sun and a shield!"

On the outside of the clasp was one solitary pearl shaped like the sun and one purple stone shaped like a shield, the exact symbols I had drawn in my art journal to represent God providing what I had missed from not having a mother and a father!

I was so elated I could hardly contain my excitement.

Michael had taken the boys out on an errand. The few friends who would understand were on a ski trip. Who could I tell who would get it? It was all so completely personal and intricate and totally amazing!

About to jump out of my skin with exhilaration, I cranked a Josh Groban CD from my backyard speakers and danced in the snow. I suppose it was good it was dark so no one could see me. As the snow fell delicately on my shoulders, I couldn't miss the sense of God's presence.

A couple of years earlier the tidal wave had loomed above me and threatened to sweep me into the darkness. On this end of the processing journey, everything looked white . . . pure white.

Lifting my hands to the genuine set of pearls around my neck, I methodically ran my fingers over each uniquely shaped bead.

In the stillness I felt God all around me. I closed my eyes. In my mind's eye was the most beautiful gate I had ever seen. I knew immediately what it was. I walked through the gateway in my mind and was ushered through the rite of passage into womanhood.

Once inside, I heard a whisper in my heart say, *Make a circle.*

In the freshly fallen snow I traced my footprints, forming one large circle.

Stand in the middle.

I did.

As I looked at the circle that surrounded me, the currents of the last few years merged into the new place where I stood as God began to reveal the meaning of my gift.

Each pearl on your strand represents someone who has been a Pearl to you in some way along your journey. Because they crossed your path you have been encouraged to fly, pursue your dreams and reach your highest potential. They spoke words that brightened your path, walked with you awhile or cheered from afar. Authors motivated you; music moved you, and unexpected strangers inspired you. Think about the people who have added value to your life. These are your Pearls. When you put them on you will carry the blessing they passed on to you.

Continue to look to me for all of your needs. I am your Sun, your Shield, and your Source of Life. By continually looking up you have allowed me to take the irritations of your life and mold you into a beautiful pearl. It is time now for you to take what you have learned and pass it on to girls coming up the road behind you.

Feeling the smooth unique shape of each bead, I thought of the women who were already represented on my strand and looked forward to the ones I would someday meet, either in person, in books, or through unexpected circumstances..

CHAPTER 29

pass it on

Another gift came soon after.

Michael had asked Kurt Kaiser (a Dove Award–winning composer) to write a piece for solo violin and orchestra based on hymns. Kurt titled it "Emmanuel: A Musical Witness of God's Presence through the Ages." At its premier, Michael asked George Beverly Shea, lead vocalist for the Billy Graham Crusades, if Mr. Shea would sing some of his favorite hymns.

I've always loved hymns, as they are really stories of people on their journeys with God put to music. Hymns have encouraged me, inspired me, and taught me to continue exploring the depths of God's love and purpose for my life.

Mr. Shea is one of the most kindhearted, gentle men I've ever met. I wasn't sure if I would connect with his wife, Karlene, since I had never spent time with her. I'm a little bit awkward at times when I'm in conservative settings. I pretty much still look like a free-spirited surfer girl on most days. I wear flip-flops and jeans all year long. In the winter when it's too cold for flip-flops, I wear my UGG boots. Although I can clean up pretty good, it's an extremely rare day when I'm seen in a dress, and I never wear a suit!

While our husbands were rehearsing music for the concert they

were about to perform, I asked Karlene if she wanted to go hang out. Though she usually stays with Mr. Shea, she seemed eager to go with me.

Karlene, dressed in a nice suit, hardly made it down the hallway before telling me she wished she had worn her casual clothes and flip-flops! That was it. Before we even made it down the stairs of the hotel and out onto the street we were both talking so fast we hardly stopped to catch a breath. She had grown up in the San Francisco area, and we had so much in common. This woman was full of energy, loved talking about lives changed by God, and was keenly attentive to the details of my life. We connected so quickly that we just kept walking up and down the street and talking. We never even went into a store!

After about an hour, Karlene bought us lemonades and a funnel cake to share. The air was cool yet the sun was out. It felt good to sit and wind down our pace. Karlene put the funnel cake on the bench between us and we dug in. Somewhere in between bites of food and conversation I heard God whisper, *Are you enjoying this?*

I looked up. I couldn't exactly answer him out loud. I didn't want her to think I was a total nutcase.

I smiled as I answered him in my mind, *Yes, I am.*

Good. I arranged this for you. She is one of your pearls.

I took a bite of funnel cake and continued my conversation. I looked at Karlene and wondered if God had just talked to her too. I wondered how she would be a pearl to me. Was it just this moment or would there be more?

Over the next few months we shared more with each other at other events and in several phone conversations. I never told her many of the details about the way God talks to me in symbols or much about the harder part of my life. We mainly talked about the vision I had of building an organization to offer support to young women.

A month or so later, another surprise came. God was still show-ing me how to keep my focus on him as the center of my star.

I went to get the mail one afternoon, and there was a little box with my name on it. It was from Karlene. *How cool*, I thought. *I wonder what she sent me.*

Inside the package was a small fancy box from a diamond store. I opened the box to find a necklace with a sterling silver star that had a sparkling diamond in the middle!

Karlene had enclosed a note and said the necklace reminded her of me and what I wanted to do in helping other girls. She encouraged me to keep pursuing my vision and not to give up because there was nothing out there quite like what I wanted to do.

I was experiencing the "immeasurably more than all we ask or imagine" blessings that I had read about in the book of Ephesians but had never encountered quite like this. God was making his presence so clear, so obvious that he could not be missed.

* * *

Elena, Katie, and I met up in San Francisco for some girl time. We talked about the last few years and the changes we were going though. As we often do, we laughed about some of the wild adventures and experiences we had had together since first grade, when we became friends.

"If you could change one thing about the past, what would it be?" Elena asked.

"That's a tough question," I said. "In all that processing I did I really learned to like who I've become. I wouldn't be the same person I am today if any of that had been different. So many of my strengths have come from what I've lived through. It's as if God turns even our suffering into gifts."

"Still, just think for fun, what would you do differently?"

"Oh!" I said excitedly. "I know! I would redo my wedding day. I'd still pick Michael, but I wouldn't let my older sisters control anything about it."

"Ahhhhh . . . those dresses we had to wear were so ugly!" Katie said, gagging.

"So was mine!" I agreed. "I can't even stand looking at those pictures; we look like a bunch of dorks. I wouldn't trade how classic Frankie was that day, but all I really wanted was to get married on the beach, barefoot, with some funky music, fun clothes, and a few friends."

"Hey, your fifteen-year anniversary is this year!" Elena said. "You ought to turn that into a party like you originally wanted."

"Do you think we could pull it together?" I asked.

"Definitely!" Katie and Elena said in unison.

"Let's do it next month down in San Diego," I said. "That way I can get my sister and her family to come also."

We all agreed on the plan: Everyone could wear whatever they wanted as long as it was blue and white. We'd all wear our pearls. I'd get the flowers and the music. All everyone else had to do was show up.

I left Katie and Elena in San Francisco and boarded a plane to San Diego for a visit with Anna and her family for a few days. It was a flight on Southwest Airlines. The first section had six seats, three facing the back of the plane and three facing forward. I sat in the middle seat facing forward, in between two women. Across from me sat one girl and two men. As the plane started down the runway I took out a book I had been reading, *Motherless Daughters*. One of the men across from me noticed the title and asked me what it was about. Now all five people were looking at me. As the plane took off, so did I, telling them a little of my story. Then they told me theirs. The entire flight we talked, listened, and understood a bit of where we each had been.

I was particularly drawn to the girl sitting across from me. She looked to be in her late teens, with long blond hair and beautiful blue eyes. She didn't share much of her story, but she listened to everyone. I could see deep pain in her eyes. Many times she reached for a tissue to wipe the tears away.

The plane landed, and we all felt like one big family hugging good-bye and wishing each other well. There's something about sharing stories that brings people close. I wanted to talk to the girl across from me and wished there had been more time. I walked off the plane. She followed.

"Excuse me," she said. "Do you think you could recommend a few more books that could help someone who has lived through that?"

"Sure. I can think of lots of books," I said. "If it weren't for people willing to write their story, I would feel alone in mine. I have read many books that have helped me tons."

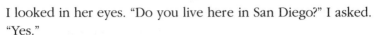

I looked in her eyes. "Do you live here in San Diego?" I asked.
"Yes."

"I don't know if you'd be into it, but can you meet me at the beach in Del Mar tomorrow for a long walk? We can talk, and I'll bring some books with me."

"Wow, that would be great," she said. "I'd love to."

"Okay, let's meet at noon at the Poseidon Restaurant on Fifteenth Street, across from the train tracks."

We said good-bye, looking forward to meeting the next afternoon. Then I realized I didn't even know her name.

She had walked down the hallway through a crowd of people heading toward the baggage claim. I caught up with her, tapped her on the shoulder, and said, "I'm sorry, I didn't even get your name."

She smiled. "Rosie. My name is Rosie."

Everything around me went into slow motion. My grip weakened, and I almost dropped my bag.

"See you tomorrow!" she said as she continued down the hallway. She moved through a crowd of people until she was out of sight.

I finally turned and walked away. Goose bumps covered my arms as I remembered my close friend Rosie from so many years before.

The following afternoon Rosie met me right on time. We kicked off our flip-flops and walked onto the white sandy beach, heading straight for the tide washing onto shore. I walked side by side with this girl named Rosie whom I didn't even know but felt an immediate connection to. I asked her a few pointed questions, which led to the core of her story.

For the next three hours we walked along the shoreline. Without hesitation, Rosie told me everything. The words came effortlessly, as though telling her story was something she had done many times before, but in fact I later learned that on this day, on this walk, it was the only time she had talked about it. Ever.

She had experienced horrible things in her life. The kind of things you can't even imagine would happen to a kid. But they did.

Rosie laughed and at times cried from the sheer joy of being understood and accepted in her experiences. As we walked back up the beach toward our starting point she asked me, "What are the things that helped you the most?"

I thought for a minute before I answered.

"Believing that God loved me. My dolphin pod of friends I travel through life with." I placed my fingers on the strand of pearls around my neck and continued, "And all the pearls that have helped shine a light for me along the way."

"I wish I could believe that God loved me," Rosie said. "I'm too messed up for him to love me. Anyway, I don't even know if I believe in God. How can you believe in a God you can't even see?"

I looked out at the water for a moment.

"I heard pro surfer Bryan Jennings once say, 'I can't see God, but I can see how he changes lives. I can see how he shows up and helps me know what to do.'

"When does he show up?" Rosie asked.

"I think he always shows up; it's just a matter of us recognizing it's him. Here, sit down. Let me show you something."

With my finger I drew an ocean star in the sand. "This is you. Your life is like an ocean star.

"When I was a child, my dad told me a story: 'A long time ago the nighttime sky was filled with bright, shining stars. All we had to do was look up to their light to help us find our way. There were so many zillions of stars to look up to that no one ever got lost. Then one day, some of the stars forgot how to shine for each other. One by one, many of them broke and fell from the sky. They landed in the sea. Some people call them starfish, but they're really ocean stars. They're on a journey to learn how to get put back together again. Once they do, they turn back into a star, shining for others the way they were meant to. So if you ever find an ocean star, make sure to be kind and gentle. It's trying to find its way home.'

"What my dad didn't know is that there is one star up there called the Bright and Morning Star. It's Jesus. He left the sky on purpose to come down here and show us the way home. Of all the gifts God has given, this is the greatest . . . it is the gift of his love. He came here to help you find your way home."

"I don't understand. What is home?"

I drew a diamond in the middle of the ocean star. "When this gift of love is received inside your heart, you find your way home to the

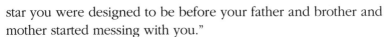

star you were designed to be before your father and brother and mother started messing with you."

Rosie looked at the ocean star.

"You were not designed to be broken," I said. "You were designed to shine!"

I explained the different parts of her star and talked about how her life now could be affected by her past experiences.

"Just as when this ocean star is connected to its source of life it can be restored, when you are connected to your Source of Life, your heart can be healed," I explained. "It takes time and it's a long journey, but if you're willing to embrace it, you will get to a place where you don't feel broken or empty anymore. He will fill you with streams of living water. Not only will you have enough light for yourself, you'll have an overflow—enough to give away."

"Do you know what else is so cool about an ocean star?" Rosie added. "Underneath each one of its five arms are hundreds of tiny suction cup feet that the starfish uses to propel itself. At the end of each arm is an orange eyespot. The starfish can't see, but it uses its eyespot to sense light and dark."

"It sounds like a journey of faith," I said. "That's really what walking with God is like."

"How do I start?" Rosie asked.

"You just did," I said as we both stood up. "The first step is talking to someone who can be trusted. The next thing I want you to know is that God does love you."

We brushed the sand off our legs and began to walk back up the beach. "You don't have to figure out how God could love you. You just have to believe."

"Okay," Rosie said. "Okay, I'll try."

We hadn't taken five steps when I noticed something written in the sand. It was written so big I had to take Rosie's arm and lead her away so we could read it. Each letter was about four feet tall. First I read the *G*, then the *O*, then the *D*. I moved back even farther to see it clearly: *GOD LOVES YOU!*

I looked at Rosie. Hot tears were already streaming down her face.

I started swinging her in circles and shouting right there in the middle of a crowded beach. "Rosie, this is just for you! God sent this just for you!"

"You too!" she said as she wiped her tears.

"I already believe. I didn't need this. Rosie, do you realize that someone wrote this before you and I even started talking? See? God wants you to know that he loved you even before you knew it. And think of the person who wrote it. God must have whispered, *Write it bigger. No, bigger. No, bigger. I want to make sure Rosie sees it.* Look at this, Rosie, I've never seen anything written so big in my entire life!"

Rosie stood there staring at the words.

I took hold of Rosie's arm and gently turned her to face the ocean waves rolling into shore. "Do you come to the beach often?"

"Yes, I've been coming here ever since I was a young child," Rosie said. "I love to come and watch the waves. It's so peaceful. I read one time that the symbol for *mother* in many languages is the waves of the sea. Somehow when I come here I feel like I'm getting something I missed."

"Me too. Since I was young, I've learned so much about life by listening to the ocean's currents and vibrations. It has taught me when to go after the wave and when to let it carry me where it wants to take me. Whenever I don't know what to do or I feel out of sorts, I just have to get back to the water and everything becomes clear for me."

"Sometimes I get confused about what kind of woman I want to be," Rosie said. "Just looking out at the water teaches me to try to have a balance of both strength and gentleness."

"Kind of like a mermaid?" I said with a wink.

Our laughter danced over the water, sending its vibration out to sea.

For a few minutes we stood at the water's edge and let the foam lap at our feet. We listened to the wind and the soothing rhythm of the roll waves.

Gently turning her head, Rosie studied my face with her eyes before calmly asking me, "Do you think you can help me figure out how to put the broken pieces of my star back together?"

"The cool thing about God is that he knows everything about you. He's really the only one who can put a broken star back together again. But Rosie, I will definitely share my story with you and some of the things that worked for me. As you start your own journey, you will find what works for you. Everyone hears God a little differently. Everyone needs different things along the way. And God will send you some pearls too!"

"Like he sent me you?"

"Yeah, like he sent me. Other women will come at different parts of your journey."

"How do I find them?"

"You don't have to go find them, you only have to open your eyes to the women who are already in your life in some way or who cross your path in an unexpected way. Keep your eyes open and be aware; signs of his presence and helpers are everywhere."

CHAPTER 30

celebrate life

"Can a mother forget the infant at her breast,
walk away from the baby she bore?
But even if mothers forget,
I'd never forget you—never.
Look, I've written your names on the backs of my hands.
The walls you're rebuilding are never out of my sight.
Your builders are faster than your wreckers.
The demolition crews are gone for good.
Look up, look around, look well!
See them all gathering, coming to you?
As sure as I am the living God"—GOD's Decree—
"you're going to put them on like so much jewelry,
you're going to use them to dress up like a bride."

(ISAIAH 49:15-18, *The Message*)

I had been reading through the book of Isaiah the week before my family headed out to San Diego for our wedding anniversary. I felt like this passage summarized my life journey.

I really wanted the day of celebration to focus on being thankful for those I do have in my life and how important they are to me.

The anniversary provided a good reason to do something tangible to express the gratitude I had overflowing inside my heart.

I didn't want there to be any stress in the day, but there was.

Elena and Katie arrived safely but Katie's baggage was lost. We rushed to the store to find something for her to wear that was blue and white and still reflected her personality.

I ran to get the flowers. I had ordered one white magnolia for each girl to wear in her hair and enough to make a bouquet for me to carry. They didn't get my order right. There were enough for the girls but not for me.

The day flew by. Half of us were dressed; the other half were still not home from running errands.

There was still the food problem. Food or no food?

And the car problem. How would we cram everyone into two cars?

Anna said she had a boom box for me to play the music, but someone had borrowed it and hadn't returned it. What was I going to do for music?

We were supposed to start at 5:00.

It was now 4:30.

We weren't even at the beach.

Katie and Elena looked at me as if maybe I'd better accept that this whole thing wasn't going to happen.

That's when it hit me. *Maybe no one else is really into it.* Katie and Elena would pretty much do anything I wanted to do, and vice versa. Other than that, maybe I was expecting the others to go along with this whole gig and they really didn't want to.

I looked at Katie and Elena.

Elena looked her hippie, free-spirit, artist self, in a dress made of fabrics she had designed. Katie, who was much more conservative than the two of us, wore a preppy-looking sundress. I wore a long, royal-blue satin skirt I found rummaging through Anna's closet looking for something special to wear. It was a little big for me, so it hung extra long and looked as if it had a train. With a simple white tank top and a sheer multicolored blue scarf around my shoulders, I was set to go.

"I feel like we just played dress up but no one else wants to play," Elena said, breaking the ice.

"Well, what should we do now?" Katie asked.

That's when we heard the horn blast as a car sped into the driveway. We rushed outside.

Anna had gone to the grocery and bought enough food to do a cookout at the beach. Within ten minutes everyone was ready to go.

After a whirlwind of running around gathering what and who we needed to pull this thing off, I found myself standing just where I wanted to be . . . barefoot on the beach.

Anna grilled up some killer chicken burgers and then cleaned up the mess as the rest of us finished getting ready. She said she was already a maid of honor for me once and would rather be the photographer the second time around. Her husband said he'd do pictures too.

"When are we going to start?" Trevor asked.

"In about fifteen minutes!" Elena said. "Your mom said once the sun gets a little bit lower, we'll begin."

"You better hurry up and change, Anna," Katie said. "Christina said everyone has to wear blue and white no matter what!"

"I'm just going to wear this sweatshirt; it's white," Anna insisted.

"It's not white!" I said. "That logo takes up the whole front! You'll mess up all the pictures."

"I'm not going to be in any of the pictures. I'm taking them, remember?" Anna said.

"Oh, come on! Don't pull a Frankie on me. You brought something nicer than that, didn't you?"

"She's kidding," Elena said. "We better get down to the water; it's almost time! We still need to put the flowers in the girls' hair."

As we ran toward the water, I turned around, and Anna lifted up her sweatshirt to flash me the blue shirt she had on underneath.

Anna's daughters—then sixteen and twelve—and their friends, whom I had known since they were small, agreed to be my flower girls.

Katie and Elena put the fresh magnolia flowers in the girls' hair as well as in their own. Elena pulled my hair back to one side and placed a magnolia flower behind my ear.

Then it was time.

The three of us knelt down in the sand and reached deep into our bags. I pulled out the blue satin pouch that held my treasure. Katie and Elena watched as I carefully lifted out my genuine strand of pearls. Elena moved my hair to one side, and Katie attached the clasp together in the back. My hair fell back in place over my shoulder.

I helped Katie and Elena put on their pearls next.

Then we put on our matching friendship anklets made out of royal blue daisies on a thin, clear chain.

Michael stood at his place near the water's edge with our boys on either side of him. All three of them were in khaki shorts and white polo shirts with strands of long puka shells hanging around their necks.

The sun was about to set. "Okay, it's time!" Anna shouted excitedly as she ran toward us with her camera.

Knowing that the vows couldn't take more than five minutes and there wasn't much else planned, I decided I'd better make the most out of the procession. So we started about half a mile down the beach.

Though most of the hard-core sunbathers had cleared out, the beach was still about half full of people and birds involved in a montage of activities. Surfers were catching a few last waves; seagulls were aggressively looking for food; and power walkers, joggers, and golden retrievers were running along the surf. Children were making sand castles along the water's edge, small lifeguard aircraft were flying low over the water, lovers were kissing, and families were spread out on blankets eating dinner.

First the volleyball game to our right stopped to watch, then the children playing king of the sand mountain looked on, then the lifeguard on the tall chair behind us asked if we wanted him to announce it was time to start the procession up the beach.

One of my niece's friends, dressed in Hawaiian board shorts and a Rip Curl T-shirt, stood halfway down the beach holding the boom box, waiting for the signal to push play. I didn't take into consideration how loud the sound of the surf would be, and there was no way the sound of my voice would travel. I turned to the lifeguard and took him up on his offer.

Loud enough for the whole beach to hear he shouted, "Start the music!" Now everyone was watching, even the seagulls!

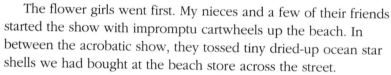
The flower girls went first. My nieces and a few of their friends started the show with impromptu cartwheels up the beach. In between the acrobatic show, they tossed tiny dried-up ocean star shells we had bought at the beach store across the street.

Families that had been sitting on blankets were now standing. Joggers stopped jogging. Walkers stopped walking. Even the surfers straddled their boards and sat in the roll waves watching the procession.

Before the flower girls even made it to Michael and my boys, the crowd started cheering.

Katie, Elena, and I were laughing so hard I thought we'd all stop breathing before it was our time to walk. I turned to them. "I'm not walking up there by myself! You both have to walk with me."

"No way, sister," Elena insisted. "You're on your own."

"You have to stay here," Katie said as she took Elena's arm and started up the beach.

The surfer boys howled and cheered. *Oh no!* I thought.

In all the craziness of the day I had not even prepared what I was going to say when I got up to Michael and the others.

Way down the beach my nieces and their friends stood next to Jake. My girlfriends stood next to Trevor. Anna and her husband each had a camera in their hands.

I'm sure my face was completely red as most of the beach stood at full attention, waiting for me to walk.

The sun was right where I wanted it. The clear blue sky formed a crisp backdrop as the huge orange ball ever so gently touched the surface of the ocean far in the distance.

I whispered in a soft voice, "Ten, nine, eight, seven, six . . ." I stopped and then began again. "Five, four, three, two, one. Look up!"

The ocean was calm with only a few sets of baby waves rolling in to shore. A glossy pink hue blanketed the water, reflecting the changing light in the sky.

I steadied my feet upon the cold, wet sand. The bottom of my silk skirt dragged behind as I took my first steps toward my husband, my children, my sister's family, and my lifetime friends.

Half of me was completely embarrassed that everyone on the beach was watching me, but the other half didn't even care. Life is

short. I wanted to do this to celebrate my sister, my friends, my husband, and my children. I wanted them to know how much I love them and appreciate them.

As I got closer I could hear Bob Dylan's voice blaring from the boom box: "Shine your light. Shine your light on me. Ya know I just couldn't make it by myself . . ."[6]

I had already been smiling, but now I was smiling bigger.

I could see my family and friends standing in a half circle watching me walk up the beach. Not all of them were smiling. They were doubled over, no, tripled over, laughing harder than I'd ever seen a bunch of people laugh. Then I started laughing too. The crowd joined us and soon the entire beach was filled with joyous laughter.

I had about ten more steps to take and I'd be standing in front of Michael. What would I say? I couldn't even think straight. All there was, was laughter. That is until my sister screamed.

She screamed so loud. So loud.

We snapped out of our laughter and looked up at her. What could it be?

"Look!" Anna screamed with all her might, pointing out at the water. "There's a dolphin!"

We quickly turned our focus toward the water as a dolphin fin broke the surface right in front of us. Then another fin and another until I screamed, "It's a whole pod!" I jumped up and down, shouting, "There's a dolphin pod in the roll wave!" No one could speak. They looked as if they were in the middle of a miracle. Everyone there knew the significance of a dolphin pod in my life.

"This is God, Anna. He sent them here!" I told her while I grabbed her by the shoulders.

"I haven't seen a dolphin pod since we were young and said we would be a pod for each other," Elena added.

"Wow, this kind of stuff always happens to you!" Katie said as she stared out into the roll wave.

Michael, Jake, and Trevor were smiling as they watched the dolphin pod show off, flipping in and out of the wave.

I ran to the water's edge, shouting, "Thank you, God! Thank you so much!"

"Don't get my dress wet!" Anna shouted after me.

Good thing she stopped me. I would have dived in the water fully dressed, I was so excited.

Everyone followed me. "Hurry, form a circle," I said without even thinking. "The dolphin pod wants to be part of the ceremony."

With everyone holding hands in a circle, I began, "I know we started this thinking it was about a wedding anniversary, but it's not just that. It's about all of us. You are all my dolphin pod," I said, getting choked up.

My boys looked as if they were afraid I was going to start bawling my eyes out.

"I know this is not something I planned, but I just want this moment to be about being thankful for all of you." I first looked at Anna and through the tears starting to form, I said, "Thank you for everything you did for me when I was a child. I want you to know now that you don't have to take control of everything anymore and this can be a season for you to enjoy just being at peace and enjoying your life. I wish you much happiness."

"You both have been the best friends anyone could ever ask for," I said as I looked toward Elena and Katie. "I never understood when girls would get jealous of each other, talk bad about each other, or compete with each other. The older I get, the more I realize what we have is unique. You both have made me feel like I'm never alone, and we have had so much fun together. Look at us, even standing here today."

Then I turned to Michael. "Wow, can you believe we've been married fifteen years?" We all laughed, which was good since we needed to catch our breath. "Being married has been really hard at times and really good at times. Thank you for being a man of integrity. There are not many guys out there who are committed to love their wives and children like you love us."

"Look!" Jake screamed. "The dolphins are getting even closer!"

We all stood at the water's edge watching the dolphin pod. As majestic strokes of color spread across the horizon, a warm, comforting peace surrounded me. Deep in the stillness, I remembered the promise I heard at the beach during the darkest point of my life: *Don't focus on the darkness of the disappearing sun. Look up at the color I can paint with your life.*

The ongoing sound of the soothing waves rolling in to shore filled my soul with renewed energy. The earth below me shifted as the tide receded under my feet. I surrendered to the movement, embracing a new balance, anchoring deeper into the sand with the changing tide. In the calmness, I heard nothing but the fresh rhythm beating inside my soul.

A dolphin rose, standing on its tail. Then it dove back into the sea to play.

"Mom, this is your gift from God," Trevor said, breaking the silence.

"I think you're right," I said as I locked eyes with Trevor. "But you know what? You are a gift. You and Jake, Jessie and Jamie, all of you," I said, looking into the eyes of each child there. "It is the greatest privilege on the face of the earth to be a mother. I pray before God today that I will always connect with you and invest in your hearts. That I will help you unwrap the gifts that God has placed inside of you. I love you so much!"

My husband wrapped his arms around me, then grabbed me and both of our boys in a big bear hug.

The first stars of the evening dotted the darkening sky far off in the distance.

"Look up and find a star," I said to all of the kids. "When I was young I read a book that said, 'If God can know about each one of the stars in the nighttime sky, and know them each by name, how much more can he know and care about me?' Always remember that God will walk with you no matter what you face on your journey."

Elena broke away and blasted the music. Even though it was dark, Anna started taking more pictures.

Anna's husband, Brett, started laying out bases for a makeshift baseball game in the sand, with no light except from the stars and moon above. Everyone ran off to form teams.

I stood alone, barefoot on the cool sand glistening in the moonlight, my eyes fixed on the dolphin pod in the wave. "Thank you for coming!" I whispered out over the water.

I rolled my skirt up and ambled in the calm shallow water. The last remnants of color faded from the horizon, and the nighttime sky blazed with zillions of glowing stars. My hair blew in the salty, wet

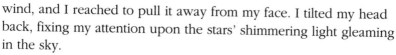
wind, and I reached to pull it away from my face. I tilted my head back, fixing my attention upon the stars' shimmering light gleaming in the sky.

And thank you too, God.

Your spirit hovers over the water, and it is here that you have shown me how to find my way home. You are the one I hear when I listen to the quiet whispers of the changing tide. You are the one I sense when the water's vibration rolls over me. You are the one I recognize through the symbols of the sea. When the thrashing waves threatened to take me down, you showed me how to find my rock and hold on tight. You are the great comforter and healer. Through the powerful and gentle work of your Living Water, you have healed the broken pieces of my star and filled me with your light so I can shine for others.

ENDNOTES

1. Kurt Kaiser, "Oh How He Loves You and Me," 1975.
2. Margaret Wise Brown, *The Runaway Bunny* (New York: Harper & Row, 1942).
3. Raphael Cushnir, "Two Questions That Could Change Your Life," *O: The Oprah Magazine*, November 2002, 113–114.
4. Hope Edelman, *Motherless Daughters* (New York: Delta, 1994), 171.
5. Gary Smalley and John Trent, *The Blessing* (New York: Simon & Schuster, 1986), 23–24.
6. Bob Dylan, "Precious Angel," © 1979 Special Rider Music.

CONTINUE READING
TO FIND OUT WHAT
CHRISTINA'S DOING NOW!

If you know someone who would enjoy *Ocean Star*,
please share yours or buy one to give away.

for the most current printing, make sure to get the "Third Edition"

MY DREAM...A PEARL FOR EVERY GIRL!

From every community, every tribe, every nation

A surfer can feel a set of waves coming long before he or she actually sees them. They don't plan for them. They feel them. That's how it is with my dreams. I feel them coming long before I ever see them. Then I position myself as best I know how to ride the wave when it comes.

The Bible says in Hebrews 11:1, "Faith is the confidence that what we hope for will actually happen; it gives us assurance about things we cannot see." In whatever creative way we can define our dreams, they give us confidence to work toward our goals.

Since the release of *Ocean Star* in 2006, I have not stopped reaching for the dream that God has given me. The dream that every girl from every nation would understand she is a pearl of much value, every girl would have a pearl who was willing to shine light into her life and she would be a pearl for another girl.

It is now 2011 and much has happened that I will share in the following pages:

1. You're Designed to Shine!

2. Pods Forming around the World

3. Gathering of the Pearls

4. The Fountain of the Water of Life

5. How You can be part of the Dream!

ENCOURAGING GIRLS TO SHINE!

Events and workshops for all ages

Soon after *Ocean Star* was released I started doing workshops and events for girls in communities all over the United States. I remembered what it was like to be in high school and also in college, and I thought to myself, "What would I have gone to that would have been a source of encouragement and inspiration?" I would not have gone to something that was boring. I would have gone to something only if it inspired me. With that in mind, I created a workshop/event experience called *You're Designed to Shine!*

Pro surfer, Shannon McIntyre and musician, Jessica McLean, joined me in shining for the girls. We did our first event in Laguna Beach, CA. I wanted the event to be outside where the girls could feel the wind and the waves, and be exposed to the amazing powerful presence of God that is revealed in nature. We talked about life, their dreams, their friendships, their families, their Pearls, their relationship with God, and how they can make a difference in the lives of others.

Together we integrated inspiring stories, art, and music in encouraging the girls on their journeys. I would often step back and watch the girls thinking about their lives, talking about their dreams, and sharing with each other lessons they learned that they can pass on. My whole heart fills up with joy to watch these girls who are full of potential as they celebrate their uniqueness and look up to the color God desires to paint with their lives!

YOU'RE DESIGNED TO SHINE!

6 Lessons that will change your life!

"Make a careful exploration of who you are and the work you have been given, and then sink yourself into that. Don't be impressed with yourself. Don't compare yourself with others. Each of you must take responsibility for doing the creative best you can with your own life." GALATIANS 6:4-5

Each girl who attends the workshop gets a copy of her own *You're Designed to Shine!* workbook/journal. The study includes 6 sessions:

MY DREAM – Defining what you want your life to be like.

MY STAR – Find healing and restoration as you learn how to shine.

MY POD – Travel with supportive friends.

MY PEARLS – Discover mentors to encourage you on your journey.

MY GIFT – Develop your relationship with God.

MY WAVE – Shine for others in unique and creative ways.

Visit us at www.oceanstargifts.com to find additional resources

A CALL FOR HELP

Sending out an SOS to all who have a heart to shine!

I read an article in a San Francisco newspaper that explained how a diver discovered a whale all tangled up in fishing line. He realized if there was any hope of setting it free he would need help. So he immediately sent out an SOS. Help came fast. Five boats surrounded the whale as a rescue team tried every tool on their boat to try to cut the lines free. It soon became clear that there was only one way to save the whale. They would have to dive in. For hours they surrounded the whale, carefully cutting the fishing line until the whale was free to swim back to open waters.

We don't need the media to show us that girls are tangled up in more than fishing line. My dream has been that girls and women all over the globe would be willing to dive in and take the risk of being real with other girls, sharing their stories, taking time to listen, coaching them to wide open waters of God's love so they can discover the pearl of great value that they are.

As I sent out my own SOS, many girls and women responded saying that they were willing to dive in but they didn't have the tools needed to make the connection with the girls and coach them as I did in my workshops.

Simple Solution!

I wrote a very easy-to-follow guide in the back of *You're Designed to Shine!* Immediately, help arrived for girls! We started to hear from girls and women all over the world who were gathering girls in their own neighborhoods, churches, college campuses and communities to lead them through the sessions in *You're Designed to Shine!* The dream started to spread…fast!

art by Shannon McIntyre

PODS FORMING AROUND THE WORLD

Girls diving in and making a difference

Over the past few years we have heard from girls all over the United States, Europe, Panama, Peru, Puerto Rico, Israel, South Africa, South America, Costa Rica, Brazil, Australia, New Zealand, Belize, Indonesia, Aruba, Jamaica, and on and on the letters come.

Lisa in Barbados started with ten girls and led them through the six sessions of *You're Designed to Shine!* When they were done, those ten gathered ten more, and it continued to grow so that now over 200 girls have been touched just in a small area of Barbados! One of those girls, Melanie, started a surf camp called Surf 'n'Shine. She reaches out to the young girls on the island by teaching them how to surf in the morning and how to live life in the afternoon. Another Lisa on the island uses her art to teach and inspire girls. Rachael paints murals in the children's wing of the hospital and teaches the children to have dreams for their lives through art.

Diana in Puerto Rico started by gathering her daughter's friends and has now spread to reaching out to girls all over the island.

Ellima lives in Indonesia. She went to the mountains of Java for a healing retreat and the woman leading the entire weekend started by reading out of a book, called *Ocean Star.* This led her to starting her own pod in Indonesia which has now spread to hundreds of others.

Letters continue to pour in over email and Facebook sharing how they found *Ocean Star* and *You're Designed to Shine!* and how people are using these tools to set girls free in their own communities. We love hearing from you!

Find us on Facebook under Christina DiMari and/or *You're Designed to Shine*

GATHERING OF PEARLS

When I met Irene Neller, vice president of communications and marketing at Biola University in Southern California, I knew I found a genuine pearl!

I had been praying about doing an event each year where Pearls could come together from the nations to be encouraged, equipped, and inspired to go back and shine in their own communities. I had been reading Revelation 21 and 22, envisioning bringing girls to the fountain of the water of life. As they came to the water, their stars were restored, their pearls were transformed, their bodies were refreshed, and their dreams encouraged. I imagined girls coming from the north, south, east, and west. Coming together from diverse backgrounds and nationalities to form a circle of unity around the fountain of the water of life. Coming together like pearls being strung together on a strand with a common vision to shine value into the lives of other girls.

Like always, when I have a dream or something I am thinking about I draw a picture of it in my prayer journal. Then I play around with it until it becomes clearer and takes shape. So I drew a picture of a fountain, labeled the N, S, E, and W, and drew girls from every nation coming together in unity. Then I wrote out the verse from John 4:14, "Whoever drinks of the water that I shall give him will never thirst. but the water that I shall give him will become in him a fountain of water, springing up into everlasting life."

Irene invited me to speak at an event on Biola's campus called Pearls in Process. After the event I was walking around and noticed a fountain off in the distance. As I approached the fountain the first thing I noticed was a tile in the ground with an S at the base of the fountain. I looked to the left and there was a tile

continued

with W. I looked to the right and there was a tile with E. And one at the other side marking the North. The fountain looked just like the one I had drawn in my prayer book. My eyes looked through the water hoping to find sign of any words that would confirm my initial feeling that this was meaningful to me. Nothing. No words in the fountain. No words on the ground around the fountain. I walked behind some tables where students gathered alongside the fountain to study. There were some pillars. With words! The first explained the vision of the fountain, which was donated from a lady named Marjorie. It explained her heart for creating a place on campus where students could gather in unity to be encouraged and equipped! The second tile read, "Whoever drinks of the water that I shall give him will never thirst. but the water that I shall give him will become in him a fountain of water, springing up into everlasting life."

I could hardly contain myself. This fountain meant something and I had to tell someone! Irene listened with tears in her eyes as I told her all these things. She looked at me and said, "I believe we have been brought together for a reason, what is your dream for how Biola University can become part of what God is doing to encourage girls? If we can do something soon, what do you envision?"

I explained, "To host an event here, around the fountain. To invite the pearls to come from all over the world. Pearls who have been diving in and helping girls. To encourage them, equip them, inspire them and connect them with each other."

"Lets do it!" Irene says, "Let's do it in the fall of each year!"

The first "Gathering of the Pearls" was held in the fall of 2010. Pearls flew in

continued

from all over the world! It was everything we both had imagined and even better. The highlight of the whole event for me was Friday night at the candlelight service around the Fluor Fountain of Faith on Biola's campus. Shannon McIntyre was painting the drawing what I had in my prayer journal from two years earlier, with girls from every nation surrounding the fountain.

Irene chose 12 girls (Pearls) from a variety of cultures. Each dressed in a different color representing the 12 jewels in the fountain of the New Jerusalem. All 12 of these girls are standing spread out in a circle around the fountain facing outward holding a blue container filled with freshwater pearls.

I asked all the girls attending to form lines in front of each of the 12 girls holding the pearls. Each girl received a pearl and a prayer of blessing over them as they reached the front of the line. During this beautiful moment Jessica led us in worship with her song she wrote specifically for this aspect of our vision landing, called "The Fountain."

Several girls wanted to speak to me afterward, so I had them form a line and I sat at the fountain edge. I wanted to hear a bit from each one. Then standing in front of me was a beautiful Spanish girl. I asked for her name. She replied, Marjorie. In the back of my head, I was thinking "Oh! That's cool, her name is Marjorie, like the lady who had this vision to build the fountain at Biola." Before I could ask her another question, streams of tears start flowing from her eyes. She tells me how much tonight means to her and how all of the lessons I shared about the meaning of the pearl are so significant…because…her name, Marjorie… means *PEARL*.

FOUNTAIN OF LIFE

Come to the water that will satisfy your every thirst

I have heard that there really is no way to kill an ocean star unless you take it out of the water, away from its source of life. As long as the ocean star stays in the water, it will heal and restore the pieces that were injured or cut off along its journey. But what is even more amazing, if you take an ocean star and cut it in a hundred different pieces and put it back into the ocean, each one of those pieces has the potential to grow into its own star. When we stay connected to God as our Source of Life, he will take the broken pieces of our lives and multiply them into hundreds of blessings that shine light, love, and hope for others.

I hope as you have read the pages of my journey you have heard the whisper of your own name being called, saying, "Come! Come to the Water!"

The Spiritual Water I connect to is referred to as the Fountain of Living Water that flows from the throne of God. It is there I have found everything I have ever searched for.

"Whoever drinks of the water that I shall give him will never thirst. but the water that I shall give him will become in him a fountain of water, springing up into everlasting life." JOHN 4:14

"I, Jesus, have sent my angel to give you this message for the churches. I am both the source of David and the heir to his throne. I am the bright morning star." The Spirit and the bride say, "Come." Let anyone who hears this say, "Come." Let anyone who is thirsty come. Let anyone who desires drink freely from the water of life." REVELATIONS 22

If you have been touched by what we are doing I hope you will read the following pages to see how YOU can be part of the dream!

art by Shannon McIntyre

HOW YOU CAN BE PART OF THE DREAM
Donate

Consider placing your gift into the water and know that God is taking your gift on His Mighty Wave to shine for girls all over the world.

Partner with us to help girls shine! Your tax deductible gifts provide:
Gifts of $25.00 to $5000.00 provide discipleship materials for girls.
Gifts of $5,000 to $10,000 help us run our events and outreach programs.
Gifts of $20,000+ larger gifts provide for all items listed below.
To accomplish our 5 year plan our dream would be to raise $1,000,000. Or more!

How we use the money that is donated:
View our website for more details: www.oceanstargifts.com
- Training future *You're Designed to Shine!* Pod leaders through inspirational events
- Provide discipleship workbooks to girls all over the world who cannot afford the costs
- Establish mentoring programs on every college campus
- Outreach in surf culture and inner city through sponsored events
- Mission trip opportunities for girls leading YDTS activities in countries outside the U.S.

Thank you for your donation!
To partner, visit our website for detailed information.
www.oceanstargifts.com

art by Shannon McIntyre

HOW YOU CAN BE PART OF THE DREAM

Form a pod on your campus or in your community!

Consider gathering girls on your campus or in your own community and lead them through the *You're Designed to Shine!* experience!

TESTIMONIES

"Even though I don't "feel capable" to lead my pod, I keep on going because I can see how much it means to the girls. No matter what their age or background, we all learn from each other."

"*You're Designed to Shine!* is truly a gift from God. I walk with more confidence now and the lessons I have learned have helped to heal me and now I know how to follow God's dream for my life."

"I enjoyed taking the journey of *You're Designed to Shine!* with my friends because we grew together in our relationship with each other and with God. Our leader was so kind and caring. She really showed us what it means to make a difference if the life of another girl. I hope to do the same for others now that I am done."

"My world has opened up tremendously, to the vastness of God's love, and the amazing power within us, to encourage and shine God's light. A love that I have come to embrace, that has no boundaries, and knows no age, colour, class nor creed."

HOW YOU CAN BE PART OF THE DREAM

GIVE THE GIFT OF PEARLS

Our signature necklace of a single freshwater pearl on leather has become a very special way you can bless another girl. Consider buying the necklaces and looking for girls you can bless by telling them they are a pearl of much value. They will never take it off and never forget you for calling out their value and worth.

How a pearl is formed?

When a single grain of sand enters into the living membrane of an oyster, it causes the oyster fits of conflict and irritation. The oyster's reaction to it continually coats it and over time, the grain of sand is eventually transformed into a pearl. The pearl symbolizes deep inner change that now shines with beauty outward to the world. The Latin word for pearl literally means "unique", attesting to the fact that no two pearls are the same.

Why I wear my necklace?

When I wear my pearl necklace I am reminded that I belong to God and he created me unique for a special purpose to fulfill while I am on this earth.

HOW YOU CAN BE PART OF THE DREAM

PURCHASE FROM OUR ONLINE STORE!

Portions of the proceeds from all sales in our online store help us keep the dream alive! All items in our online store are made from girls who have been touched by the dream in some way. This includes our pearl necklace!

CARRY OCEAN STAR GIFTS IN YOUR STORE!

Resorts, gift stores, boutiques, bookstores and surf shops all over the United States and the Caribbean Islands carry the full line of our products, Ocean Star Gifts.

It has been very exciting to watch buyers not only love the products but get super excited about having their store be a light to shine for the girls coming in who are buying the cards, books and jewelry. Many of the stores actually buy cases of *Ocean Star* and give them out to girls in their community as a way to give back and make a difference.

We cannot thank you enough as this is the main way resources continue to flow into the fountain so we can continue to pour out and bless girls all over the world!

Visit us at www.oceanstargifts.com to purchase from our online store

CHRISTINA DiMARI is a writer and artist who draws inspiration from the ocean, an environment that has great meaning in her life. She loves to use her gifts to bring hope and encouragement to girls all over the world.

Christina received her BA degree from Simpson University where she studied Inter-Cultural Communications. An adventure girl with a strong missions heart, she spent several years after college working with street children in third world countries and traveling the world. Christina went on to get a Master of Corrective Body Work Therapy from National Holistic Institute where she integrated nutrition and holistic health in her work with encouraging and coaching others to live a whole and healthy life. She then completed her studies in Art Therapy. For thirty years she has been helping young women, through creative processes, find wholeness and purpose early on their journey. Christina is the author of four books. She enjoys spending time with her husband and two boys either by the sea or exploring mountain trails.

OCEAN STAR (MEMOIR) Christina's inspiring memoir continues to shine for girls all over the world. *Ocean Star*, which reads like a gripping novel, brings to life hope filled transforming life lessons through the symbols of the sea. <u>Age appropriate</u>: 14 and older.

You're Designed to Shine! —*an outreach to girls all over the world*
Thousands of letters came in from girls around the world who were encouraged by reading *Ocean Star*. Christina wanted to do more to help the girls look at their own lives: where they have been, where they are and where they want to go. So she created *You're Designed to Shine!*, a six week interactive journal/workbook based on the six main lessons she wove throughout her memoir, *Ocean Star*. In a fun and thought provoking study, she coaches others how to become the shining stars God designed them to be.

Ocean Star Gifts
Christina then founded Ocean Star Gifts with the vision to create a company that could fund her vision to shine for girls all over the world. Her dream began as a seed, a seed that was watered with faith and cultivated with hard work. It has now become a flourishing reality!